REVOLUTIONARY
FORGIVENESS

REVOLUTIONARY FORGIVENESS

FEMINIST REFLECTIONS ON NICARAGUA

The Amanecida Collective

Carter Heyward   *Anne Gilson*

Laura Phyllis Biddle   *Kirsten Laura Lundblad*

Florence Gelo   *Patrick Michaels*

Susan Harlow   *Laurie Ann Rofinot*

Elaine Koenig   *Margarita Suárez*

Virginia Sapienza Lund   *Jane W. Van Zandt*

Carol Vogler

ORBIS BOOKS

Maryknoll, New York 10545

The Catholic Foreign Mission Society of America (Maryknoll) recruits and trains people for overseas missionary service. Through Orbis Books Maryknoll aims to foster the international dialogue that is essential to mission. The books published, however, reflect the opinions of their authors and are not meant to represent the official position of the society.

Copyright © 1987 by the Amanecida Collective
Published by Orbis Books, Maryknoll, NY 10545
Manufactured in the United States of America
All rights reserved

"It Could Have Been Me" by Holly Near © 1974 reprinted by permission of Hereford Music (ASCAP).

Portions of "Lessons Learned in Nicaragua," by Anne Gilson (February, 1985) and "Whose Freedom of the Press?" by Carter Heyward (March, 1984) reprinted by permission of *The Witness*.

Library of Congress Cataloging-in-Publication Data
Heyward, Carter.
   Revolutionary forgiveness.

   Bibliography: p.
   1. Liberation theology.   2. Feminism—Religious aspects—Christianity. 3. Amanecida Collective.
4. Nicaragua—Military policy—Religious aspects.
5. United States—Military policy—Religious aspects.
6. Communist strategy.   I. Gilson, Anne.   II. Amanecida Collective. III. Title.
BT83.57.H49   1986   277.285'0828   86-5434
ISBN 0-88344-264-7 (pbk.)

We dedicate this book to everyone
who responds with courage and compassion
to suffering—
and to all who suffer today
the violence wrought
by our own nation

It always seemed to me that the roosters would act up more on evenings when there was constant mortar fire. Some nights I would lie in bed and listen, not being able to sleep. I remember how often the sounds they made would sound like human moaning.

FLO GELO

The true American goes not abroad in search of monsters to destroy. . . .
[America] well knows by once enlisting under other banners than her
own, were they even the banners of foreign independence, she would
involve herself, beyond the power of extrication, in all wars of interest
and intrigue, of individual avarice, envy and ambition. She might become the dictatress of the world: She would no longer be the ruler of her
own spirit.

JOHN QUINCY ADAMS
JULY 4, 1821

Dios es amor, Dios es solidario, Dios es solidaridad. Donde hay solidaridad ahí está Dios hablando eficazmente. . . .
Dios habla en Centroamérica por la solidaridad. Dios habla donde hay
solidaridad con Centroamérica. Y Dios pide solidaridad con Centroamérica, con sus pueblos, con sus pobres que sufren.

JON SOBRINO, S.J., AND JUAN HERNANDEZ PICO, S.J.,
Teología de la Solidaridad Cristiana

Contents

Foreword

The Revolution Fights against the Theology of Death

by Dorothee Sölle

One of the principles of liberation theology states that "the poor are the teachers." This book written by thirteen North Americans testifies to this hermeneutical advantage of both knowing and teaching. The poor from Central America teach their visitors from the north things unknown in the context of the rich or, even worse, things that religion completely distorts and takes out of context inside the culture of the rich. The title of this book names what a variety of people in Nicaragua, but mostly the poor—children from El Salvador, Comandante Tomas Borge, some nameless mothers who lost their children in Reagan's war against Nicaragua's rural population—have taught the members of the Amanecida Collective. In some ways all the people who surface in this work teach revolutionary forgiveness.

But, as the Collective demonstrates, revolutionary forgiveness is difficult work. What was possible in the historical momentum of the Triumph of the revolution in 1979—namely that the torturers and the children trained in torture were forgiven by those who put justice, not violence, at the base of their commonwealth—becomes more difficult today under the violent actions of the United States, a superpower that respects neither law as acknowledged by most peoples, that is, "international law," nor God's commandment: "Thou shalt not kill." One aspect of the ongoing killing is that it twists the indigenous generosity of the Nicaraguan Revolution whose first official, legal act was to eradicate the death sentence. Like some of the authors of this book, I am a pacifist. Arriving from Europe on two visits to Nicaragua, I had difficulties with the increasing militarization of the society. What effects would it have? Doesn't the gun change the hand that touches it? Has any nation, once militarized, ever demilitarized? The Sandinista Revolution used to celebrate the literacy teachers as the heroes of the revolution; would Nicaraguans revise the history of the revolution? Like the Amanecida Collective, I could not simply push these concerns to one side. And, like these authors, I too learned in Nicaragua much that has caused me to reflect critically on some of my own assumptions about the ethics of armed struggle. Is armed struggle *always* wrong?

I would like to share two observations that are important to me in this context. One observation has to do with the role of the soldiers I saw. For example, I remember the way one soldier carried and rocked his baby while his wife danced, and the way another helped an old woman cut through some red tape with the authorities. In a society with less division of labor than our own, soldiers are also teachers and social workers, technicians and artisans, and students who are learning to read. The newspaper *La Barricada* expanded on the slogan "All arms to the people" to urge the people, "Arm yourselves by reading!"

My other observation has to do with weapons. Nicaragua has armed itself for its defense; it has no plans for conquest and no first-strike strategies! The people are fighting for their survival, for the simple defense of their territory. The leadership is extremely anxious not to cross into Honduran territory while pursuing counterrevolutionaries, an action that would offer an excuse for invasion. "We must swallow our pride and tolerate the artillery firing; we must explain to our own soldiers that they have to exercise self-discipline," Captain Federico Zerda informed us near Estelí. The revolution must fight if it is to survive. The Amanecida Collective's work helps us see in what ways this is the case.

North Americans may not take the Nicaraguans' motto "Free Homeland or Death" seriously—but the Sandinistas do. The violence is not a matter of one army making war against another, but of mercenary troops fighting an entire people, and the actions of the government and people in carrying out their defense are based on a profound faith and theology. The contras who have been captured by the Sandinistas have to admit that, to their surprise, they have not been tortured or starved by "those communists."[1] This fact testifies to an aspect of the war that I would like to highlight in this foreword, for it is of vital concern to the authors of *Revolutionary Forgiveness*: the theological dimension. The relationship between politics and faith is a key to understanding the Nicaraguan Revolution and the efforts of the U.S. government to crush it.

TELLING THE TRUTH

The Amanecida Collective realizes that, in the United States as well, there is strong historical confluence between dominant currents of politics and faith. The turbulence of "coming of age" in these currents gives this book a political urgency and spiritual agitation. These authors become more astute politically as they become more aware spiritually. We, the readers, become witnesses to their corporate process of political and spiritual awakening, which is not complete but which is well under way. To read this book is to catch a glimpse of what it means to share a feminist liberation commitment.

Like these thirteen, I too learned much in Nicaragua that caused me to reflect deeply on the meaning of Christian faith. Let me tell you something of what I learned.

I recall a conversation that I had with Tomas Borge in 1983 in Managua that deeply impressed me. One is aware of Borge's presence as soon as he enters a room. Everything focuses around this small man who looks very Indian. He is wiry, thinks and speaks quickly, and is incredibly intense. I had seen a number of other ministers and members of the government who I can easily picture, under quite different circumstances, as social-democratic civil servants. Not Borge. The people call him "Tomasito." He is a leader of the people. He does not inform but instead uses knowledge as a spur to action. Perhaps one can measure the power of a person by how quiet one becomes in that person's presence, how attentive, how serious.

Our conversation revolved around the question: Will the United States intervene because it cannot achieve its aims any other way? Can the United States win without an invasion? Borge said: "The attitude of the United States toward Nicaragua is nothing new: the history of Nicaragua is a history of resistance to the United States, which believes it determines what happens in Central America. The last freely elected president of Nicaragua, Zelaya, received a letter from the North American government telling him to resign. He submitted; he resigned. Aside from minor nuances, for example under Carter, this has always been the case. With the triumph of the revolution that is over—but the United States does not accept that."

Borge talks himself into a passion; I could hardly get a word in edgewise. What will happen if the United States government does not intervene directly? Borge responds: "They will go on supporting the contras, but that poses no danger to the revolution. The contras have bragged about taking Managua, but in reality they can't even get a little place like Jalapa under their control. Jalapa, a little village on the border—a geographically unfavorable place for us, where the contras have backing and supplies from Honduras." When asked what help Nicaragua could get from other countries in case of invasion, Borge takes another tack, asking, "How many people does it take to get a revolutionary process under control? We never had as many armed people as the National Guard. Our strength lies in the participation of the people. How many people does the Salvadoran army need in its confrontation with the guerrillas? In El Salvador five thousand freedom fighters are facing fifty thousand government soldiers. If we compared that situation with Nicaragua, the North Americans would need five million soldiers. . . . If the United States were to invade Nicaragua, we would make the Yankee soldiers' lives impossible, and we'd keep it up twenty-four hours a day—they'd never have a moment's rest; they wouldn't even be able to count on the air they breathe. They might be able to drive us out of the cities, but certainly not out of the countryside. And how long could they last here? One shouldn't underestimate the power of international opinion. They might stay here six months, set up a government of National Guardsmen—and *that* would last about as long as an ice cream cone at the schoolyard gate."

According to Borge, Nicaragua must keep its defense in its own hands. Even if they wanted to, neither Cuba nor the Soviet Union could intervene in the conflict. "We are not so irresponsible as to let the conflict in Nicaragua turn into a threat of World War III or a nuclear war. So we will defend ourselves by our own means, although we won't do without international solidarity on the level of public opinion and protests, which may of course also turn into actions. For instance, who can guarantee that the Panamanians will not occupy the Panama Canal? Who can guarantee there won't be attacks and acts of sabotage in other parts of the world? Who can guarantee the lives of U.S. diplomats in Latin American countries? We can negotiate about a lot of issues—but not about our revolution, not about our solidarity with the peoples of Latin America, not about our anti-imperialism and our sovereignty. We can negotiate about all kinds of things, but our revolution is a nonnegotiable issue."

Borge spent five years in Somoza's prison; he lived for nine months beneath a hood painted with tar. It took all the strength he had just to draw a breath, to survive the torture.

To the question of how many CIA agents there are in Nicaragua now, Borge responds, "Fewer than before. But there are two kinds of CIA agents—the professional and the ideological ones. I won't say that Monsignor Obando is a CIA agent, but he has gotten money from the CIA." The comandante cannot reveal his source or the details lest his informant be endangered. But later I heard of the existence of a photocopy of such a check made out to Obando.

Borge turned to the topic of the papal visit that had taken place the previous spring and on which the government had spent four million dollars. "There was great naiveté on our part about the pope's visit. We were so naive that we told the organized masses not to shout political slogans on the square. The Sandinista youth were posted along the streets to protect the pope. When the people finally shouted 'We want peace,' the hierarchy considered that an insult. The call for 'a prayer for our dead'—and that was what the mothers of the fallen were waiting for, in tears—was fended off with '¡ Silencio!' Since when may a priest refuse to pray for the dead?"

Borge sees the political outcome of this dramatic event—the pope was booed down—as a loss of the pope's aura, above all among the many young people in Nicaragua. "There is a new religious skepticism, and while the papal visit may have affirmed the church hierarchy, it weakened Christianity."

I asked what we can do for Nicaragua when we return home. Borge's answer is disarmingly simple. At the same time it is sharply critical of a culture that he believes will never reach liberation and truth through "development," but which rather must be challenged and overcome: "You can tell the truth, in a convincing way. The truth will set you free, as the Bible says. The European peoples have fenced in the truth, and have no access to it anymore. How can the people who produced European culture remain on the level of the *Reader's Digest*?"

The strength of *Revolutionary Forgiveness* is that its authors are attempting to tell the truth not only about Nicaragua but also about the United States.

AGAINST THE THEOLOGY OF DEATH

Tomas Borge also said that the revolution fights against the "theology of death." What does this mean, I ask myself. Do I live and work for a "theology of death"? Similarly, the Amanecida Collective asks, are we in the First World obsessed with a theology of guilt and powerlessness, of believing in sin but not in being freed from the necessity to sin? Are we dominated by a theology of sadness and cynicism? I see it in so many faces of my pastor brothers, not so much though in my sister priests. Does the capitalist system require a theology of death? It certainly requires an economy of war in which the rich become richer and the poor poorer; it certainly needs the militarization of the globe and beyond, so that it can maintain its economic world hegemony by controlling the prices of raw materials; it certainly needs rapid-deployment special units to use against any groups it declares to be "terrorist"; it needs torturers and those who train and equip them because they maintain the insurmountable mountains of injustice it needs to blind and deafen its subjects, to keep them in a spiritual form of apartheid. It is here, on the cultural level that has its economic, political, and military interconnections, where theology becomes a theology of death.

It is encouraging to one like myself, a teacher of Christian theology, to meet a collective of U. S. theologians who are moving against the theology of death. The tradition of the Protestant Reformation distinguishes between the living God and the dead idols. God, so the distinction goes, promises life and gives life, whereas the idols promise life and give death. As these authors point out, God promises a life that is never to be possessed and hoarded and kept for the individual. The life that God gives and promises is essentially shared life—as the poor share their food, though little it may be. The idols of the "free enterprise system" promise life for the happy few that will "trickle-down" to the many. But this promise is false. That system does not feed the hungry; it needs to exploit them. As soon as the poor claim their rights, as the people in Nicaragua did with their revolution, the idol shows its other side and brings death to the people. A theology that does not clarify the distinction between God who promises and shares life and the idols that bring death to two-thirds of the human family is de facto and often even expressly a theology of death. It hails military escalation as "security," exploitation and slave labor as "freedom"; it calls the war in which every year fifteen million children die of hunger "peace." *Revolutionary Forgiveness* is an effort to reveal that the theology of death distorts all creative concepts of theology by making them into individualistic assumptions about the human person and her or his world. The theology of death also has to silence the death of the poor; it makes their death invisible; it silences the truth, as the Amanecida group demonstrates again and again. I shall give an example of that silencing of the truth.

On October 29, 1984, six small children in San Gregorio in the north of Nicaragua were killed by the contras. Two of the children, Carmen Rosa and Azuema, were only five; the others were six, seven, eight, and eleven years old.

I would like to share three different reactions to these deaths, three different forms of spiritual responses. The Catholic bishop Pablo Antonio Vega, when asked for a commentary, replied: "It is worse to kill the soul than the body." He and his superior, Archbishop Obando y Bravo, believe that the Sandinistas poison the souls of the people; for that reason the murdered children do not matter. The official opposition paper, *La Prensa*, had nothing to say about the murder of the six children. The headline on its front page the day after the massacre was about the transplantation of an animal's heart in a California baby. The fantastic scientific experiment was a "first"; it was judged to be more relevant and important than the killing of six children of poor campesinos. This media message reveals the attitudes of the bourgeois elites in the Third World toward the historical reality of their own people. The California baby with the monkey's heart achieves for *La Prensa* precisely what the CIA calls "neutralization." I heard a third commentary on the death of the children while I was standing in protest before the U.S. embassy in Managua. We sang, prayed, and expressed our solidarity with the Nicaraguan people. An elder citizen of the United States who has lived quite a while in Managua told me that he felt like a decent German in Berlin in 1938 after Crystal Night: he felt shame, despair for his own people, and the need to resist the crimes of his government.

THEOLOGY OF FAITH AND HOPE

From beneath the theology of death a different faith and hope arise. I shall show one image of this other theology that I experienced on my visit to Nicaragua: going to Solentiname.

The flight to San Carlos, near the Costa Rican border, crosses the great Lake Nicaragua. The islands of Solentiname appear, dark jungle green. Today we shall come to this island of which I've dreamed since 1967, when Hermann Schultz asked me to write a foreword to Ernesto Cardenal's *Psalms*. In 1966, Ernesto returned to Nicaragua after prolonged residence abroad. "That was thirteen years before the Triumph," I think, "thirteen more years under the dictatorship—longer than the Hitler era." For me, Solentiname is a kind of holy place, like Jerusalem or Mecca. "I shall kiss the earth," I think, still in the airplane. Somewhere on this planet there must be a piece of land where I can say: "Here. Now. Take your shoes off. The place where you stand is holy ground." Here a few people, artists and campesinos, brought a piece of life into being for a certain time. The intellectuals worked with their hands, and the farmers painted.

The rain begins while we are crossing by motorboat to Solentiname. Outrunning a black wall of clouds, we approach the hilly island. There are women washing clothes on the shore; their clothing glows in bright colors—indigo, red, and blue. After a forty-five minute trip across the lake, the white huts appear. On the pier stands a young soldier, a rifle in his hand. I watch him tie up our boat with his left hand, without putting down his rifle. It hurts to see this. It is unavoidable; during the war of liberation Solentiname was attacked and devastated by the Somosistas. It is necessary, I repeat to myself; but everything we do for "security," that most powerful of ideologies, shrinks our freedom—even here, where security is not an ideology but a real need. I don't want to give up my dream of a Solentiname that has no angel with a flaming sword at the gate. The pain I feel at a sight like this is part of my love for a free Nicaragua.

The cloudburst breaks as we land; we run and jump under the nearest cover, the church, a little structure with no side walls and a dirt floor. The only decoration is the ornamented altar in the center; there we lay our melons. We share one melon, and as the rain lets up somewhat, we go to Ernesto Cardenal's house. I stand once more under a big tree, and embrace it, as though I wished to touch all that is here. The brown horses, which come trustingly closer, the children of the woman from the next island. . . .

Ernesto, dressed in a white peasant shirt, an Indian headband around his forehead, greets us, a little reproachfully because we are so late. Our visit to the refugee camp was one of the many improvisations of our journey. Over glasses of white rum, we immediately begin to speak of Eden Pastora, the renowned Comandante Zero, who leads his own counterrevolutionary band and finds followers here in the South. Why has he become a Judas? Ernesto knew him well, and saw him for the last time in Cuba; there Pastora felt imprisoned although he had complete freedom of movement. Ernesto told us Pastora is a good guerrilla fighter, but has a very unclear political analysis. When the Sandinista Revolution did not offer him a leadership post, he tried going to El Salvador and then to Guatemala. But he could land nowhere—a blind, ambitious big talker. Alejandro told us in the car that Eden Pastora "confuses" the farmers: he is anti-Somosista, anti-imperialist, anti-Sandinista. He is evidently financed by the CIA.

We eat fish that were caught that day in the lake, glorious avocados—each of us gets a huge one—rice, and beans. We talk about Ernesto's understanding of culture in his capacity as Minister of Culture. His basic concern is the participation of everyone in the various forms of artistic expression. "Everyone . . . " Ernesto begins, and then corrects himself—"almost everyone is an artist." Under Cardenal's influence, the farmers in Solentiname began to paint and write poems. I try to build a bridge to a religion in which all who pray are included, and are artists who are taken seriously. Ernesto nods and smiles. Perhaps someday, after all, we shall really hold the congress, the gathering of revolutionary mystics of which we dreamed a year ago in New York. . . .

I find two dimensions of this book especially critical for all who are seriously interested in justice or Christian faith: One is the authors' refusal to view Nicaragua as if it were at a remove from us. In the best feminist tradition, they insist that the meaning of what is happening in Nicaragua must be brought home to U. S. people. They ask, what does Nicaragua tell us about our own lives in the United States? Somehow, these students and teachers of theology have understood the Gospel proclamation that we are One—all of us, in Nicaragua, the United States, Germany. . . . The second dimension of *Revolutionary Forgiveness* that seems terribly significant to me is that its authors are attempting here to do theology on the basis of their engagement with structures of injustice. The primary arena of their praxis is not Nicaragua but rather the

United States, which the Amanecida Collective has come to see more clearly through the lens of their Nicaraguan journeys.

Let me add a third dimension of the work which I also appreciate: the fact that the authors worked collectively. This book might have had a tighter coherence, a more predictable logic, a more dramatic style had it been crafted by one or two people. Instead, we are met by an assortment of theological professors and students, musicians, political activists, rather traditional Christian feminists, radical feminist theorists, parish pastors, and others who mirror *together* what they witnessed in Nicaragua: the *collective* character of creative work, love, faith, and hope.

Finally, when we reflect upon what is to be done, I would suggest praying, and so I close with a prayer that I wrote in 1983 but which is needed even more today:

Prayer for Nicaragua

Spread a big blanket
over the little country of volcanoes
that the bomber fighters may not find it
that the killer squads will not intrude
that the president of the united dead
will forget the little country.

Spread a big blanket
over the little country just four years old
that children may go to school
and even older women like myself
that coffee may be harvested
and medicines distributed
that nobody will be forgotten.

Spread a big blanket
held by all those who love that country
the Virgin Mary has a coat
and St. Francis has a robe
he threw it at the feet of his rich father
and Ho Chi Minh wore a peasant shirt like Sandino
of such cloth the blanket is woven.
Spread a big blanket
made of wishes that breathe so much tenderness
that they become prayers
to love is the word of action
that belongs to God thus the blanket comes from God.

A dark blanket
spread to protect the hope of the poor
until the night will end
until, at last, the night will end.

Preface

This book is not primarily about Nicaragua. It is about thirteen U.S. citizens who, like many thousands of people from the United States, have had the opportunity to visit Nicaragua during the last few years. Among the thirteen of us who make up the Amanecida Collective, we have made five trips to Nicaragua, beginning in January 1983 when Susan Harlow went on an Oxfam America tour. In July 1983 Margarita Suárez left for a six-week stay. In November 1983 Carter Heyward went on a fact-finding trip sponsored by the Nicaragua-Honduras Education Project. In January 1984 Anne Gilson and Kirsten Lundblad spent several weeks in Nicaragua helping lay groundwork for an on-site study program being sponsored by the Episcopal Divinity School in Cambridge, Massachusetts. Finally, in August 1984 Carter, Anne, and Kirsten returned for about a month as participants in the Episcopal Divinity School's Project Nicaragua. With them were eight other seminary-based educators and students: Laura Biddle, Florence Gelo, Elaine Koenig, Virginia Lund, Pat Michaels, Laurie Rofinot, Jane Van Zandt, and Carol Vogler.

This book is in one sense about our lives as U.S. citizens and religious persons. All of us have been, at one time or another, involved in the Christian church, some of us Protestant, some Roman Catholic. Most of us are still active Christians. We note our Christian affiliations because they are significant in the ongoing formation of our spiritual commitments, and because Nicaragua was, for each of us, an arena of spiritual transformation. We will never be the same again, and we will not be able to practice, preach, or teach our religions as if we had not been to Nicaragua.

This book is, thus, a spiritual manifesto, an offering which, we believe, has been inspired by the same revolutionary spiritual movement which empowers women and men throughout the world, and indeed in the United States, to struggle on behalf of food, shelter, medicine, education, dignity, and other embodied forms of justice for all. Because our experiences in Nicaragua are the foundation upon which our collective was built, we hope that this book will give voice to the people of Nicaragua, as we hope that our collective will function as an embodiment of our solidarity with them.

We have tried not to romanticize the Nicaraguan Revolution. Flawed, imperfect, at times erratic, the Sandinista leadership nonetheless can stand proudly on its own commitments and accomplishments. Relative to most other governments in both U.S. and Soviet spheres of influence, the government of Nicaragua is a model in terms of its humanitarian achievements and the extent of its popular support. The Sandinistas themselves are the first to admit that it could be better than it is in terms of liberties. But, like most U.S. citizens who have been to Nicaragua, we thirteen are clear that it is precisely the United States' not-so-covert war on Nicaragua which has precipitated and exacerbated the Nicaraguan government's imposition of such controls as press censorship and its military build-up—two "problems" which the U.S. State Department cites as legitimating U.S. aggression against Nicaragua.

We did not go to Nicaragua with our minds already made up, although in truth we harbored serious doubts about the Reagan Administration's attitudes toward our neighbors in Central America. All of us were "liberal," some of us perhaps "radical" by U.S. standards, but all of us were also firmly rooted in the libertarian ideals set forth in the U.S. Constitution. Such ideals as freedom of the press and freedom of religion have been precious dimensions of our lives in the United States. We took to Nicaragua a predilection for social justice and human rights, the common good and the worth of the individual. We were ready to be critical of the Sandinistas, and we spent a good bit of time in Nicaragua with people who are. We were ready also, in ways which continue to surprise us, to be critical of ourselves—not only our government (about which we have become increasingly alarmed) but also our own lives and values as members of the body politic.[1]

One of our members, Flo Gelo, discusses her own life and values and how they led her to Nicaragua:

I am a thirty-five-year-old woman recently ordained to the Unitarian Universalist ministry. I grew up in a multi-ethnic part of Brooklyn, New York. My memories include elements of the richness of the culture and the traditions of this predominately Jewish and Italian community—the grape arbors, fig trees, the aroma of foods filling the air. Eventually, however, the neighborhood deteriorated. As it became multi-racial, middle-class folks "fled" to suburbia. Crime and violence increased; property values decreased as the neighborhood became undesirable. My parents were first and second generation working-class immigrants. I was raised as a Roman Catholic in a very ethnic family (read: traditional patriarchal style with distinct gender-roles and religion as a dominant influence). Although not destitute, we lived without things that anyone living in the richest country in the world might expect, including a safe place to live. However, not unlike many in the United States, we had no other choice than to live in an unsafe, unclean, ill-policed neighborhood.
I don't remember feeling oppressed. I was very much a part of the fabric of life as I knew and experienced it. I was aware, for example, that black and white children did not often play together, but more frequently fought with each other. I was aware that I never saw a Black or Hispanic in church or in school. I was aware that it was not uncommon to see people with all of their household possessions at the curb of a street; that the morning often revealed damage to homes or parked cars; that no one went out after dark. It didn't even seem unusual to me the morning I joined my friends to inspect a building wall splattered with blood and to

follow the trail of blood one-half block, up a few steps, into the vestibule of a building where a woman who had been stabbed had died during the night. All were typical occurences. I saw no cause for alarm in any of them.

When I was twelve my family and I moved to a middle-class neighborhood on Long Island. I remember my first impressions of my new home—green trees, flowers growing wild, spaces between houses, driveways for clean, new cars, the smell of saltwater in the evening air. There was an abundance of green grass that people dared to walk and play on. Doors to cars and homes remained unlocked. Evenings were full of the sounds of children playing. For the first time, I became aware that not all people lived as I had known them to live—as I had lived.

Prior to our move to Long Island, I had no idea that my family was different from any other family. Within the context of a patriarchal ethnic family and a patriarchal religious tradition, I was like most women and female children of the day—socialized into passive, servile roles without any consciousness of our condition. However, the move to suburbia revealed the ways in which we were different. For the first time, I realized that we were poor, less educated, working-class people with limited experience of the social and cultural world around us. I also learned that this made us socially less acceptable. Long before I realized I was being oppressed as a woman, I became aware of the oppression of growing up working-class poor.

I know that one can grow up oppressed and not know it. When there is nothing against which to compare your situation, there is no way to name oppression. It is what lies outside of your life—your home environment, your daily experience—that informs you that something is wrong. Even then you are encouraged to find reasons that make you solely responsible for your condition, reasons that cause you to believe that you are to blame for your oppression, that there is something deficient or inferior about you. This is especially true when the oppressor is not visible, is outside your immediate daily experience. When you are surrounded by poverty, you don't know that there is anything else; you don't know that you're poor. You may know that you don't always have enough food to eat, or enough money to pay your bills, but you may not know that not everyone is experiencing the same problems.

On Long Island my struggle toward self-redefinition began. I had been living out expectations that were not mine—expectations of my family, church, and society that were limiting me to a life not of my own choosing. I wasn't yet able to express the uniqueness of who I was, but I knew that I did not want to confine my life to marriage after high school, husband, children, and a part-time job to earn a little extra cash for household items. Thus began a long process of breaking away from the old in spite of the fact that I had not yet found anything new to embrace. I simply felt that things were unfair, that something was very wrong, and that I could never be happy or find fulfillment unless I did something different.

I became angry about poverty because I realized that wherever there is poverty there is not only a lack of food, health care, clothing, and education, but that interpersonal tensions and self-denigration are also overwhelmingly present because of unmet needs.

I became angry at patriarchal ethnic familial expectations that encourage self-determination for male children and servitude for female children.

I became angry at a patriarchal religion that elevates everything male and claims unholy everything that is female; that informs me of my lesser being as one not created in the image of God; that denies that I am whole.

Although angry and determined to break free of these forces, I neither realized nor anticipated the pressures that would work to dissuade me. I was unaware that some forces of oppression are not as clearly identifiable as others; that some are more ambiguous, yet equally, if not more, powerful. One can defy public opinion, for example, but it is much more difficult to grasp and confront the internalized oppression of self-doubt and fear.

As I began to redefine my life, justice became a major concern. As I became increasingly concerned about justice, I became increasingly involved in actively resisting social injustice. It was my experience of class oppression that led me to understand those who are victims of other forms of oppression. It is no accident that certain groups of people in this country are the poorest, have the highest incidence of disease, alcohol and drug addiction, unemployment and mental illness. The United States has a long history of exploiting marginalized people, resulting in the mental, physical and spiritual battering of those deemed undesirable: racial/ethnic people, women, gays and lesbians. Eventually, my concerns led me to Nicaragua.

Nicaragua is engaged in a battle against a threat to the revolution that the United States and the contras pose. And it is my anger over the greed and arrogance of the Reagan administration and our government's history of imperialistic activity that impelled me to go to Nicaragua and to join in solidarity with the Nicaraguan people. And it is my rage as a person of faith at the distortion and perversion of values in the name of God that impels me to stand apart from my government or any group that views the U.S. role in Nicaragua and throughout Central America as anything other than immoral.

My political concern is for justice for all people. I don't think one has to be able to analyze root causes of injustice to know that something is radically wrong in the world today. Reason alone can tell us there is something wrong when creating bombs to protect us from the "enemy" has priority over feeding the world's hungry and healing the sick. It is an indication that we have lost sight of the aim and central meaning of human existence.

The Nicaraguans are like me in several ways. Somehow they knew they were oppressed; somehow they rebelled and won their freedom. Now someone, the United States in particular, is trying to take that freedom from them. Since self-determination and the quality of life are my criteria for justice-making, I must voice my opposition to these activities. I know how I love the new life within me—the peace and satisfaction. What motivates me to work for justice is that I know if I want peace and self-determination, then others must want it too.

—*Flo*

The members of Amanecida resonate with Flo's words. In this book, we hope to communicate, collectively and individually, what compels us to seek justice—in Nicaragua, in the United States, and in our own lives.

THE PROCESS OF WRITING THIS BOOK

We have written *Revolutionary Forgiveness* together. Our collectivity has required that we be accountable to one another in what we have written. No one of us has been able to operate on the assumption that this manuscript is a platform simply for her or his own perspective. Throughout the text we have each made our individual contributions, as will be apparent to the reader, but even in these places, each person has worked in relation to the ambience of the larger book. Our disagreements as well as our common voice come through these pages again and again, and we value the tensions between and among us.

We have had to trust that all members of Amanecida would come through when deadlines began to press and that the writing would come together in the end. Collective writing has required all of us to assume editorial duties toward each other's writing. It has also required all of us to be clear about whether we were speaking for the whole group or for ourselves as individuals. We have had to get to know one another's perspectives, biases, and styles, and we have grown in respect for one another's particular and unique contributions.

During the fall of 1984, in a theology class designed for us and by us at the Episcopal Divinity School (Cambridge, Ma.), we in Amanecida discussed and analyzed our experiences of Nicaragua. We read liberation theology. We reflected on issues, such as forgiveness, which had begun to emerge among us as the critical theological foci for our study. We presented information about Nicaragua and helped in interpreting this information to the larger religious community—in parishes, prisons, schools, hospitals. We began to develop an institutional base (at the Episcopal Divinity School) for cross-cultural education.[2] We also began to outline and work on this book.

At the same time we were overwhelmed by the magnitude of what we had begun. All of us were undergoing culture-shock, having recently returned from Nicaragua, and were having to reintegrate our lives, loves, jobs, studies, and priorities at just the moment in which Ronald Reagan was running hard and well for a second term. The contrast between the Nicaraguan society we had met briefly and our own in the United States was stunning. One nation so tiny, the other so huge; one so poor, the other so fabulously rich; one so utterly unpretentious, the other so narcissistic. We found ourselves distressed as we resumed old jobs, found new ones, revitalized or severed old relationships, began to build new ones, and in general tried to keep our balance. Again and again we asked ourselves and one another, What are we going to do about what we have seen and heard and witnessed? The stress precipitated by the power-lessness we felt in the wake of Reagan's landslide took its toll on us. Many of us experienced a profound sense of loneliness in spite of the fact that we had one another's friendship, as well as strong, supportive networks of coworkers with whom we were beginning to build solidarity. Individualism dies hard, and we are all still in this process of dying unto our own individualism and coming into our power as a people united.

Amanecida has worked together in innumerable configurations to produce this book. All of us wrote on the themes of conversion, revolution, and forgiveness that make up the core of the book. Anne Gilson and Carter Heyward, who worked as Amanecida's editors, wrote for the whole collective in weaving together into some coherent fabric the various threads that each of us produced.

Collective writing is a revolutionary business. We have begun to see this. It is revolutionary in its process and vision. No one can control or guarantee the outcome of such writing. No one can expect to enjoy individual accomplish-ment in the ways all of us have learned to recognize as meritorious—that is, when one person's talent, insights, or genius stands out above all the others. The enjoyment of collective writing is in realizing the intellectual and spiritual vitality of that which is born together and in which each of us has played a critical part. In a very real sense, each of us is brought into her or his talent by the others. And so we began this writing project on the assumption—at first more theoretical than practiced—that any attempt to transform creatively the social, political, and spiritual character of our lives must be steeped in corpo-rate vision and collaborative work.[3]

In Chapter One—"Setting the Scene"—we present briefly the history of relations between Nicaragua and the United States. In Chapters Two, Three, and Four, we write of conversion, revolution and forgiveness. These intercon-necting themes evolved from our experiences in Nicaragua and the United States and from our studying together at the Episcopal Divinity School. We see these themes not in a hierarchical, linear sense, but in terms of ongoing movements. Conversion, revolution, and forgiveness are *not* once-in-a-lifetime experiences for most people. They are interwoven processes that may continue to impact our lives.

In our discussions of conversion and forgiveness, we have attempted to expand traditional theological usages of the terms. Chapter Two—"Conversion"—speaks of our beginning to be able to see, feel, think about, and act in solidarity with a world in which most people are not white, educationally-privileged, or economically secure.

"Revolution"—Chapter Three—explores the social, political, and theologi-cal process of transformation in Nicaragua and how it relates to our lives in the United States. In Chapter Four, "Forgiveness," we examine what seemed to us to be the spiritual basis of Nicaraguan society as it is being constructed with the support and leadership of the Sandinistas. We were excited by the determination of Nicaraguan people—intellectuals and peasants, religious and secular folk, adults and children—to build their future together in such a way that all people will be accorded honor and respect. We were stunned by how little fear and hatred, resentment and bitterness, seem to fester in this nation, which has been victimized repeatedly by greedy dictators, U.S. administrations, and multi-national capitalist interests. We heard Nicaraguan peasants speaking of love rather than revenge and we witnessed the government's compassionate efforts to convert and rehabilitate Somoza's former bodyguards. Such encounters led us to ask how these people can forgive those who have tortured and mutilated their parents, lovers, children, neighbors. We began to wonder if we knew the meaning of forgiveness—revolutionary forgiveness. Our study of this question led us to the heart of this book.

A word about the "language barrier": We regretted that so few of us knew enough Spanish during our visits to be able to converse easily with Nicaraguans. Having a translator inhibited spontaneous communication. It also served as an uneasy reminder, to us and the Nicaraguan people, of the distance between North and South and of the cultural myopia in which most U.S. citizens of Northern European descent have been raised. Our visits made us realize that we must learn Spanish well if we are to live with, rather than over, our Latin *compañeras/os.*

At the same time, we learned much about Nicaragua and about ourselves, not only through the good graces of patient translators, but also through such universal "languages" as shared meals, gunfire, laughter, and death. Nonverbal sounds in the night, as well as what we saw, tasted, touched, and smelled, were as important to our meeting Nicaragua and its people as any words we were able to understand. If only for a while and only partially, Nicaragua lifted us across the language barrier and brought us, by the grace of God, to our senses.

So many people made this project possible that it is impossible to name them all. People assisted by helping to plan the trips, generously contributing money to the project, donating supplies, and offering prayer support while we were away. Others made airport runs, talked to anxious friends and families, watered plants, registered us for classes, and took care of our feline and canine companions. Without these contributions to our work, we could not have begun our dialogues with the people of Nicaragua.

The staff, students, and faculty of the Episcopal Divinity School in Cambridge, Massachusetts have encouraged many aspects of this travel and writing venture. We offer a fond and heartfelt thanks to the Very Rev. Harvey Guthrie (dean of EDS from 1974–1985), who contributed in innumerable ways to the support of our work. We also thank the International Missions Program of the Boston Theological Institute, as well as the International Missions Office of the national headquarters of the Episcopal Church.

Oxfam America, the Nicaragua-Honduras Education Project, and *el Nuevo Instituto de Centroamerica* (NICA) are the groups under whose auspices the members of Amanecida travelled to Nicaragua. Joanna Sunshower, Rachel Wyon, Natalie Zimmerman, and Scott Mehlenbacher helped us plan the last trip and were our patient and resourceful translators.

The Rev. Dr. Robert and Dr. Jeanette Renouf—United States consultants to the Anglican Church in Nicaragua—offered hospitality and advice to Kirsten and Anne on their first trip and housed eleven members of Amanecida during parts of our journey in August-September, 1984. The staff of the Anglican Institute in Managua was helpful in setting up meetings and providing us with transportation. Along with the Renoufs, Mary Darkin and Nicholas Cruz helped make our stay at the Institute a time of learning and pleasure. The families of Doña Cruz Altiminando and Doña Cristina Lopez of Estelí offered hospitality to Margarita, Kirsten and Anne.

Sarah Layton Adams and P. Celeste Deroche worked assiduously on the typing. Marvin Ellison and Beverly Harrison proofread with us.

Members of the staff of Orbis Books have worked very hard to bring this project to conclusion. We are grateful to our manuscript editor William Schlau for his sharp editorial judgments. We thank assistant editor Stephen Scharper and assistant marketing director Nancy deWaard for their professional assistance. And we especially thank our acquiring editor Shirley Cloyes for her direction of this project and belief in the aims of this book.

Our families and friends encouraged us along the way of this project, and we thank them for helping us believe in the work we were doing.

Without the people of Nicaragua who spent hours, days, weeks with us, we could not have understood the critical connections between their lives and ours. These *compañeras/os* embodied conversion, revolution, forgiveness. They witnessed to the power of love, drawing us more deeply into a realization of that which some would call "God" and others, simply "love" or "justice." To these courageous women, men, and children, we offer this book as one small sign of solidarity.

We have named ourselves the Amanecida Collective. *Amanecida* means "dawn" or "daybreak." For us, *amanecida* signals a perception of our lives in a fresh and clearer light. As Sister Mary Hartman, who has been working in Nicaragua for almost two decades, suggests, U.S. citizens travel these days to Nicaragua to get spiritual nourishment for the work which awaits them back home in the struggle to convert the United States to the God of the poor and the oppressed. We offer this book as a resource in the on-going work of conversion.

For those named and unnamed who have gone before us, who walk with us, and who will come after us, we give thanks. As we learned in Nicaragua, *"¡El pueblo unido jamás será vencido!"*—"The people united will never be defeated!"

Anne Gilson and Carter Heyward
for the Amanecida Collective
Cambridge, Massachusetts
February, 1986

Nicaragua–U.S. Relations: A Historical Overview*

| 1850 | The United States and Great Britain, without consulting Nicaragua, sign the Clayton-Bulwer Treaty, declaring that both nations will share rights to a trans-Nicaraguan canal. |

1850   The United States and Great Britain, without consulting Nicaragua, sign the Clayton-Bulwer Treaty, declaring that both nations will share rights to a trans-Nicaraguan canal.

1855   U.S. adventurer William Walker is invited by liberal Nicaraguans to head their forces against conservative elements. He is successful and has himself declared president of Nicaragua in 1856. Partly because of confiscating property controlled by tycoon Cornelius Vanderbilt, Walker is forced to surrender to the U.S. military in 1857.

1909   Nicaraguan President Zelaya resigns because of U.S. anger over his canceling U.S. concessions for a trans-Nicaraguan canal.

1912   The first of nine invasions of Nicaragua by U.S. marines takes place. The marines occupy the country for most of the next twenty-five years.

1927   Augusto Cesar Sandino begins his six years of armed resistance to the U.S. marines, who are unable to defeat him.

1933   The U.S. government agrees to withdraw its marines, but only after creating the Nicaraguan National Guard headed by General Anastasio Somoza, who has Sandino executed in 1934.

1937–79   The Somoza dynasty rules Nicaragua as a dictatorship with the support of the U.S. government. President Franklin Roosevelt once said, "He [Somoza] may be a son-of-a-bitch, but he's *our* son-of-a-bitch."

---

*This historical overview is taken from James McGinnis, *Solidarity with the People of Nicaragua* (Maryknoll, N.Y.: Orbis, 1985), pp. 5–7, with 1984–85 up-date information from the Institute for Policy Studies, *In Contempt of Congress: The Reagan Record of Deceit and Illegality on Central America* (Washington, D.C.: ITS, 1985).

1961–79	In 1961, the FSLN (Frente Sandinista de Liberación Nacional, Sandinista National Liberation Front) begins armed resistance and political organization. Its popular base widens in the early 1970s, and many grassroots Christian communities, forming especially in rural areas, give it their support. In 1977–78, the Nicaraguan Catholic church, the business community, and the opposition press side with the FSLN in opposition to Somoza. In July 1979 it is successful in overthrowing the dictator, despite U.S. efforts through the Organization of American States to retain "Somocismo" (a client relationship with the United States), but without Somoza.
1979–80	The Carter Administration provides $75 million in aid, trying to work out a constructive relationship with the revolutionary government, but all such aid is terminated when Ronald Reagan becomes president.
1982–83	"Covert" aid, in the amount of $19 million (President Reagan wanted more), to contras (anti-Sandinista guerrillas) is allocated by Congress for channeling by the CIA. For 1983 the figure was $24 million.
1984	A March 1984 request for an additional $21 million for the contras is denied by Congress. In September 1984 Congress receives a document, "Psychological Operations in Guerrilla Warfare," a manual which members of the CIA have put together to instruct the contras on how to "neutralize" Sandinistas and create "martyrs" for the contras' cause. Earlier in 1984, the United States mined Nicaraguan harbors, damaging a dozen merchant freighters from six countries. Nicaragua brings charges against the United States to the World Court, which agrees to hear the case. The United States withdraws from the litigation, claiming that the World Court has no jurisdiction in this matter.
1985	President Reagan announces that the purpose of U.S. policy against Nicaragua is to make Nicaragua "cry uncle." In April 1985 Congress refuses to allocate funds for "humanitarian" aid to the contras. A week later, President Reagan announces an embargo against Nicaraguan exports and halts all air traffic from the United States to Nicaragua. In June 1985 the Congress votes to allocate $27 million in aid to the contras.
1986	Reagan announces that he will seek $100 million in aid to the contras, including $70 million in military or "lethal" aid.

Introduction

A Feminist Liberation Theological Perspective

When we went to Nicaragua as a group, not all of us, if asked, would have called ourselves feminists, identified ourselves readily as theologians, or understood our work as connected to the aims of liberation theology. In fact, several of us were inclined to resist acknowledging our trips to Nicaragua and our subsequent work as being especially theological or spiritual at all. We have come together, however, over the period of almost a year, to realize that our work in Nicaragua, in the class that followed the August-September 1984 trip, and, in particular, on this book has been undergirded by a feminist liberation theological perspective. Thus we feel it is necessary to explain what some of the fundamental principles of that perspective are.

Feminist liberation theology stands at the intersection of at least two strong currents of contemporary theological thought: the feminist theological movement in the United States, with its explicit commitment to the value and well-being of all people—women, as well as men—and with its attentiveness to the incarnate, embodied, sensual character of all created beings (hence, its celebration, rather than denigration, of such physical resources as food and sexuality as good and holy gifts which are ours to share); and the movement of liberation theology among Latin Americans, Afro-Americans, Asian Americans, and people throughout the world who have discovered God as the heartbeat of the revolutionary work of justice-making. These two currents of contemporary theological effort converge in a theology that focuses on a number of key perceptions. During and after our trip to Nicaragua, our understanding—as a group and as individuals—of those perceptions evolved, deepened, and clarified. What follows is a sketch of our interpretations of some of the major themes of feminist liberation theology.

JUSTICE FOR ALL—AND PERSONAL INTEGRITY

Our experiences in the United States before our trips were very different, but our experiences in and of Nicaragua were surprisingly similar. Part of the reason for this stems from our common commitments. Indeed, the fact that we have all been to Nicaragua recently, despite the war being waged against Nicaragua by our own country, points toward a large degree of common concern and commitment.

Our commitments cover a vast array of issues and foci: commitments to family, friends, lovers, and the institutions in which we work and study; commitments to colleagues, coworkers, students, teachers, employers, and shared goals. Integral to these loyalties is our commitment to justice. We are inspired to work toward justice—which we define as right-relation—by the voices of all people who call us into the struggle for human dignity, survival resources, and the creation of a world in which every man and woman is truly at home. Our efforts as theological students, teachers, and ministers revolve around the work of liberation. As such, we are liberation theologians who believe that the moral relationship between human beings and God is one of cooperation in co-creating justice wherever there is oppression—so that all races, classes, nations, and persons can live as subjects of their lives. We have begun to see, as the chapters which follow will demonstrate, that the co-creation of justice is our corporate vocation. It is God's call to us, as a people, not simply God's call to each of us as individuals.

Inspired by liberation theology's emphasis on praxis, we began composing this text on the assumption that theology must be done, not simply talked about and studied, and that it must be done together, in community. We realized that the validity of our work must be borne out in our own lives. This has necessitated some genuine soul-searching on the part of each member of Amanecida, as well as within the group as a whole. It has entailed steady engagement with one another, as well as with people elsewhere in our lives, at school and work, and in families. Again and again we have been challenged, and have challenged others, to show forth what we and others actually mean in our theological discourse about God, Christ, church, world, self, others, good, evil. . . .

Throughout our work together, each of us has nursed a variety of questions and doubts about her or his own place in the struggle for justice, including Amanecida's collaborative attempt. Each of us asked, sometimes silently, sometimes aloud: In what way can I make any difference in this work? Can I disagree and still be part of this group? What can I learn from and teach the others? How does my spirituality fit into our theological work? Because we do not live together or work on the same jobs out in the world, who are "we"? Some answers to these questions, and others, are borne out in the chapters which follow. More and more Amanecida's members realized that our unity had begun to be enhanced by our honest conflicts and differences. We began to see that unless people embrace their distinct and sometimes tension-inducing individual experiences and perspectives, they cannot hope to work together creatively. This seems to us a valuable lesson not only for Amanecida, but for all people who are attempting to work together for justice in the world.

FEMINISM: A LINK TO OTHER STRUGGLES

Feminism is a controversial movement. It signifies Amanecida's lines of continuity with the abolitionist and women's rights movements of the nineteenth and twentieth centuries. The feminist movement has never gained a foothold among those white males who hold authority in the religious and secular spheres of public life. Nor has feminism been popular in the United States among those who see their well-being as inextricably bound up in the lives and values of the Anglo males who constitute the ruling class of U.S. society. Feminism has been, and continues to be, a genuinely popular movement among those women and men who have helped one another learn the extent to which sex- and gender-roles inhibit the creativity of all people and block the possibility of economic security for women, as well as for all except ruling-class men. Many white feminist women and men have far to go in ridding themselves—their values and commitments—of the racism and class elitism which too often have turned feminism into a movement of white, upwardly-mobile females.[1] Amanecida hopes that this book will illustrate, in some small way, the extent to which a feminist commitment—to be truly on behalf of all people—necessitates struggling against white supremacy, economic exploitation, imperialistic activities, and "compulsory heterosexuality,"[2] as well as male gender superiority.

In a very personal way, Amanecida's participants began to voice a feminist commitment in our work as a direct result of our own experiences of white male domination in U.S. society. The twelve of us who are female began to hear one another speaking painfully, and boldly, of these experiences. The one male among us testified that his own life has been distorted frequently by gender expectations. We began to realize that to ignore the effects of sexism at work among us was to cut ourselves off from the possibility of any intelligent study of our lives as U.S. citizens and religious people. If we cannot recognize the details of our own lives, how can we honestly examine structures that shape our lives and the lives of others, whether in the United States or in Nicaragua? In doing feminist liberation theology, we must begin where we are, attentive to the empowering and disempowering, benign and malevolent forces in our own life together. Amanecida cannot do liberation theology without paying careful attention to the ways in which we ourselves have been formed, and deformed, by unjust social and theological constructs. It is in restudying our lives that we find links between the forces which have oppressed the people of Nicaragua and those which continue to break the bodies and spirits of many women and men in the United States. As in Central America, South Africa, and other parts of the globe, most people in the United States have been deprived historically of having any basic right to shape their own destiny.

People deprived of this right—this life-enhancing power—live as objects of other people's agendas. Much more than any member of Amanecida, most oppressed people in the world live in situations in which those who rule their lives have determined life and death conditions for them: hunger, cold, homelessness, poor health, joblessness or lack of meaningful employment, illiteracy, torture. People do not *choose* to live in poverty or hunger. These conditions are imposed on them. As we in Amanecida have begun to recognize ways in which we share the power that oppresses most of the human family, we can begin to seek ways of challenging and changing the structures of our own lives. At the same time, as we begin to see ways in which we also live outside the realm in which life and death decisions are made for us, we can begin to join our voices, minds, and bodies with people throughout the society and world who struggle for their own liberation.

A FEMINIST UNDERSTANDING OF SEXUALITY

Amanecida is committed to the well-being and human rights of gay men and lesbians in the United States and elsewhere. We cannot, in good faith, dismiss the injustices done to lesbians and gay men as a trivial issue relative to the urgent matters of our time. Lesbians and gay men are dying because of the forces of heterosexism (compulsory heterosexuality) and homophobia (fear of sexual relations between members of the same sex). Our commitment to the liberation of lesbians and gay men requires that we confront those people and policies which proclaim sexual relationships between men and women, heterosexual marriage, and nuclear family constellations as normative for the health of society. In confronting the heterosexism that is embedded in our society, we discover how deeply the homophobia which holds heterosexism in place runs among us all, and we discover that this pervasive homophobia alienates each of us from him or her self—as well as from one another.[3].

Sexuality cannot be adequately understood or addressed as simply a private matter. In the United States, as throughout the world, vast amounts of public policy have been constructed for the purpose of controlling human sexuality—specifically of limiting its expression to heterosexual marriage (and, according to the Roman Catholic church, primarily for the purpose of procreation). The purpose and effect of such public policy is to hold in place the control of males (usually white and propertied) over the lives and bodies of females (usually nonwhite and nonpropertied). Thus, the problems of heterosexism and homophobia cannot be separated from those of gender, racial, and class oppression. To try to do so is to underestimate the systemic nature of the forces of oppression in the world and to miss altogether the key questions in any adequate analysis of injustice: Who controls whom? Who holds the power over whose lives? Amanecida trusts that, in the illustrations of how our lives are linked to the lives of the Nicaraguan people, it will become clearer that race, class, gender, and sexual preference are not personal and separate issues, but rather constitute, together, an expansive terrain for the work of liberation.

A FEMINIST UNDERSTANDING OF SPIRITUALITY

Amanecida is a diverse group. This diversity looms large in our spiritualities, as we represent different ecclesial backgrounds and foregrounds. Carol is

Moravian. Flo is a Unitarian Universalist minister. Margarita and Kirsten belong to the United Church of Christ, and Susan is a United Church of Christ minister. Six of us are Episcopalians: Laura, Anne, Carter, Virginia, Laurie, and Jane; Carter and Jane are Episcopal priests. Pat is a musician in an Episcopal church. Like several of us, Elaine is a former Roman Catholic. She is now postchristian and also is wrestling with the possibility of joining the Episcopal church. All of us are, or have been, located in the seminary communities in the Boston area. Even before this particular writing project, most of us brought explicit feminist sensibilities to our work in the church.

Several of us join our voices with other feminist theologians and identify ourselves as christian/postchristian feminists. This is not entirely a question of where we stand in relation to the institutional church although that is, to be sure, a question with which many of us find ourselves struggling. Rather, our christian/postchristian identity is steeped in our realization of what we believe and with whom we stand in solidarity. We believe in a deity of justice, and we stand with women and other marginalized people within and beyond the institutional church. We must denounce the life-denying deeds done in the name of the patriarchal Christian god, and we refuse to have our lives and faith and dreams defined by those Christian men who see themselves as special bearers of the image of God in this world. In moving beyond the definitions of woman which have been shaped by Christian misogyny, we claim our power as subjects of our own lives. Our christian/postchristian faith becomes increasingly an advocacy posture for the self-determination of all people who have been objectified and damaged by the imperialistic, racist, sexist, heterosexist, classist, and anti-Semitic deeds done "in the name of Christ." The Jesus of whom we speak in these pages, the one most of us in Amanecida call "Christ," is no imperial sovereign. He is one who stands beside us, by the power of the Spirit, and helps move the struggle for justice and peace along.[4]

Some of us are more comfortable than others with patriarchal religious terms, such as "God," "Christ," "Lord," "conversion," and "forgiveness." All of us are aware of the power of words to evoke strong memories and feelings among us, as among others. We know that language can function in the service of either subjugation or liberation. We have not used religious language carelessly in our book, and for that reason we have employed it differently from time to time in these pages. We have tried to honor one another, working to use words on behalf of empowerment and liberation. We have used words to reflect our historical experiences and to address our need for liberation from oppressive forces. We have attempted to use language in such a way as to illustrate our new experiences of conversion, revolution, and forgiveness—and to invite our readers to share in these experiences.

Most of us understand a commitment to nonoppressive God-language as involving an avoidance of racist, male-dominating, or hierarchical words. The main theological issue for us in our language has been a growing sensitivity to the historical and current ways in which God-language has been used to perpetuate injustice. This means that we in Amanecida have attempted to be clear about the particular contexts and meanings of our religious language. It has meant also that we have not tampered in any way with the language employed by Nicaraguan people as they spoke to us of God.

In our spiritual commitments, we share a concern with justice as the norm for living our lives. Throughout our book, we seek to reflect this concern in our use of religious language by referring to God as imaging women as well as men. The deity illuminated in these pages is both God himself and God herself. She is our sister, our lover, our friend, just as surely as he is our brother, our lover, and friend. The Jesus of whom we speak is at once our liberator, a revolutionary, a peasant, an advocate. Our holy one is God of the poor. It is she who moves the struggle.

Where the word *God* is capitalized, we mean to communicate the traditional understanding of God as well as our feminist understandings of the one who is inclusive of the lives of women and racial/ethnic minority men. Where we do not capitalize the definite noun *god*, we refer to the perversion of the concept of god that has kept in place structures of injustice, resulting in our worship of false gods or idols: for example, the god of the status-quo, the god of white male wealth, the god of the National Security Council.

When we capitalize *Christianity* or *Christian*, we allude to the institutional, historical character of a particular religion. Where *christian* is not capitalized, we refer to those persons who may or may not be in the institutional church but who are inspired, in some explicit way, by the life of Jesus. By not always capitalizing *christian*, we attempt to signal some awareness of the often gross effects of Christian imperialism. A final note on capitalization: When we refer to the faith of Nicaraguans, we have kept the traditional capitalization because we think it is not our place to interpret our Nicaraguan sisters' and brothers' understandings of their faith for them.

The eleven members of Amanecida who were in Nicaragua in August-September 1984 shared daily rituals—from silent periods of meditation around a burning candle, to calling on the names of friends and loved ones we had left at home, to sharing bread and wine in an informal eucharistic setting. These brief rituals, led by different members of the group, helped keep us centered in our faith and purpose—and sometimes in our differences. We concurred that these periods of meditation were vital to what we were doing in Nicaragua.

Along with these rituals, the eleven of us drew strength and joy from playing together. We played cards. We sang, swam, and hiked. After about three weeks of eating beans and rice, we had a fiesta together on a bucket of potatoes which a Salvadoran refugee collective had given us. In Estelí during our last week we had a talent show. We relished our silliness, play, togetherness, and we knew well that they, too, were dimensions of our spiritual imaging of a God who enjoys her people.

We in Amanecida understand spirituality as inseparable from our daily lives. Our spirituality is the ground on which we stand, the arena in which we live as we move with growing determination to resist the life-denying domestic and foreign policies of the U.S. government. Our spirituality compels us actively to seek justice in our various communities—our local communities as well as our global village. Members of Amanecida have worked in the feminist and gay/ lesbian movements within and beyond the churches; we have worked in U.S. prisons, cities, suburbs, shelters, abortion clinics; we have been involved in the civil rights movement in the United States, the anti-Vietnam War movement, and South African, Filipino, and Central American solidarity movements (including Sanctuary). We continue to discover that God is the connecting link between and among these activities and between and among our lives. We thank the one who is our sister and mother, father and brother, our lover and friend for bearing with us and carrying us on.

CHARITY OR SOLIDARITY?

As persons schooled in liberalism, we have found ourselves at times torn between the assumption that we should "help the poor" and the opportunity to stand with poor and marginalized people. This tension, between charity and solidarity, marks our work in these pages as elsewhere in our lives. Day after day it arose in Nicaragua, as it arises in the United States. In the following passage Laurie describes one instance of this tension. Stylistically, we illustrate here what becomes prominent in the rest of the book: allowing each of us individually to speak in her or his voice by italicizing the person's contribution and indicating at the end of each passage whose it is:

Our group was eating a late dinner in the Hotel Meson in Estelí. I was just finishing up a huge chicken dinner, with salad, rice, fried bananas, when a small (age 6?) boy in torn dirty clothes tugged at my arm and asked me if he could have the scraps of my dinner. His eyes were hurt, angry, haunted. Stunned, I gave him my plate and watched as he took it and then sat at another table and hungrily ate, bypassing the rice and salad I had left and picking the remaining meat off the bones.

For ten minutes I struggled with an overwhelming sense of guilt, shame, horror, wondering what my responsibility was in that situation, and I felt great sadness for this child who was in the streets late at night begging for food. I wondered if the revolution would help this child's extreme need, if it had, in fact, enabled him to survive up to age six. This experience really numbed me at the time, as did other encounters with children who were suffering.

—LAURIE

Faced with the tension between charity and solidarity with the people of Nicaragua and their revolution, the group's commitment to solidarity deepened, an issue Anne addresses in the following paragraphs.

Do-gooders. The focus of do-gooding has traditionally been on the doer. Doing a good deed, as most people in the United States conceive of it, is a way to keep the lives of the poor and marginalized at a safe, comfortable distance. Taking food baskets to needy families and making tax-deductible contributions to charities have become hallmarks of privileged citizens of the United States. Doing good becomes a superficial effort designed more to ease the consciences of those who hold power than to actually challenge the economic disparity in our society. Doing good, we manage to silence the voices of protests because we appear to fix that which is hurting, all the while ignoring and suppressing movement toward systemic change.

Some people saw our trips to Nicaragua as acts of charity or do-goodism; however, we were not sent to evangelize Nicaraguans; our purpose was not to convert left-of-center Nicaragua to the increasingly right-of-center U.S. way. The do-gooder image implies doing something to or for—not with—Nicaraguan people. It becomes a trivialization of the relationship between Nicaraguans and U.S. people.

Our understanding of spirituality has led us to recognize the necessity of solidarity—the standing with those who struggle for justice, a process that enables us to discover God working within us as individuals and communities. More than one of us has felt guilt and shame about what our country is doing in Nicaragua. Some of us may even have personalized that guilt and shame. To do authentic good we must first move beyond that guilt and shame that breeds separation and fear. We must be converted to one of the essential elements of solidarity: trust that empowers us to see that our experiences are not ours alone, that the problems in our society, and their solutions, are corporate, and that those problems are ours, not simply mine or yours. This trust can open us so that we may be touched, maybe even moved, by poor people, women, people of color, lesbians and gay men, people of other faiths, differently-abled people, the elderly, and people of nations we have been told are our enemies. Charity emphasizes the distinction between the privileged and the marginalized. We must move beyond it to solidarity, which is the foundation of revolutionary and systemic change.

—ANNE

The solidarity of which Anne writes is one of the principle themes of Latin American and feminist liberation theology. This is why, for instance, every major Latin American liberation theologian is engaged with a basic Christian community. Those communities are the places in which solidarity is grounded, and that is the reason that many of the key experiences described in this book occur in basic Christian communities. For it was there, in the midst of relationships of solidarity and trust, that we deepened our understanding of something we had been learning in our work in various groups in the United States: to foster systemic change, we must stand with the poor and marginalized. We learned more deeply that making changes in our lives and systemic changes in the United States and Nicaragua are all interrelated processes.

This process of moving from charity to solidarity is not simple. Pat points out that the first step is to understand something of the history and contexts of other people's lives. It involves becoming better informed.

What must happen is for the U.S. people, the electorate, to become better informed about the lives of people elsewhere in the world and how the lives of the people of Nicaragua, for example, are connected to our own lives as U.S. citizens. In a democracy, it is we the people who must be held accountable for the morality of public policy, whether foreign or domestic. Only if we act and elect on the basis of what we actually know about how others live can a foreign policy be shaped which will be beneficial both to persons in other countries and to us at home.

Tragically, the knowledge we have of the rest of the world is minimal. What do we actually know about Nicaraguans? Hondurans? Salvadorans? Guatemalans? Russians? Cubans? Peruvians? South Africans? Ethiopians? Chileans? Irish? Puerto Ricans? What do we actually know about Canadians or Mexicans? Most of us know very little. We get our information primarily from TV and mass media journalism. Realizing that most U.S. citizens know very little about the rest of the world, those who control the media attempt to explain to us the context of the news stories we are watching or reading about. But who, we must inquire, controls those who control the media? The United States is quick to condemn Nicaragua for its censorship of the press, but does the U.S. government not have some control over what we hear, or do not hear, about life in the Soviet Union? Nicaragua? The Philippines?

Simply finding out the truth becomes revolutionary work for us here in the United States. Simply to ask for more than we are given on the major news networks is to make a revolutionary inquiry and to take the first step toward solidarity with people under siege in other nations. We are not a well-informed nation. We are as widely-propagandized as any other nation. And so our revolutionary responsibility may well begin simply in our search for our own history as a nation and for some actual accounting for how people live and work and play in Nicaragua and elsewhere in the world. This strong desire to know is what prompted our trips to Nicaragua.

—Pat

Feminist and Latin American liberation theologies impel us to move beyond charity, to be converted to revolutionary forgiveness and solidarity. This process, as Pat establishes, begins with a rigorous search for an understanding of the contexts of the lives of peoples different from ourselves. For this reason the opening chapter of this book explores the context and history of the lives of Nicaraguans and of the grim history of the relationship between the United States and Nicaragua. This book is in part a record of our dedication to change that relationship and to deepen our relationships toward justice.

1

Setting the Scenes: Relations between the United States and Nicaragua

It's essential—we want to make it clear—that our objectives are to reconstruct our country. We want to be ourselves. Increase the standard of living of our people. And maintain relations with all the countries of the world. . . . Our interests here are interests for peace. We have had war in our country and we don't want war anymore. And we will do whatever we need to do to avoid this war except humiliate ourselves. We will struggle for the rights of the majority until the end.

—CARLOS MANUEL[1]

Carter recalls a conversation in Managua:

"I came here the same year [1956] that 'the old man' [the senior Somoza] died," replied Mary when I asked when she had left her native Bluefields on the East Coast to find work in the Spanish-speaking western part of Nicaragua.[2] A Black, English-speaking housekeeper and cook at the Anglican Institute about ten kilometers south of Managua, Mary Darkin greeted us the night of our arrival from Miami with a table spread with fresh mangoes, rice, beef stew, beans, and unbelievably potent Jalapeño sauce. For the next six days, as we were introduced to Nicaraguan people, culture, and politics, Mary spoke quietly with us around the edges of each day, as we would take turns in the dish-washing and table-setting routines of early morning desayuno *(breakfast) and late night* cena *(dinner).*

She volunteered little opinion about the changes in Nicaragua since the junior Somoza's fall in 1979. In fact, she said little at all, except when spoken to directly, conjuring up for me an image reminiscent of growing up in the U.S. South—the Black woman who cooks and serves but does not join white people at the table and who speaks only when spoken to . . . .

"What is Bluefields like?" I asked.

"Nice," Mary smiled.

"Why did you leave?"

"To work."

"Do you like it here?"

"Yes."

"What especially do you like?"

"I like this house and the Renoufs [Bob and Jeannette Renouf, the U.S. couple who had directed the Anglican Institute since early 1980]. I like the people who come here. I like where I live [a small private room off the kitchen], and this house and grounds. It's beautiful."

The Anglican Institute has become, over the years, a center for study and relaxation for members of Anglican and other churches who are working or visiting in Nicaragua. Since the 1979 Triumph, and under the Renouf's direction, the institute has become increasingly a place in which people learn about the revolution and the church's work in relation to it. From the brochures available near the door to the thoughtful, analytical perspectives of Bob and Jeannette Renouf, the house reverberates with a low-key, well-considered appreciation of what has been accomplished in Nicaragua since the Sandinistas came to power.

Members of Amanecida enjoyed strolling with Mary and Nicholas Cruz, the Spanish-speaking grounds attendant, in the tropical gardens in which the Anglican Institute is nestled. This property, on which trees heavy with bananas and persimmons lean into one another and varieties of thick foliage abound (especially during the rainy season of our fall 1984 visit), once belonged to an affluent Nicaraguan family and has only, since the revolution, become the property of the church.

Nicholas had an elfin quality. A bone-thin, barefoot man with curly grey hair, a light rough beard, and bronze skin, he donned a wide-billed cap and knickers, and seemed always to have one yard tool or another in his hands. Speaking Spanish and with broad, swooping hand gestures, Nicholas conveyed a passion for the land, this piece of property on which he had grown up as its attendant. He literally sprang, both feet off the ground, from tree to tree, naming each and plucking pieces of fruit to offer us. Sensing our pleasure, which we felt we could relate only inadequately through our language-barrier, Nicholas more than once would wave his spade or machete in the air and, with his other arm as well, point toward the sky in praise of "el Creador"—the Creator.

Unlike Mary, Nicholas was eager to tell how he felt about Somoza, the revolution, and the Sandinistas. With Mary as translator, Nicholas spoke emphatically, with arms flailing and black eyes snapping.

"Somoza was no good. No good. He hated the people. He hated the land. He did nothing good."

"And the revolution?"

"Yes. It was good. Thanks be to God, the Creator! We are happy, a joyous people. Can't you tell it!?"

"Are you happy with the Sandinistas in power?"

"I am happy. It is good. Praise God! Can't you see—the land is good!" Nicholas fell to his knees and rubbed the earth and, in an instant, jumped up and raised his hands, all covered with dirt. *"You see, it is so beautiful."*

Back in the house, Mary cooked up some meat and beans. Standing at the sink, washing several pots left over from breakfast and lunch, I was a little anxious about asking Mary what I wanted to know—What did she really think of her country and the government? She so obviously steered clear of our group's "political" conversation. . . .

"Mary," I managed to begin, *"what do you think of the government of this country today?"*

"I don't like it very much."

"Why?"

"We spend all our time waiting in line, and then we can't get what we're waiting for—toilet paper, milk, sugar. Everything costs too much now . . . . "

"It wasn't this way before, during Somoza's time?"

"No."

"It was better?"

"No," Mary hesitated. *"It was worse."*

"In what ways was it worse?"

Mary was silent for a moment. Then, for the first time in the conversation, I felt her looking directly at me. I put down the sponge and stared back as she spoke slowly:

"Somoza, the old man, and the son, the last Somoza, were tyrants. They kept everything for themselves. They were greedy. Especially the son. He was much like your president."

"President Reagan?" My voice no doubt conveyed surprise at the suddenness of her indictment.

"Yes," she nodded, then turned back to the stove and was silent.

It took a minute or two for me to gather my thoughts. . . .

"Well, Mary, are the Sandinistas different from Somoza?"

"Yes."

"How are they different?"

"I don't know. . . . They're just not at all the same. I think they are trying to do what's good. This is different from Somoza."

"Are you saying that, even though the lines are long and everything costs too much, this is a better place to live now than before?"

"I think so."

"Mary, what do you think about the United States government's attitude toward Nicaragua?"

"It is wrong."

"But, Mary, President Reagan also tells us that the lines are long and everything costs too much in Nicaragua. And he also says that the Sandinistas are racist—that black people and Miskitos are being oppressed by the Sandinistas. And that there's no freedom in Nicaragua. And that that's why the United States should be trying to get rid of the Sandinistas. . . . "

By this time Mary and I were standing face to face.

She nodded, "Some of what he says is true and some of it is untrue. But he is wrong in his attitude. The United States should keep out of our affairs. People here can handle our own problems."

"Do you think the up-coming [fall 1984] elections in Nicaragua will make any difference in how your country is being led?"

"I hope so."

"Can you vote for anyone you want to?"

"Yes."

"Who do you want to win?"

"I don't know."

"Do you think the Sandinistas will win?"

"Yes."

"Then what difference do you think can be made by having the elections?"

"Some other people will also win, and the Sandinistas will be okay. They are not awful. Some of them are even good."

"And so it's okay with you if the Sandinistas continue to govern this country?"

"Yes."

"But you also want some changes to happen?"

"Yes."

"And you want the United States to leave you alone?"

"Yes."

—CARTER

Like the above conversation at the Anglican Institute, the experiences that are described and reflected upon in this book took place against two settings: Nicaragua and the United States. While in Nicaragua, the members of the Amanecida Collective witnessed the tangible effects of the long history of U.S. involvement in Nicaragua, and our experiences informed our understanding of our country, of the vision of the Nicaraguan people, and ultimately of ourselves. We feel it is necessary, then, to begin by sketching the history and current state of the relations between the United States and Nicaragua. Following a historical overview, this chapter will focus upon current U.S. policy toward Nicaragua and the justifications the U.S. government offers for making war against the people of Nicaragua.

FROM WALKER TO THE SOMOZAS

The Spanish colonized Nicaragua in the sixteenth century. The year 1821 is celebrated throughout Latin America as the year in which the continent won its independence from Spain. But this independence was to be short-lived in Nicaragua. In 1855, William Walker, a U.S. entrepreneur and friend of Cornelius Vanderbilt, went to Nicaragua under the banner of Manifest Destiny to help defray a possible civil war between the liberals of León and the conservatives of Granada. Walker was successful in his intervention and he set himself up as president of the country. One of his first acts as president was to reinstitutionalize slavery in Nicaragua. Two years later, as a result of his falling out of the grace of his U.S. financial cohorts, Walker had to flee Nicaragua.

In 1898, José Santos Zelaya, a liberal, revolted against the conservatives who had held power since Walker's ouster and became president. Zelaya began a process of modernization and reform but in 1909, when he refused to grant canal rights to the United States, the U.S. State Department supported a revolt by the conservatives. Following Zelaya's forced resignation, the conservatives came back into power, bringing U.S. control with them.[3]

In 1912, the U.S. marines landed in Nicaragua to secure their control of Nicaraguan finances, railroads, and communication. From this point on, the U.S. military was prepared to assist the Nicaraguan government in putting down a host of uprisings and revolts by liberals who were seeking a more humane national government.

In 1927, a young general, Augusto Cesar Sandino, refused to sign a peace treaty designed to end the guerrilla war between the liberals (led by Sandino) and the conservatives (backed by the United States). The other liberal leaders signed, but Sandino said: "I am not prepared to surrender my weapons even if everybody else does. I would rather be killed along with the few who accompany me, because it is better to die as rebels under fire than to live as slaves."[4]

Sandino wanted the United States out of Nicaragua. Having divorced himself from the aims and strategies of other liberals, he assembled a rag-tag army of peasants and continued fighting the marines. They could not defeat him and his small band of peasants. In 1933, the marines left, but not until they had been replaced by a new police force, the Nicaraguan National Guard, headed by U.S.-educated General Anastasio Somoza, a liberal. Following the marines' departure, Sandino signed a peace treaty with the Nicaraguan government and returned to the mountains to help the peasants organize cooperative agricultural centers. On February 21, 1934, Sandino was assassinated on the orders of General Somoza.

As head of the National Guard, Anastasio Somoza seized power in a coup in 1937. He and his sons were to rule Nicaragua as a family fiefdom for forty-two years, and the National Guard served as their personal army. The elder Somoza was assassinated in 1956 and was followed by his older son, Luis Somoza Debayle, who ruled until his death in 1967. Finally, Anastasio (Tacho) Somoza Debayle took power and ruled until 1979 when he was overthrown by the

Sandinista-led insurrection. After his downfall in 1979, even some of his closest cohorts (people living today in Miami, San Juan, and elsewhere) admitted that Tacho Somoza was "mad on greed," "a pig," "a terrible man." With guns, money, and the United States on his side, he had held Nicaragua in his grip until he fled the country on the eve of the revolutionary victory. With him he took his wife, his mistress, the coffin bearing the remains of his dead father—and all but a few dollars of Nicaragua's national treasury.

The Somozas' rule of Nicaragua was characterized by oppression of the poor, injustice, and violent and ruthless repression of any form of dissent. The use of violence by the National Guard, the Somozas' instrument of repression, grew to horrendous proportions when the insurrection against Anastasio Somoza Debayle gained strength in the 1960s and 1970s:

> Bombardment of villages, cutting of children's throats, violation of women, burning huts with peasants in them, mutilation as torture— these were the study courses which the U.S. professors of civilization had taught the National Guard during the period of the guerrilla resistance led by Augusto Cesar Sandino from 1927-1932.[5]

These atrocities, perpetuated by funds from the United States, had continued for forty years and were instrumental in the Somozas' relentless drive for complete control over all economic interests of the country. The atrocities were to begin again when the United States established and began to fund remnants of the National Guard—the contras.

THE ROOTS OF REVOLUTION: CONDITIONS UNDER SOMOZA

Often in the United States, when we hear or speak of revolution, we think about wars and the possibilities of totalitarian communist regimes taking power against the will of the people. We seem to have forgotten U.S. history and the history of France, in which revolutions took place in order to liberate people from a tyrannical, hierarchical power. We seem to have forgotten that it is when people are living in oppressive conditions that they will rise up to claim life rather than to live in conditions which appear to produce only death. Change is inevitable, yet many governments and principalities will try to hold on to absolute power by means of control and terror rather than to see the inevitability of the people making their own decisions for their lives.

In order to understand the revolution in Nicaragua, it is important to understand the roots of oppression which held the people in chains for years. Nicaragua has a history of domination and imperialism which, until the Sandinistas' victory, had kept 80 percent of the rural population illiterate and 5 percent of the population owning 58 percent of the arable land (of which the Somoza family owned 23 percent). Fifty percent of the people had an average income of about $90 a year. Eighty percent had no running water; 59 percent no electricity; 47 percent no sanitary facilities; and 69 percent lived in houses with dirt floors. Over the last several decades of Somoza's rule there had been epidemics of malaria, polio, tuberculosis, typhoid, and gastroenteritis. By the time of Somoza's last years in power, more than one hundred babies died out of every one thousand born; and six of every ten deaths of these children were from curable infectious diseases.[6] Such reprehensible social conditions were bound to precipitate social unrest and, finally, revolution, since the Somoza dynasty demonstrated a transparent refusal to create justice.

VISIONS OF A NEW NICARAGUA:
THE FSLN AND CHRISTIAN BASE COMMUNITIES

In response to the repression, oppression, injustice, and detestable social and economic conditions under Anastasio Somoza Debayle,some in Nicaragua organized and worked toward a vision of a country devoted to the uplifting of the poor. During the 1960s and 1970s the group that led the struggle against Somoza was the Frente Sandinista de Liberación Nacional (FSLN). The FSLN was formed in 1961, and during the 1960s the group combined military and guerrilla actions with organizing among the poor, students, unions, and other groups. In the early 1970s the FSLN stepped up the level of armed combat.

In December 1972 an earthquake jolted Nicaragua and killed some ten thousand people in Managua alone. Somoza and his cronies syphoned off vast amounts of the relief money that poured in and, in short, used the widespread devastation as a source of profit. In the wake of the devastation and the Somocistas' blind greed, the FSLN stepped up its aid to and organizing among those hardest hit, the poor. The FSLN continued its popular guerrilla war, and the level of indiscriminate repression by the National Guard increased. During the early and mid-1970s various groups, such as the *comunidades de base* (Christian base communities), began working openly with the FSLN until the revolt grew to a point that the insurrectionists were able to overthrow Somoza in July of 1979. Throughout the struggle, the Sandinistas' vision had been of a just Nicaragua in which the poor and marginalized—turned away and oppressed by U.S.-backed dictators—would inherit the land and food and necessities of life that they needed to become subjects of their history.

United with the FSLN in this vision were the Christian base communities, a major force in bringing Somoza's reign to its end. The base communities had been organized by priests, nuns, and laity—largely peasants—in the mid-1960s. The community in Solentiname (an island in Lake Nicaragua), which Father Ernesto Cardenal had helped organize, was one such group among the many which joined their voices with the FSLN in calling for justice and for the removal of Somoza from power. The base communities were composed of peasants and workers, mostly Roman Catholics, who came together in people's homes to study scripture and to discuss the gospel message as it pertained to their lives. They searched for answers in scripture which would help them make sense of their lives in an oppressive situation. They began to see Jesus as the liberator who had come to teach a new way of living in the world in which all persons would treat one another with respect, because no one was greater than anyone else in the eyes of God. Seeking not vengeance but equality and justice, these Christian peasants and workers began to understand that the rich also needed liberation from the powers of death which kept them from knowing how to love their neighbors. Thus, the Christian base communities provided a valuable resource to the revolution which toppled Somoza. Still today many of these groups meet regularly to carry on their work for justice against the U.S.-backed contras, who threaten to undo all the accomplishments which have been made since 1979.

AFTER THE TRIUMPH: RECONSTRUCTING A NEW NICARAGUA

After the fall of Somoza, the members of the new government continued to work for the goals they had pursued during the insurrection: a just nation in which the needs of the poor are of paramount importance. The Nicaraguans, 80 percent of whom had lived in abject poverty under the Somozas, had begun to build their nation on behalf of the common good. Education and health care for all Nicaraguans—but especially for the poor who for so long had been denied them—became two of the foremost priorities of the new government. Susan, who was on the Oxfam America study tour in 1983, has written about the Sandinistas' focus upon education and health care for the poor:

> *Just eight months after the FSLN had defeated Somoza, the new government organized a major literacy campaign. Using seventeen thousand volunteer teachers (mostly women and teenagers from urban areas), Father Fernando Cardenal, the National Director of the Adult Literacy Campaign, organized an effort which reduced the illiteracy rate from 50 percent to 12 percent. Cardenal described the process as "social awareness" building. Speaking to the Oxfam America study tour group in January 1983, Cardenal explained: "Through the literacy campaign in Nicaragua, the people learn the history of the country and that they are destined to be the owners of this country. While learning social awareness, they also learn to read."*
>
> *Using workbooks developed in pilot projects in the field, the literacy campaign of 1980 enabled people in remote rural areas to reach a fourth-grade level of reading and writing. They began with passages such as the following from the book El Amanecer del Pueblo (The Dawn of the People):*
>
> *Austerity*
>
> *Our country has many debts. It is broke.*
> *Many citizens are unemployed.*
> *We don't have many crops.*
> *Somocismo is to blame for all of this.*

In spite of these conditions, we can improve the economy.
With more dedication, we will increase the country's resources.
We are sharing what little the Somocistas left.
Austerity is necessary.[7]

Through sharing the resources they did have, the Sandinistas were able to provide teachers for regions of the country never before reached.

Fernando Cardenal also told us, "The exploitative systems of Latin America need illiterate people." Democracy is dependent on an educated constituency, an informed and participatory public. The Sandinistas began to realize this goal. The literacy campaign laid the groundwork for the Adult Education Program. Over 1,400 schools were built between 1980 and 1983, and 70 percent of all Nicaraguan adults and children were enrolled in some kind of educational project.[8]

Health care was also a high priority for the newly formed government. Before the Triumph, there were eight to ten new polio cases each year. There was a very low life-expectancy and a high infant mortality rate which surpassed most other countries in the region. Because health care students were among the most vocal opponents of Somoza, the training of health care workers had been severely curtailed prior to 1979, producing a shortage of doctors and nurses.

The Sandinista government is committed to casting off the oppression of illness and epidemics. The government implemented immunization programs throughout the country. The result has been the eradication of polio from Nicaragua since 1981. The government initiated programs in malaria control and rural sanitation, built new health care clinics, and increased training opportunities for doctors, nurses, and other health care workers. Enrollment in medical schools increased by 600 percent between 1977 and 1983.[9]

Despite the war being waged against Nicaragua by the United States, the Nicaraguan Revolution continues to take place on behalf of the poor. The hungry are fed. The homeless are sheltered. The nation is no longer depleted by epidemics and illiteracy.

—SUSAN

The health care and literacy campaigns have been extended into the workplace, where the Sandinistas and workers have made significant improvements. Anne describes a cigar factory she visited near Estelí:

Three hundred workers. The average age is 16. They work from 7 A.M. to 3 P.M.. seventy-five percent of the workers are women because, in the words of our guide, it takes a "finer touch" to do this kind of work. Before the revolution, Somoza owned the factory. The workers were not paid. During the insurrections it was burned down. After the revolution, the workers built the factory back up. Somoza had been shipping the

tobacco off to Honduras. Now the workers have health benefits, includ-
ing a doctor who holds a clinic there weekly. They are working on plans
for a day-care center in the factory which will have the capacity for 500
children. The head of the workers' union is a woman. The workers get 1
paid month off a year. There is a 3-month paid maternity leave. The
factory has a library, as well as an adult education program where the
workers who know how to read and write teach the ones who don't. The
adult ed program takes place in the night: 2 hours/night. The minimum
wage: 44.17 cordobas/day (at the time of our visit, 28 c. = $1.00). There
are benefits for people who produce more. Most people make around 100
c./day. They have vigilantes to defend the factory as it would be a target
for contra attacks.

—ANNE

The goals of the Nicaraguan Revolution—to forge a system that gives to all people the necessities of life that are fundamental to freedom, justice, and true democracy—are at odds with the way the leaders of the United States view their country and its role in the world. The people of Nicaragua have demanded the right to determine their own economic, political, and social system. This demand and its implications have so infuriated, intimidated, and frightened the U.S. government that it has responded by unleashing an economic and terroristic war against the people of Nicaragua.

U.S. POLICIES TOWARD NICARAGUA

Who Are the Contras?

This is a critical question. Ronald Reagan refers to the contras as "freedom fighters," "our brothers," comparing them to our own "founding fathers." Gerry Studds (D—Mass.) has called them "a bunch of thugs." For an answer to the question, Who are the contras?, we turn to an "in-depth research report" prepared for the Arms Control and Foreign Policy Caucus of the U.S. Congress (April 18, 1985). We present the summary of this report almost in its entirety because we believe this information essential to a fair-minded assessment of U.S. involvement in Nicaragua. Some of the statistics in the report may vary slightly between the date of its publication and the publication of this book, but we believe the basic contentions of the report are true and accurate. The report, in part, reads:

The United States has been supporting armed opposition to the Nicaraguan government since 1981. Over $80 million reportedly has been spent to build and maintain a force of from 10,000 to 15,000 contras.
The purpose of this report is to analyze the leadership and membership of the contras and the nature and goals of the private organizations which provide their financial and material support. . . .

Information published by the Nicaraguan government has not been used in this report. Instead, the report is based primarily on extensive interviews with former high-ranking officials of the Frente Democrático Nacional (the primary contra force), literature published by the FDN, and interviews with representatives of organizations that aid the contras. While we recognize there are limitations to this approach, the [U.S.] executive branch has thus far failed to respond to our requests for specific information on the structure and leaders of the FDN military command. . . .

SUMMARY OF REPORT

1. While the "foot-soldiers" of the FDN army are largely peasants, the army is organized and commanded by former National Guardsmen. In the first publicly available organizational chart of the high command of the FDN military force, the report finds that 46 of the 48 positions in the FDN's command structure are held by [Somoza's] Guardsmen.

2. While the FDN's civilian directorate has been cleansed to minimize the role of former Guardsmen and Somoza associates, the military leadership has not been. As a result, the key military strategist positions, including the Strategic Commander, are held by ex-National Guardsmen; as are all of the General Staff; four out of five of the Central Commanders; six out of seven of the Regional Commanders; and probably all 30 Task Force Commanders.

3. Up to 20 private groups in the United States have provided the contras with substantial financial and material aid (apparently some $5 million) in the past year. Most of these groups are not traditional relief organizations or other established groups recognized as providing humanitarian aid, but rather are ultra-conservative or paramilitary groups on the fringe of American political opinion.

4. These groups are largely operated by a small group of about half a dozen men, mostly with military or paramilitary backgrounds, whose close association often means that the groups work in tandem.

5. A major "relief" effort for the Miskito Indians living on the Nicaraguan-Honduran border has had the effect of maintaining the MISURA contra army. One of the groups contributing to this effort is funded in large part by Rev. Moon's Unification Church.

Ex-members of Somoza's National Guard are the foundation and core of the contra army. Under the Somozas, these men committed innumerable atrocities, and they continue to do so. Men and women are tortured and murdered; women are raped; children are murdered. And this is supported by the U.S. government. In June 1985 the U.S. Congress voted further funding for these acts of terrorism. But that was not enough.

The Economic Embargo

In the last several years, the United States has done its best to destabilize the Nicaraguan economy. Nicaraguan economists estimate that U.S. pressure deprived Nicaragua of hundreds of millions of dollars in lost trade and loans in 1983 alone. The United States has also blocked Nicaragua's access to international credit. When Nicaragua attempted to reschedule $560 million of its external debt, U.S. banks were urged to cut Nicaragua's access to loans. Since then, only $11 million in loans has been forthcoming.[10]

During the weeks (May 1985) in which Amanecida was completing this manuscript, the U.S. president unilaterally imposed economic sanctions on Nicaragua. These sanctions will mean the loss of hard currency from agricultural exports to the United States (20 percent of Nicaragua's total) and the cut off of U.S. imports (18 percent of the total). According to *El Esteliano*, the Nuevo Institute de Centro América (NICA) newsletter from Estelí:

> Many private businesses, 60% of the Nicaraguan economy, will be bankrupted; basic medicines will become more scarce; seeds, fertilizer and farm credit will be late or unavailable; and parts for U.S. industrial and agricultural machinery will become almost impossible to replace.[11]

During the spring of 1985 the U.S. economic aggression tightened its stranglehold on Estelí's economy:

> NICA's staff and participants have reported an inflation rate of over 100% over the last several months. For example, the Managua-Estelí bus fare is now 48 cordobas [the official exchange rate was 28 cordobas to $1 U.S.]; a bottle of beer is 100 cordobas; a liter of milk is 30 cordobas; eggs are 60 cordobas a dozen; mangoes, in season, are 20 cordobas apiece; while a single box of corn flakes in the supermercado costs 1500 cordobas or $24! In April (1985) there was no cooking oil or cigarettes in Estelí for two weeks while toilet paper, toothpaste and other basic items have disappeared from many stores altogether. . . .
>
> [In April 1985 the calculated price] of a chicken [was] three days pay for an ATC [A;sociation of Rural Workers] farmworker; a pair of plastic flip-flops was four days wages; and a pair of pants costs three months pay. Black market exchange rates for U.S. dollars have been reported as high as 1,000 cordobas for $1 while 500 to 1 rates have become common.[12]

Why has the United States unleashed an economic and military war against Nicaragua? Carlos Manuel, an FSLN regional representative in Estelí, commented that the problem is that Nicaragua does not want to be another state of the union.[13] Thus, the Reagan Administration is hard at work to dismantle the revolution and justify U.S. policies and intervention.

U.S. JUSTIFICATIONS FOR ITS POLICIES

The Reagan Administration is trying to convince U.S. citizens that the United States must come to the rescue of Central America in the name of freedom and democracy. It justifies its policies toward Nicaragua on a number of false or unfounded suppositions:

1. Nicaragua is exporting revolution to other Central American countries, e.g., by sending arms to El Salvador;
2. Nicaragua is a "communist" threat to the United States—"a second Cuba";
3. Nicaragua is undemocratic, tending toward "totalitarianism," newspaper censorship, violations of human rights, and restriction of religious freedoms.

Exporting Revolution

As illustrated above, the Nicaraguan Revolution was and is a response to an extremely repressive U.S.-backed regime under Anastasio Somoza which resulted in widespread poverty. It is in these conditions that revolutions are born, not by receiving arms from other countries. If Nicaragua were sending arms to neighboring countries (and there is little evidence to substantiate the charge), repressive conditions would have to exist in those countries along with a high consciousness of the problems in order to fuel any revolution. The "spread" of revolution in Central America is viewed by Reagan's Administration as a threat to the United States, undoubtedly because it might eventually engulf Mexico or Panama—two countries in which the United States has vested major strategic military interests.

Carlos Manuel responded to the charge of exporting revolution to El Salvador:

> The patriots of El Salvador were fighting before we had the Triumph. It is also true that the tradition of armed struggle in El Salvador predates armed struggle in Nicaragua. The first armed insurrection in El Salvador was in 1932. It also had a class base to it. Or in the language of Reagan— "communist." It might be easier for us to export revolution to Honduras, which has its borders right next to ours. What I'd like to say about this charge is that revolutions are the effects of problems *within* the country. It's nothing but a pretext that we are giving help to one revolution or another.[14]

A Communist Threat

The Reagan Administration calls Nicaragua a "Soviet surrogate," a "communist threat." Before we can even consider the charge, we must ask—What does Reagan mean by "Soviet surrogate" or "communist threat"? The United States makes no distinction between communism, Marxism, and socialism. Our Administration holds that communism is both a political and a moral threat to the so-called free world. Communism is ungodly. Thus, it is immoral for the United States to lose control over nations that demonstrate socialist commitments, such as Nicaragua's commitment to eliminate poverty. As several Nicaraguans said to us, the Nicaragua/U.S. tensions are not a result of an East-West antagonism, but rather a North over South domination.

If we were seriously to engage Reagan's charge, we would have to say that there is scant evidence to support it. The leading factions in the Sandinista party coalition were formed over the objections of the small, Moscow-oriented Communist Party in Nicaragua. The Nicaraguan pluralist economy bears no resemblance to the Soviet model of centralized planning.[15] The Sandinistas have begun to create a new class of landowning small farmers, moving in exactly the opposite direction from Soviet collectivization of agriculture. The latitude accorded the Catholic church and the religious elements of the revolution itself are dramatically different from Soviet attitudes and practices toward organized religion.[16]

Nicaragua has intentionally avoided becoming dependent upon the Soviet Union, although how long this can continue is open to question. In 1982, France sold $11 million worth of arms to the Sandinistas. Because of U.S. pressure, France has not made any further arms deals with Nicaragua. As in the case of Cuba, U.S. policy is forcing Nicaragua into the East-West conflict. Because of U.S. economic and military pressure, Nicaragua may not be able to remain unaligned for long. Thus the superpower tension is escalated. Up to 1985, however, the bulk of Nicaragua's nonmilitary trade has remained with Western and Third World countries. The future of such trade is uncertain.

Carlos Manuel commented:

> We *do* have relations with communist countries. We try to have relations with *all* countries. No one *ever* mentions that our basic programs, our basic economic structure is financed by the European community and that our petroleum supply depends on Mexico and Venezuela. The only thing that is ever mentioned is that there's this interest between Nicaragua and communist countries—another pretext for intervention.[17]

Lack of Democracy and Freedom

Essential to the Sandinista government's accountability to the poor is democracy. Democracy in Nicaragua is not the same as it is in the United States. Democracy in Nicaragua has a bias for the poor, while in the United States it has a bias for white, middle-to-upper-class men. Daniel Ortega articulated a Nicaraguan understanding of democracy:

For us democracy is literacy. For us democracy is health care for our people. For us democracy is rights for workers. For us democracy is agrarian reform. For us democracy is sovereignty, independence, and self-determination.

We do not want the kind of democracy that the North American administration wants to impose on us; because here we do not want the kind of democracy that denied its own citizens the right to vote simply because they were black . . . . We do not want that democracy where barely 30 percent of the population participates in electing its own president; here we do not want the democracy of the Ku Klux Klan. That kind of democracy we have already known, in the times of Walker, in the times of Diaz and Moncada, and in the times of Somoza.

For us democracy is to truly love one another; which is to say, to bury self-centeredness, greed, and the thirst for gold. That is to say, to bury the exploiter and to raise the exploited up out of their graves.[18]

While walking the streets of Estelí before the 1984 elections, Flo caught sight of an example of the kind of grassroots, participatory democracy that President Ortega spoke of:

When I passed the doorway to the headquarters of the Communist Party in Estelí, a man sitting behind a desk in the corner of a large area that looked like the inside of a barn noticed my curiosity and motioned me to come in. As I came closer to him I saw that he was drawing a campaign poster for the election. There was nothing else in the room except a large poster panel on the wall behind the man.

What impressed me was the fact that, given the contrast to a major political campaign in the United States, here sat a man drawing a campaign poster.

—FLO

And Carlos Manuel was very clear about what he believes democracy is and about the contrasts between the U.S. and Nicaraguan conceptions of democracy:

We're doing what we said we would do. We said that we would take power through armed struggle, and we did that. We said that we would make agrarian reform, and we're doing that. We said that we would give land to the campesinos/as, and we're doing that. We said that we would try to wipe out illiteracy, and we're doing that. And we're continuing. We said that we would give better living conditions and health care to the people and we're doing that. The majority of the property in this country is private property. More than 50 percent of the land is still in private hands. The majority of business is still in private hands. Private property will exist but it will exist for the benefit of the majority of the people.

Therefore, our project is a national project. It is a project of justice and of democracy—*popular* democracy. When we're talking about democracy, we're talking about it from its Greek roots. It means the power of the people. The North American objective is to pretend that democracy is elections. We *believe* that it's elections and many more things. Popular democracy is not democracy of the rich. We didn't say we wanted democracy of the rich; we said we wanted *popular* democracy. After the triumph of the U.S. revolution, how many years passed until the final copy of the constitution? And they want that we should have everything done in less than 5 years. The problem of Nicaraguans is that the U.S. wants that we shouldn't be Nicaraguans. The U.S. only understands Nicaragua as another state in the union.[19]

After her November 1983 trip to Honduras and Nicaragua, Carter responded to Reagan's charges that the Sandinistas are inhibiting peoples' freedom in general and, in particular, their freedom of press.

Pedro Joaquin Chamorro agrees with Reagan. As editor of La Prensa, *a Managua daily, Chamorro protests vigorously against reference to* La Prensa *as an opposition paper: "Opposition? That's a compliment to the Sandinistas. We are not an opposition paper, because that implies freedom. We are not free to print, to say what we want."*

Demonstrating his complaint, Chamorro hands us copies of columns and editorials which have been censored by the Sandinistas. Included are articles on ARDE (Eden Pastora's groups of contras who are organizing to overthrow the government); a recent trip of Sandinista leader Daniel Ortega to Mexico; a quote from the New York Times *in which the Nicaraguan censor had insisted, in reference to the movement to topple the government, that* La Prensa *change the words "rebel," "insurgent," and "dissident Sandinista" to "contra"; and finally some editorials calling for the Sandinistas to return to the democratic goals of the revolutionary movement.*

Gustavo Parajon, president of CEPAD (Evangelical Committee for Aid and Development) and a medical doctor who worked in rural Nicaragua before assuming a Baptist pastorate in Managua, spoke passionately of the U.S. government's attempt to "destroy Nicaragua." In Parajon's view, the freedom of the press argument is simply one more tactic the United States is using to discredit the Sandinistas. "If we're going to talk about freedom of press," Parajon suggested, "let's talk about the U.S. press. About the news blackout during the Grenada invasion. About the Voice of America or the U.S. Armed Forces radio. Have you listened to them recently?" he inquired. "Pure propaganda. That's all. The United States will do anything and say anything right now to further its own interests."

As for the Sandinista censorship of such papers as La Prensa, *Parajon insisted, "Of course, there is censorship, and that's not to be desired. But you must understand that Nicaragua has Goliath on its back. We are in a state of national crisis, which your government has created. We are at war. I would refer you to your own history—the censorship measures that have been imposed upon your press during times of war."*

When pushed as to whether, even so, it is legitimate to limit peoples' freedom, Parajon responded, "I think it is illegitimate to attempt to bring down a government at the expense of the poor. And not only illegitimate, but unpastoral. Because what can be more pastoral than to be for justice and life?"

A day earlier our delegation had met with about 150 members of a Christian base community in Estelí. "What is this 'freedom' about which your president speaks?" a woman asked us. "For the first time, we are free to have the food we need to eat. For the first time, we are free to have babies who will live past one year of age. For the first time we have free health care, which means that our children do not die of polio."

A man rose to join in, "Is it freedom, if you have a warehouse full of food and I am starving? Is that what Mr. Reagan means by freedom?"

Juan, a young farmer carrying a rifle to protect himself, his family, his land and, for the moment, our delegation from the possibility of a contra attack, walked with us through a field of tomatoes. "What is your country trying to do to us?" he wondered out loud. "To bring democracy and freedom to those of us who, for the first time in the many generations of our families, have land that we can work, crops that we can sell, the possibility of an income that we can save? Are there not people in your country—black people and Indians and other poor people—who are not yet as free as we have become? It seems to us that your government wants to keep all poor people in Nicaragua and in the United States unfree. It seems to us that the only people whose freedom matters is the rich peoples' freedom to live as they want."

This is precisely the point, according to Peter Marchetti, a Jesuit priest and U.S. economist working in Managua. Agreeing with Gustavo Parajon as well as with the farmers and the members of the Christian base communities with whom we spoke, Marchetti condemns U.S. aggression against Nicaragua as a "war of the rich against the poor." In Marchetti's analysis, the United States "will not tolerate the emergence of a neighboring state which is committed to a mixed economy and a posture of international nonalignment" (dependence upon different spheres of influence for different needs). In this way, Nicaragua represents to other Third World nations the possibility of actual freedom from the competitive hegemony of the superpowers. In Marchetti's opinion, this is the reason the United States is bent upon the destruction of the Sandinista vision.

"Even if the United States bombs this country back to a million people with a Somoza and a vicious National Guard," Marchetti asserts, "Nicaragua will have served as a model to Third World countries of how an actual democracy can come into being in the world among the poor." *"Yes," concurs Monica Baltodaño, a guerrilla leader against Somoza and today a leading Sandinista. "What you see today is a flawed system which needs to be much better than it is," she acknowledged. "But rather than being able to make our nation better, to solve the problems we admit we have, our entire nation is having to accelerate preparation to win this war with the United States. Your political, economic, and military assault on us has affected all sectors of our lives, not just the military. Everybody and everything is affected. And all of our people are prepared to fight to defend our freedom from U.S. domination.*

But is it true, we asked, that you are now getting military help from the Soviet Union? "Of course. We will take assistance from anyone who will offer it. We did not start this war. We asked for friendly relationships with your government but it shut the door in our face and announced its plans to destroy us. We will not be aligned with either of the superpowers, but we will take help from anyone who provides it in order to defend our country."

Rita Delia Casco was the Nicaraguan ambassador to the United States after Somoza's fall, during the last year of the Carter Administration and into the Reagan Administration. Casco reiterated Baltodaño's charge: "Please point out to your people that, from the beginning of our new government, Nicaragua has sought good relations with the United States. What we have said is that we will not be your slaves. And that is why your current administration refuses even to dialogue with us. Under Carter, we could at least engage in conversation. Under Reagan, we are told that our role is to listen, submit, and follow. Under the pretext of dialogue, your government sends a group like the Kissinger Commission, which informs us that either we will do things your way or be destroyed." *Casco recollects the visit of the Kissinger Commission: "They were to be a fact-finding body. Presumably their role was to listen. But all they did was talk to us about our lack of freedom, our being a closed society, our being unwilling to listen to anyone but communists. And when Comandante Daniel Ortega finally got up to speak, Mr. Kissinger removed his earphones, and we heard one of the commission members say to another, 'Stop listening to this son-of-a-bitch.' "[20]*

—CARTER

The Reagan Administration charges that there is a general lack of freedom in Nicaragua. The administration evokes images of constant surveillance and a lack of freedom of movement and speech, but we and the people we met moved about freely. People spoke openly to us—whether they were critics or supporters of the Sandinistas. We hitchhiked. The people who picked us up spoke openly about the government. They were not afraid. We went to any churches we wished—Pentecostal churches, Catholic cathedrals, Episcopal churches—and watched the people worship as they wished. The following piece by Laurie evinces some of the variety of people with whom we spoke, the freedom of movement we had, and the freedom with which people, whether criticizing or supporting the government, spoke to us.

During an FSLN forum in Estelí I got into a conversation with a group of men who were disagreeing among themselves about whether the government was doing a good job. Later during the rally, a boy, age fifteen or so, approached me and told me he was studying English and asked if I would talk to him. Clearly a middle-class kid, he went to a private, middle-class school in another town and was proud of his good grades. English was his favorite subject, and he wanted to be able to visit the United States to see relatives in Los Angeles and, of course, to go to Hollywood and meet some stars.

He crooned popular North American songs to me, tried out entire pages of his memorized English workbook on me ("The pencil is on the desk," etc.), and when I pulled out my dictionary, he nearly went crazy. Apparently good ones are very hard to come by, and he coveted mine.

Toward the end of the rally there was a short rainstorm. I pulled out my plastic poncho, and several kids ran over and asked if they could get under it with me. Within five minutes there were a dozen of us, adults and children, all sharing the sheltered space, laughing, trying to talk and keep warm, and just enjoying it under there. And the rally went on in the rain.

Afterward I walked toward "home" with my fifteen-year-old friend, and as we parted ways I handed him the Spanish-English dictionary that I had owned and used for fifteen years and that was a great source of security for me in this strange land. He thanked me, simply and quietly, and I never saw him again.

—LAURIE

People are free to visit Nicaragua and speak to anyone they wish—in fact the Sandinistas have repeatedly invited high-ranking U.S. officials, including President Reagan, to visit Nicaragua. While in Nicaragua we mingled with whomever we chose and we openly criticized aspects of the revolution and the government. When the openness and trust of the government became clear to us, we were reminded that Nicaraguan officials, like Tomas Borge, are often not allowed into the United States or—as with Daniel Ortega's visit to New York in the fall of 1985—are restricted by bureaucratic means from speaking freely throughout the United States. Writers and intellectuals are free to visit Nicaragua. But major figures such as the Nobel Prize winner Gabriel García Márquez are, for ideological reasons, not allowed into the United States. The Reagan Administration's charges about a general lack of freedom should, it would seem, be leveled against itself.

U.S.-NICARAGUAN RELATIONS: BACKDROP TO CONVERSION

Because Nicaragua is determined to establish an economic system that is beneficial to all its people, it has implicitly challenged the hegemony of the United States in Latin America and the vision that the United States has of itself and its role in the world. The U.S. government has responded to this challenge with violence. Foremost in the Nicaraguan government's agenda is responsiveness to the poor. The U.S. government, on the other hand, has stopped listening to people who are poor, oppressed, and marginalized struggling for sustenance and liberation throughout the Third World and within the borders of the United States. With Nicaragua as a backdrop, the members of the Amanecida Collective began to understand the close links among the U.S. government's policies toward Nicaragua; the oppression of the poor, women, and other marginalized groups within the United States, and our own lives. This understanding propelled us further into the process of conversion we had begun unaware long ago.

2

Conversion

Nicaragua is more than a symbol of the poor, the rejected, the outcast, and the silenced. It is a real, historical, geopolitical community of people. The Nicaraguan people do not live the same patterns as we do. The juxtaposition of our lives and values in relation to theirs gives us an opportunity to see more clearly who we are as a people, a realization that can be ours only in relation to others. And, as U.S. people—the powerful in relation to Nicaraguans—we must listen well and hard. Otherwise, our prejudices will stand in the way of our seeing and hearing either the Nicaraguan people or ourselves.

—PAT

FOUNDATIONS BEGIN TO SHIFT

Three A.M., our fourth night in Managua: We woke to the shaking of ground beneath our bodies. By the third ominous shake we were wide awake. "Holy Shit!" yelled Virginia, "It's an earthquake!" Mary Darkin was quickly at our door to tell us we must go outside because the walls of the house could cave in. And so we dressed hurriedly, packed a few valuables, and went outside. Some of us remember the night outside as hollow . . . so still and quiet. Others remember it as noisy, with more than occasional rumblings of the earth, howling of dogs, chattering of birds.

The Nicaraguans with us were worried. This brought back memories of the devastating earthquake of 1972. Some of us heard a woman down the road chanting and wailing. And so we waited, nervously clustered together. Some of us lit a candle and sat silently; others of us paced to and fro. Communication to the outside world was non-existent. For all we knew, Managua could be in ruins. The "earthquake," as it turned out, was merely a tremor, which did little damage in Managua, although several villages in northwestern Nicaragua were badly affected. We heard later that parts of Chile had suffered the worst devastation in this quake. Finally, we were told it was safe enough to go back into the house, but the rumblings continued throughout the next day and night.

This experience was jarring. On what could we depend if the very earth under our feet was moving? The tremor had begun literally to shake us up and to loosen our feelings of security. For Flo, the key to the earthquake experience was that we automatically reached for what was most valuable before leaving the house: passports, plane tickets, traveler's cheques, watches, medicines, toilet paper—the very items least accessible to most Nicaraguans. We knew that there was no sure way to save ourselves, only our belongings.

> *Standing in the night with trembling beneath my feet, in anger and fear . . . I had thought lots about dying in Nicaragua, but not like this. I came to Nicaragua because I believe that justice belongs to all, that the right to choose the way we want to live belongs to each of us. This I had planned to say with my presence in that country. I had thought about dying, but not like this . . . not right now.*
>
> *At that moment I realized that, yes, I was intellectually committed to justice, but that the actual fight for justice, out of the head and onto the human plane, requires emotional strength. I was afraid, yet it was this fear that was my first experience of bonding to the people of Nicaragua. You see, I realized that it was this fear, the loss of life, that they faced each day. Their fear is not of natural disaster, but rather of U.S. supported aggressors.*
>
> *Conversion is the moment when you can acknowledge what has already happened in your life and know you will be totally committed to it. I was living the reality I was seeking before the earthquake happened to bring it all together. As a believer in justice, I knew I would need the emotional strength to meet the unexpected . . . over and over again. I wanted to be wholly committed to what I rationally knew.*
>
> —Flo

The next day most of our group decided to have a swim in Tiscapa Lake, an ancient half-mile wide volcano crater located in the heart of Managua. Viewed from above, which is the only view one has of this deep green lagoon from the edges of its lofty circumference, Tiscapa seems enchanted, a bottomless resource of memory as well as the public swimming hole. We had heard that the decaying buildings, which line the edge of the steep hill surrounding the lake, not so long ago had housed Somoza's National Guard, and that the water had been a dumping hole for the bodies of Somoza's victims. We had not heard, as we did later, that most Nicaraguans do not swim in Tiscapa and that, therefore, it is really a place for tourists and others whose friends and relatives are not buried somewhere in or under this deep lagoon. To swim in the lagoon was a sign of our initial separation from the Nicaraguan people.

Only later did all eight of us who took this swim admit to having been leery about this exercise. Swimming in a bottomless lake was enough to evoke spasms of aquaphobia among us. Add to this the occasional glimpse up the long hillside to the old buildings and the harsh memories of what terror must have ruled this land and this lake. Several of us sensed images of the dead with us, *presente* in the water which seemed so warm and thick. Our sense of security having been undermined the night before, it was as if, without fully understanding it, we were beginning to feel something of what the Nicaraguans feel: the constant presence of the dead as a source of sorrow, but also of hope and solidarity. Around and under us the earth continued to quake periodically. Half way across the lake, several of us turned back while several swam on toward the other side.

Five of us were heading back to shore when we heard a dog yelping. Not being able to see anything, we climbed up on the shore trying to follow the sound. Suddenly, through the undergrowth on the hill, some-thing half slid, half tumbled and a puppy's head appeared. Not caring if it bit me or not, I started slowly toward it talking gently. She willingly came to me—an injured doberman puppy with her tail cut and sore with an open wound crawling with maggots, and partially paralyzed hind legs.

—JANE

Meanwhile, three of us moved on slowly across the lake. Our swim was silent and eerie. Not only was the earth around us tremoring but also the sky was dark and a storm seemed imminent. About three-quarters of the way across, lightning lit up our view of the cliffs and buildings, and we quickly turned around and headed home. I was afraid. I feared for my life. I felt surrounded by dead bodies—and powerless. We were swim-ming for our lives, still in silence and still afraid. When we arrived safely back at the diving rock, the three of us laughed off our fears and immediately joined the others in their concern about the dog they had found. I was relieved to be able to take care of something other than my own fear of death.

—LAURA

One of our translators talked with us about the possibility of finding a vet on a Saturday evening in a country where it's difficult to get an aspirin for a sick child. She explained that the kindest thing would be to put the dog to sleep— that the Nicaraguan people just would not understand this obsession of North Americans to get the best care for a puppy. Our bus drivers knew of a couple of vets, neither of whom turned out to be home. At this point, there seemed to be no way we could leave the dog, so we took her back to the Anglican Institute. We hovered around the dog trying to make her comfortable. We named her Terremoto after the earthquake. Laurie stayed up with her all night.

When we got up the next morning, the dog looked better, though she was walking unsteadily. Soon she began to fall sideways and in a short period of time grew noticeably weaker, beginning to foam at the mouth, and finally lying in the sun half dead. When she began to seizure, it was apparent that to kill her would be best. Nicholas Cruz, the caretaker, took her behind the house and beat her head with a stick. Our reaction to finding the dog, her illness, and her death was mixed. All of us were upset: some of us, about the dog; others, that we were upset about a *dog*.

Rabies is epidemic in Nicaragua among the growing numbers of dogs who roam the streets, and health officials had begun coping with the problem by setting out poison. After Terremoto's death, we realized that she had been poisoned and/or had rabies. As Flo had pointed out with the earthquake incident, our reactions to the situation had betrayed our North American presuppositions. We had acted as if we assumed that the resources we were accustomed to having in the United States would be available in Nicaragua. In a situation of stark poverty, where food and medicine are in short supply and where human resources are being spent fighting a war against a superpower, the choice between a sick dog and a hungry child may be a very real daily dilemma. We had the privilege—time, money, van, food, medicine, shelter, and human resources—to care for Terremoto. We were not wrong to care for her, but we would be wrong not to understand that our class privilege enabled us to do it.

To a person, each of us was becoming more aware of the various assumptions we bring to each day—whether about swimming holes, pets, or the process and significance of dying. Many of us had begun to talk about a "clash of cultures." We had begun to understand better our lives and values in relation to those whose world and worldviews are unlike our own.

CONVERSION FROM FEAR TO TRUST

Susan had gone to Nicaragua about a year before the rest of us. She tells a story that reveals a series of emotions and thoughts that many of us experienced in Nicaragua: a turning from an ideological affirmation of the Sandinista revolution to a thorough-going belief in the people; a turning from fear to trust and the beginnings of solidarity; a turning from gods of alienation to a liberating God at work in the lives of the poor:

> *While I was in Estelí, my group of thirty-two North Americans met with a Christian base community in a large hall which serves as both the site for religious services and community meetings. Soon after we had exchanged greetings with the people, a woman left crying. She had just been told that the body of her eighteen-year-old son had arrived from the northern border region. He had been killed by the counterrevolutionaries while guarding the coffee pickers near the Honduran border. This was the second son this woman had lost, as earlier another son had been killed in the struggle against Somoza.*
>
> *Our meeting continued. There was a very moving exchange of requests from the Nicaraguans for us to help the U.S. people understand that the poor of Nicaragua are organizing themselves to improve their living*

conditions, their health, and their lives. They pleaded with us to get the U.S. government to leave them in peace.

Two nuns, one Mexican and one North American, living in Jalapa on the northern border, described to us the atrocities they had witnessed committed by the contras, Reagan's "freedom fighters," against the peasants of that region. In story after story, they told of the contras gathering the community leaders—the teachers, the health care workers, the lay religious leaders—torturing them, often brutally murdering them as an example to those who remained. In the midst of such suffering, the nuns spoke of the solidarity among these people as they share their scarce resources with those who flee their homes in fear of their lives.

At the end of our meeting, we were invited to the wake for the woman's son. We went to the simple, mud-floored, almost bare dwelling of the family. Flowers and palm tree leaves were hanging on the wall and a cross was over the door. Many had gathered in the street, including one inebriated man who kept hugging us and exclaiming, "¡Amigo! ¡Amigo!"—friend.

The body had been moved to the Sandinista Hall for the one o'clock funeral. (The cathedral in Estelí had been damaged during the last days of fighting against Somoza and was still under repair.) So, boarding our tourist bus, we left the house and went to pay our respects to this slain compañero.

The auditorium was crowded with townspeople and militia men and women in their green uniforms. As we entered, we saw two caskets at the front of the auditorium and a long line of people processing past the coffins. As we waited in line to view the body, the odor of death surrounded us. Off to the left in an open courtyard was a large group of armed militia. Behind us, standing in the rows of benches, townspeople and militia were shouting. The sound of their anger was frightening. I could not understand the Spanish. I did not know what they were shouting, and the intensity and volume of sound made me fear for my life. My heart was in my throat! Was it safe for me, a "gringa," to be in this place? Why were they shouting, when funerals I had attended in the United States were solemn, silent occasions?

The caskets were of a brown wood with a glass window over the head and chest region of the body. As I got to this window, the appearance of the young man was ghastly (without the benefit of embalming and cosmetic reconstruction). This young man had been wounded in the head and face, and his nose and forehead were stuffed with cotton to fill in the large gashes and wounds. The sights and the smells of death were overwhelming.

Thinking that the second casket contained the body of one of the two 13-year-old children killed by the contras two days earlier as they harvested coffee, I got into the next line. Instead this was the body of another soldier, a very young man with a handsome face, not yet old enough to grow a beard! All I could think of was that it had been bullets from the United States that had killed these young people.

The shouting had not subsided. Still not understanding what they were saying, I feared they would take out their anger at the United States on me and my companions. I hurriedly tried to get away from this place of death and back to the safety of our bus. It was on the bus that I learned their angry shouts had been of defiance and determination to not be overcome by those who seek to destroy the gains of the revolution:

"The revolutionaries didn't say we must die, they died!"
"¡Estan presente!" (They are here, present!).
"People, army, united!"
"We will not be stopped from picking our coffee!"
"¡Estan presente!"[1]

In the face of death, these Nicaraguans had set on a new way for life. Even when the U.S.-backed contras daily remind these people of the closeness of death, their faith enables them to go forward, to pick the coffee that is so important to the Nicaraguan economy, to defy the overwhelming odds against living. Holly Near's song kept going through my mind:

It could have been me, but instead it was you.
So I'll keep doing the work you were doing as if I were two.
I'll be a student of life, a singer of songs
A farmer of food and righter of wrongs.
It could have been me but instead it was you.
And it may be me dear sisters and brothers before we are through.
But if you can live for freedom . . . I can too![2]

Until I had come this close to death in Nicaragua, I ideologically understood and supported what the Sandinistas were doing. But when I experienced their anger and outrage at U.S. backed contra aggression channeled into defiance and determination, I was profoundly moved. My ideological affirmation of the Sandinistas became deeply rooted in my own faith and experience.

—SUSAN

Young people from the town had just been killed by contras supported by the United States, and yet at the Christian base community's meeting the members spoke to North Americans of the need for understanding, and at the auditorium the people shouted of solidarity and hope. With the knowledge that our country was waging war against many of the villages and towns we visited, we all, like Susan, feared hostility and revenge from the Nicaraguans.

We had carried a set of North American presuppositions into Nicaragua. We had carried with us many of the values of a culture rooted in fear and alienation. We had come from places in which alienation rules our daily lives. Alienation, and the resulting fear, have become the well-defended, logical norm in the United States. We have built our society, our very lives, on fear. We are afraid to touch or be touched, move or be moved, see or be seen as human beings who, despite our protestations, hold something in common with one another. When Margarita went to Nicaragua to study Spanish in July 1983, she went through a series of experiences which reflected North American presuppositions based on fear and alienation. The experiences are also indicative of how those presuppositions began to give way in the midst of the Nicaraguan people.

After I had been in Managua for a week it was time to meet with the rest of the session, so I went to the airport—as was designated—and our group of students left for two days of orientation, after which we took the drive north to Estelí. When we arrived at the Casa Popular de Cultura (Popular House of Culture), many Nicaraguans, women, men, and children, were waiting for us. There were a few welcoming speeches in Spanish, translated for us. Then we responded with a few speeches in English, translated for them.

Now it was time for us to be joined with our families. Each family's name was announced, as was the name of the North American who would be their adopted daughter or son for the next five weeks. It was a time of great anticipation. None of us as a group knew any of the others very well, and now we were being separated to live with the Nicaraguans. So then my name was called but my family wasn't there. I was told that the mother in my house was sick in bed and she couldn't come. So another family had been asked to bring me to my home.

When I arrived, my mother, Doña Cruz, was in bed, her daughter of eighteen, Marisol, was there as were two men who were family friends. At the same time I met the last member of the family, Carmen María, a girl of twelve who was not Doña Cruz's daughter. It was quite a bit later that I learned her story, which I will tell in time.

I was apprehensive at this first meeting with Doña Cruz. I couldn't understand when she told me what was wrong, and I didn't push to get information, especially since the language barrier was very great. Marisol showed me to my room. I was to share a room with Carmen María. I had what appeared to be a new cot. I began to unpack. One of the things we were told during orientation was that our families would be very curious to see what we had brought with us, and they told the truth because they "ooed" and "aahed" over everything I took out of my bag. They were particularly interested in the tampons, never having seen them before. They touched everything and asked questions incessantly. I could answer sometimes, but often I felt quite stupid and wondered how long it would be before I could have a real conversation with them. I asked them where I should put my clothes. I was given two drawers in the bureau and some nails on the wall for hanging my clothes. There was also some space on top of the bureau for my toiletries, while I kept all my extra toilet paper and medications in my suitcase under my cot.

After I'd unpacked, I asked to see the rest of the house. It was a one-story cement building, terra cotta and tan. In the front of the house was a small store that didn't seem to be used very much. There were also a living room, a family room (with a TV and one of the six hundred phones in a city of forty thousand), and a bathroom (with a shower, toilet, and sink). Doña Cruz's bedroom, my room (which I shared with Carmen María), a kitchen (with a two-burner propane stove and a refrigerator), and a large courtyard. The indoor bathroom, phone, and refrigerator indicated that my family was better off than most, and yet Doña Cruz was not wealthy. In our barrio there were houses made of wood with dirt floors and only one room partitioned with cardboard walls. Houses like that were only a half-block away. My family did not have the money to live in the center of Estelí where there were houses that were two stories high with more modern appliances, but I knew that I was very lucky to have gotten such a place to live. I had been prepared for much worse.

The courtyard was filled with plants and flowers and there were clotheslines hung from the overhang of the walkway to the fence on the other side. It was a wonderful house. But I should have known that such comfort would not come without a price.

Doña Cruz ended up in bed for three weeks, and during that time Marisol cooked for me. She didn't cook very well. I grew up on rice and beans, loving every morsel. But beans must be cooked for hours before they are done, and Marisol didn't cook them long enough. I couldn't eat the beans that she cooked. There wasn't much else. Each morning I had black coffee with sugar and pan dulce (sweet bread). The first few days I came home for lunch after Spanish class to rice and beans with crema (which is like sour cream but more like sweet sour cream). It made me gag! So I asked not to have the cream, but I also had a tough time with the rice and uncooked beans. So I began to have lunch out with friends from school. It gave me a chance to speak English and get some food. For dinner I'd have a tortilla, rice and beans, and an egg. Unfortunately I couldn't eat the beans or the tortilla (it also was inedible), so I tried to pick out the rice to eat with the egg. There were many nights I went to bed hungry, but I kept telling myself that I needed to make this sacrifice, after all now I could say that I had experienced hunger. So I didn't say anything about my situation to the "responsibles" of the school or to any of the other students. I felt guilty about living in such a nice house when some of my friends were living with cardboard walls.

But finally I told the staff that I wanted to move, and I explained that Doña Cruz had been in bed since I arrived and I wasn't getting enough food. My liberal limit had been reached! I wanted something to be familiar. I was tired of incompetency and waiting all the time for buses or people or things to happen. I was tired of Spanish all the time and not being able to feel at home. The culture was driving me nuts. Forever shouting slogans, the incessant mosquitoes, flies, rain, dirt, mud. Even Carmen María whom I found out was a servant who had come to Doña Cruz from a very poor family, possibly as payment of a debt, even she, as sweet as she was, began to grate on my nerves. She cried often; she wet her bed; and she went through my things when I wasn't home. I wanted to go home, back to the United States where I could eat cottage cheese at midnight or anything else that I wanted. I wanted to see the dirty streets of New York. I wanted to go to a movie or smoke a filtered cigarette. So Joanne and Ro (NICA's staff) came out to my house one evening and we all spoke with Doña Cruz. That night I realized that she had come close to death with a terrible vaginal infection. She had been in intense pain, and only now was she regaining her strength. She had even felt that I had not contributed enough to family life because I wasn't home very much. She felt hurt and I felt terrible.

I hadn't realized any of this and didn't know how to respond. She understood my need for food, and as she was recovering, she would see to my welfare. And I, well, I apologized for not being more sensitive to her pain. I told her that I hoped to be a better member of the family from then on.

We had some group discussions that week about how we as North Americans were adapting to life, and I discovered that there were many of us who had experienced similar walls. Walls that emphasized our liberal limits, walls that needed to be broken through if we were to be profoundly moved by the experience of living in Nicaragua. I realized that my frustration was nothing when compared to a Nicaraguan who had to live day after day, month after month, with food shortages, paper shortages, no toothpaste, no toilet paper, never knowing when there would be soda or milk or cheese or meat or eggs or chicken. Never knowing when the plane that flew overhead might drop another bomb, or the gun shot heard in the middle of the night might mean a contra invasion.

Doña Cruz's only son, Erasmus, was an electrical engineer who worked up north putting in electrical lines for roads and hospitals and schools. She prayed each day that he would come back alive from his journey northward. She prayed that he would live to sing another song and to see his six-month old son grow up to be a man. How does a mother or a wife or a sister or a brother or a father live with such uncertainty every day? I changed after this realization. I could leave and go back to my comfort any time it got too tough, and I would leave and begin a new life as a seminarian at Harvard, of all places. But Doña Cruz and Erasmus and Marisol and Carmen María would remain, forever hoping for an end to war and a chance at a peaceful, decent life.

I love them all very much. They gave me music and laughter the last two weeks I was with them. They taught me joy and love of family. My mother painted my finger and toenails the last night I was there because she saw me put make-up on for the first time and wear a wild outfit, and she wanted to add something to my appearance. I was amazed and overjoyed. I sang a song in Spanish that night at our going-away party. She was so proud—as if she had been my blood-mother. I cried when Marisol took me to the bus the next day. We both did. We hugged and kissed. I was leaving my family who had shown me another side of life, the side that most of the world knows. I thank them and God for letting me experience this so profoundly.

—MARGARITA

In the United States we have failed to see that the barriers erected among us have historical, social roots. Like Margarita, who had begun to understand the barriers that exist among North Americans and between North Americans and Nicaraguans, it was when we in Amanecida began to understand those roots that we began to turn from fear. We began to trust. We began to understand the faith of the Nicaraguan people. Like Susan during her visit to the Christian base community in Estelí, we saw peasants who have little or no formal education come together and speak about their lives, joys, pains, and fears. They speak of Jesus as a liberator, one who advocates a just society and world in which there are no contras who kill innocent children. Jesus shows a way to liberation in which all persons have a responsibility to participate. The gospel message enables many people to see their own alienation and then to join with others in community to overcome alienation and fear. These people have found God located in the struggle of the poor. Their faith gives them strength to continue to struggle toward revolutionary change. Their faith has given us strength to begin to overcome our fear and unite with them.

One of the first nights we were in Managua, we attended a campesino Mass. It was dusk, and we were in a poor barrio. I remember that I was overwhelmed by being in a new and different country, still trying to assimilate all that we had seen and heard that day. I was looking forward to some "quiet time" in a worship setting. What I experienced was totally different from the "Mass" I expected. Luckily I was sitting next to one of our interpreters, who gave me the literal interpretation of what was happening. Most of the format of the service was as one would expect, except that after scripture was read, the priest sat down with the people and listened as three or four folks—who had been sitting with the congregation—stood up and responded to the scripture, relating to what was read through their own experiences. It was very touching, and literally brought the scripture to life. After an elderly woman had spoken, a young man in army fatigues stood up and in a gentle, soft-spoken manner explained that he had just returned from the border region where there was much fighting and bloodshed. He spoke about the shortage of rations and equipment on the front, and how so many young men and women have kept a strong faith in the midst of the struggle for freedom.

He said that sometimes there is only one tortilla and one canteen of water for fifteen or twenty compañeros. Then he said, "If there is one tortilla for twenty people, then we share one tortilla twenty ways. If there is one canteen for twenty people, we pass it around till each one has a drink. We don't share because we have to, or because someone tells us we should; we do this because we are Christians, and that makes us brothers and sisters working together." This turned out to be the first of many instances where I was taken aback by the character of the Nicaraguan people. Their quiet strength and genuine faith comes alive in their relationships with each other and their common struggle, a struggle which is not just a military one, but which includes a continual battle to meet the most basic of physical, emotional, and spiritual needs.

—Carol

CONVERSION TO SOLIDARITY AND LIFE

It was a bright, sunny morning when we began our hike to the Well of Death. Our Nicaraguan Spanish teachers were taking us on a field trip to a remote spot outside of Estelí called Buena Vista where, on March 19, 1979, six hundred National Guardsmen and mercenaries massacred thirteen civilians. We retraced the path the thirteen and the six hundred took and, after winding our way up what seemed like an unending hill, slogging through mud and crawling through bushes, we came to the site. One of our teachers, who was living in the community at the time of the massacre and had lost a cousin in it, told us the details of the story.

We sat and listened at this beautiful place with rolling hills, rocks jutting out of the land, a cow grazing nearby. On top of what had once been a well was a small shrine. Inside were a crucifix and a plaque with the thirteen names affixed to it. There, on the very earth on which we were sitting, eleven adults and two little girls were tortured and sexually abused. Puddles of blood and pieces of bodies were found the next day—including a breast hanging from a tree branch. The bodies were then dumped into a well and a bomb was exploded on top of them. Some of the local people who were able to hide behind the bushes reported that there were mercenaries among the six hundred soldiers and that many of them had glazed-over eyes, suggesting the use of drugs. After the telling of the story, we North Americans and the Nicaraguans together moved closer to the shrine and to one another and as each name was read, we responded "¡Presente!" (They are present!).

How odd to be in such a seemingly peaceful and lovely setting, while listening to this horrifying story. At that site I was filled with sadness and pain, and my tears came uncontrollably. It was not so much that one particular story affected me so deeply, for we had heard so many stories of pain and suffering, and countless numbers of tears have been shed for lost loved ones. As I look back on that experience now, the story told at the well that day was a culmination of all I had heard and seen. It was the catalyst for sensing and experiencing the pain inherent in all the stories we had heard and in the reality of the present evils taking place within the country.

—CAROL

Going to the Well of Death was a conversion experience for me. Standing in the place where the massacre had taken place, feeling the ghosts in that place, meeting a brother of one of the dead, evoked such pain within me, such deep sorrow and anger that human beings can treat each other in such a way. At the same time it evoked a passion and a commitment to confront and transform such evil.

—KIRSTEN

The Nicaraguans had made such a transformation. They had transformed death into life—their dead were present, symbols of hope and struggle. Like Susan at the funeral in Estelí, what we had experienced at the Well of Death was a widening of our experience of solidarity and community. We had had difficulty comprehending the massacre that had been described to us. How could human beings do this to one another? We were met by evil at the Well of Death, and we couldn't turn it off like TV. It is not, of course, as if this were an isolated incident, a rare occurrence in our world. It is not as if this only occurs in *other* countries. It happens on our streets, in our prisons, in our homes. . . . Not to see, hear, feel, and believe is to devalue the lives of those martyred in Nicaragua and elsewhere. It is to devalue the lives of Nicaraguans as well as our own. It is to devalue the lives of children who will come after us. How long must the *fear* of losing our own personal gain immobilize our capacity to realize both the evil of such atrocities and the inestimable value of that which is lost?

Our visit to the Well of Death was a conversion experience for us because it was one of the places at which we strongly felt a unity among ourselves and between the Nicaraguans and us: together we had had the experience of uniting to call "presente" and to sense the dead giving hope and renewing commitment. At Tiscapa Lake we felt alienated and afraid of Nicaragua and the ever-present dead. We had felt alienation among and within ourselves. We had begun to move through our fear of Nicaragua into solidarity with Nicaraguans. In so doing, we were becoming more deeply involved in the global movement from despair to hope and from fear to a faith in God at work in the community of the poor struggling for justice. As participants in that widening community, we are less alone and afraid:

"Your solidarity gives us strength." That statement has echoed in my memory since the moment a woman said it to Anne and me in a meeting of the Mothers of Heroes and Martyrs that we attended during our first visit to Nicaragua in January 1984. The women had gathered that night

to present their stories, a description of their work as an organization of mothers, and to deliver a plea to North American mothers. We broke into small groups, which gave us the opportunity to ask questions, dialogue, and listen. I was impressed by the diversity of age in this group of women, which is certainly not always true in women's organizations in the United States. They are all linked by a common experience—the loss of sons and daughters to the hands of Somoza and his National Guard, and/or to the contras. Together they share their pain and losses, as well as their courage, and they collect provisions and bring them to the border towns, visit the sick, help in the fields, and give support to those women who have recently lost children to the war.

One mother said to us, "Our hearts are of steel. We are not afraid of death anymore. If it happened to one, it happened to everybody. . . . We're going to resist. We're not afraid anymore. We're used to it. . . . We old people know what has happened. . . . "

They recounted to us tales of the atrocities, the stories of how they lost their children. They said, "We have already felt so much pain. We don't want other mothers to feel that pain. If the aggression continues, North American mothers will experience that pain." They encouraged mothers in the United States not to send their sons to die in Nicaragua. "Nicaragua is not a threat to the United States," they told us. It was toward the end of our evening together that one of the women in our small group said to us, "Your solidarity gives us strength."

During our second visit to Nicaragua we went back to visit the Mothers of Heroes and Martyrs and renewed our bonds with them. When we were introduced to the group, they all stood up and began to clap. We in turn began clapping for them, and for a few moments we were all clapping together for each other.

Those Nicaraguan women, and others, awakened me to a powerful sense of responsibility, to the meaning of the word solidarity. They opened me up to a deeper understanding of sisterhood, a profound realization of my kinship with the people of Nicaragua (and elsewhere), a kinship involving responsibility, which is not simply felt but acted out.

How these Nicaraguan people with whom we met and talked understood their relationship with one another and with us, and their relationship to death, has transformed my understanding of my own life and my sense of purpose. "If it happens to one, it happens to everybody." There is no such thing as individual, personal salvation. Our fates, our lives, and the meaning of our lives are intimately linked. I can no longer perceive and value my own life as having meaning simply through personal gains, successes, and possessions. Rather, my life has its value in relation to others' lives.

When I contemplate the meaning of resurrection, I think of the graffiti which marks the walls in Nicaragua—the names of those who have died in the struggle for liberation, followed by the word "presente". I think of *the words that the people shout together in rallies, "After fifty years, Sandino lives! Sandino lives! The struggle continues!" I think of Archbishop Oscar Romero's words, "If they kill me, I will rise again in the Salvadoran people." It is a vision of our lives as not being individual, solitary struggles, but as holding value in relation to all those who struggle for liberation. It is a vision of our lives as a part of a whole human fabric.*

—KIRSTEN

FROM ALIENATION TO A GOD OF THE EXPLOITED AND POOR

When we returned from Nicaragua to the United States we knew that each of us had undergone a change. We understood, of course, that each person's conversion to life happens differently. For some it is a moment of awakening in which we see the world differently. For others it is a process that occurs slowly over time and involves much pain. And there are those of us who experience both. We had been shaken by the particular experience of the Nicaragua journey. As Flo had stated in her reaction to the earth tremors, for each of us the journey served to underscore the value of the justice-making that we had begun *already* to realize in other times, places, and situations.

Back in the United States and in light of our experiences in Nicaragua, we began to reexamine our culture and ourselves. When we examined life in our country, we found that in spite of the popular mythology about the United States as the land of plenty, of freedom, of democracy, of our being "one nation under God with liberty and justice for all," life in this country is withering away. This "land of the free and brave" is dying because, with the passing of each day, we are becoming less fully human, more out of touch with one another, more encased in cloaks of denial. We fail to see what is happening to those closest to us at home in our cities and suburbs, much less to our sisters and brothers elsewhere in places like Nicaragua. We are entrenched in cycles of wrong-relation. In these cycles, the lives of people of color, poor people, women and children, lesbians and gay men, differently-abled people, and people of a *living* faith (those who do not worship the deities of the status quo) are expendable.

As we looked more deeply to try to find the cause of the deep alienation and divisiveness in the United States, we discovered a complex of values and attitudes rooted in fear. We came to understand more deeply than we had before we went to Nicaragua that our government is promoting a set of attitudes that—as they pervade our culture—are dangerous to our nation and to the rest of the world. The core of this set of attitudes is: (1) a false pride in the nation, a my-country-right-or-wrong mentality stretched far beyond the bounds of either morality or common sense: thus, brutal regimes—such as Pinochet's in Chile—that sing the praises of the United States are supported, while people—like the Nicaraguans—who try to further their own unique vision of justice, are condemned and attacked; (2) an obsession with propriety, with good looks and good order; appearance is more important than morality: national political conventions with celebrities and entertainment catch the nation's eye while the same political parties promote and finance contras, death squads and the murder of innocents throughout Central America; (3) a sanctification of injustice for the good of the nation: leaders insist that civil and equal rights legislation is dangerous, that affirmative action is unnecessary, that women's procreative choice is murderous, that a strong labor force is bad for all, and that giving full rights to gay men and lesbians is against the will of god; and (4) a belief that behind all evil in the United States and the world lurks Marxism.

To promote these beliefs, leaders employ a form of soul-control—they try to coopt leaders and celebrities from minorities and marginalized groups, and all the while they sow seeds of divisiveness among diverse groups and peoples. What the four attitudes above have in common is that they are rooted in fear and insecurity, and especially in fear of any people who look or think or act differently than those in the dominant groups in the United States. Our journey to Nicaragua helped us see the extent to which this complex of attitudes is creeping into and controlling life in the United States. What is taking hold is the institutionalization of our fear (and, finally, our hatred) of those whose lives do not mirror our own, the systemization of the unwillingness to love anyone except those who are most like us. It is the politicization of our narcissism. It is the total perversion of our worship of the God of love, whose faces, names, and colors are as varied as the peoples and other creatures on earth.

As we began to reexamine our lives when we returned to the United States, we saw with increasing clarity to what extent these attitudes—though we might intellectually reject them—had become entangled in our own suppositions and worldviews. For example, the United States as a nation seems obsessed with being the best, the most powerful, the most righteous, the most exceptional of nations. As we pondered that, we asked ourselves which woman among us, strong and intelligent, sensual and sensible, has not known the temptation to be hailed as the Exceptional Woman? The One who isn't like all those others—the *Nice* One. The One who can show the others how to make it if they really try:

> In the past few years, in the context of living my life as a privileged white, U.S. citizen and also as female in a male-dominated world and lesbian in a land of heterosexist coupledom, I have learned about my own complicity and participation in the cycle of wrong-relation. I have numbed myself to the point of being unable to speak, hear, see, or touch. In my life I have worshiped the god of the status-quo because I have not known any better and because I have been afraid.
>
> I have bowed before this god by caring too much about established expectations—needing to be a people-pleaser, to measure up, to push the limits of perfection. And then there is the horrible part of my own homophobia and sexism in which I want to be an exception—to be the

One who is liked, accepted, advanced, ordained, even though I'm female
and lesbian (and divorced, left-wing, prone-to-arrest, and vegetarian). I
have been withering away—afraid of being present.

—ANNE

We U.S. citizens have gorged ourselves on these myths of our being exceptional and best, deluding first and sometimes only ourselves. What we have
failed to notice for so long is that the very category of the "exceptional"
woman, man, child, or nation suggests the separation of person from person,
of nation from nation, of the "best" from the run-of-the-mill. This separate-
ness seems to us so familiar, but it is utterly foreign to the prevailing national
consciousness in Nicaragua today. The war in Nicaragua is really between a
superpower that is held together by its people's struggles to be exceptional and a
small nation being built by the common people for the common people, no
exceptions permitted, lest the hungry be forgotten and the hope of the poor be
taken away.

We came to realize that there is no health in the assumption that in order to be
good, strong, worthy, well-loved and respected, either we or our country must
be best. For where there is a best, there is a worst. Where there is a worst, there
is an enemy. And, more often than not, where there is an enemy, it is hard to
know whether the tales we hear about our enemies are fact or fantasy, real or
projected, rooted in love or steeped in fear. Nicaragua helped us to understand
better our country and ourselves. Our visit threw our lives and the contorted
values and fear in our nation into sharp contrast against the struggle taking
place in Nicaragua:

One of the turning points in my life, a time when I feel a change took
place within me, came the second time we joined the Witness for Peace
people and others protesting in front of the U.S. embassy in Managua.
The protest is held every Thursday morning between 7 and 8. People
bring colorful banners and signs, wear T-shirts with a message, and sing
songs together like "Down by the Riverside" and "We Shall Overcome."
They have a sound system set up, and groups and individuals are wel-
come to make a public statement. Carol and Virginia had written a
statement the night before expressing our position and feelings about
what the U.S. government is doing in Central America. Carol read it on
our behalf, then read each of our names. It felt really powerful for me to
hear my name, followed by "Episcopal priest, Diocese of Massachu-
setts." I could feel my heart pounding and my eyes filled with tears as I
realized that I had reached the point where I was willing to take a risk in
order to make this commitment to the people of Central America, willing
to speak out publicly against my own government. It's odd how the fear
just melts away or sometimes gives energy to the one who has finally
mustered the courage to make a decision and act on it. Since our trip I
have frequently been the victim of verbal abuse from strangers and even

*acquaintances (yes, even in my parish) when I have worn a pin that states
my position, or a T-shirt with a pro-Central American slogan, or have
preached the gospel and used as illustrations anything whatsoever to do
with Nicaragua. It can feel very isolating and frightening. But I'm
convinced that I'm doing the right thing and, for the most part, it feels
good.*

—JANE

We were converted in Nicaragua, but our conversion was very different from
what most people in the United States consider when they hear the word
conversion. In the United States most people think of conversion as an inner,
private experience. It is an experience that turns us inward and away from the
Holy One who meets us in relation to our neighbor. Our "faith" in the United
States has been synonymous with our acting and thinking *in conformity* with
the dominant moral ethos of society. In this individualistic/anti-social way,
"conversion" to such "faith" has been an effective instrument of social control, wielded by rulers of church and state to the same end: the maintenance of
a status quo that serves to keep the power in the hands of those who have it.

The movement to the political Right in the United States has been embraced
and, in ways, led by architects of the religious Right under the rubrics of
"faith" and "conversion." The prevailing moral ethos in our nation, signaled
by the Reagan landslide in 1984, testifies shamefully to the perversion of the
moral character of love. To actually love is to treat our brothers and sisters in
exactly the same way we would hope to be treated ourselves—with respect,
dignity, and justice.

The individualistic form of faith practiced by many people in the United
States is not, however, limited to the conservatives or the New Right. It is also at
the very core of liberalism—that very set of values and attitudes on which many
of us have been nurtured. Thus, most of Amanecida's members share the
spiritual and political dilemma of all *liberals*. As typical persons of good-will,
we have been raised and educated on the false assumption that if each of us,
individually, leads a good life, doing the best she or he can, our problems
eventually will be solved—or, if not solved, at least brought under control.
From a liberal religious perspective, conversion is a gradual process: We learn,
over time, to think clearly and well about ourselves and God. We "mature"
spiritually and psychologically. We become more and more self-affirming and
self-respecting. And our god becomes more and more like us. Beverly Wildung
Harrison, professor of Christian Ethics at Union Theological Seminary in New
York, illuminates the dilemma of liberals:

Liberal ideology goes astray not because of its concern for people but
because of its portrayal of people as individual monads and the overwhelming tendency of liberals, now often among the affluent and privileged, to assume that guarantees for individual welfare are already
embodied in our political-social structure. The truth is that in this society

one's "individuality" is respected in direct proportion to one's wealth, social standing, race, gender, and age.[3]

The moral inadequacy of liberal theology, rooted in our failure to understand the *social, systemic* nature of oppression, has begun to push a number of us onward in our journeys for spiritual depth and meaning. The faith of Nicaraguans we met is not individualistic. It is a faith acted out in community. It is rooted in solidarity.

> *The people of Nicaragua have committed themselves to what matters most: a real and simple life, in which bread and poetry are for all. If this is, as many U.S. skeptics contend, a "romantic" view of life, what then do these same men and women make of the simple charge to love our neighbors? A "romantic" rule of thumb? Would these surrealists turn us over to those who have proven that they have no time for such fanciful goals as feeding the hungry and comforting the afflicted—men like Pinochet in Chile and Marcos in the Philippines?*
>
> *Here in this war-torn situation, met by the witness of Nicaraguan campesinas as well as Sandinista leaders, I recognize in these people what I value in us all. U.S. citizens are wounded by our lack of solidarity, our failure to realize that we are a common people. It is not my particular failure, or anyone's, but rather ours together. Those who come bearing good news that there is a better way, a more caring, less cluttered way, are always folks who have found this way together, working for some form of justice to which they are passionately committed. I delight in the liberation that can come when people act together, living and working cooperatively rather than as self-sufficient monads. I am beginning to turn further from those people-eating, self-denying, god/ess damning rituals of being "exceptional" in the great society, great religion, great movement, great anything.*
>
> —CARTER

Listening in Nicaragua, Amanecida hears words of trust spoken by people who know what they believe. They believe in themselves and in us as bearers together of blessing to this world. Turning to us, the Nicaraguans bear God: One who trusts us. We U.S. citizens are not condemned. We are affirmed, blessed by the assurance that we are received in Nicaragua as friends. We are embraced as a gift to the people of a nation which our own has pledged to destroy. "How can this be?" we ask. "Because we know that you care," they have replied.

In Nicaragua, we hear echoes of the same radical affirmation, at once collective and individual, which some of us first heard clearly and unequivocally in the women's movement. For a number of us, a feminist consciousness-raising group was a place in which conversion began to take hold. It was a place in which we began to come to life, as we realized our collective power as women. As Laurie testifies, "It was when I began to see that something was wrong and to connect that sense of wrongness with a growing, empowering anger." It was through feminism that we began to refuse to apologize for our inquisitive minds, resonant voices, strong bodies, vocational abilities, political commitments, and woman-centered spirituality. According to Laura, "As each day passes I grow in my ability to reject the mentality which asserts that I am less adequate, less informed, less important, less everything than my white, middle-class male counterparts." Turning *proudly*, we meet the One who has been with us all along—from the beginning, the source of a radical sense of self-worth. She has never been more fully present to us than in Nicaragua.

Traditionally, justice-seeking Christians have named this One the "Christ"—specifically, Jesus Christ, our Lord, the One who holds authority over all earthly rulers. More recently, liberation theologians have built upon the same christological foundations a suggestion that Jesus Christ, this Lord of all, is the God of the poor: the One who is with the poor and like the poor and, only in so being, is God of all. Today, the Nicaraguan Christian people draw afresh from a wellspring of spiritual images: Jesus Christ Liberator has come to Nicaragua through the life and struggle of General Augusto Cesar Sandino who lives forever and is embodied in *el pueblo*: *the people*.

Nicaragua had helped us to begin to move from fear to solidarity; it had helped us to continue our turn from alienation and an individualistic faith to a faith rooted in community and the God who lives among the poor and exploited. Gustavo Gutiérrez has written that conversion "means thinking, feeling, and living as Christ-present in exploited and alienated [human beings]"; he says conversion "involves a break with the life lived up to that point . . . and presupposes . . . that one decides to set out on a new path"; he says that it is "a break with sin and [as such] will have to have both a personal and a social dimension. . . . [Conversion] does not exclude but rather calls for . . . an encounter [with the Lord] in the depths of the wretchedness in which the poor of our countries live."[4]

Like Gutiérrez, many liberation theologians have stated that conversion is not an individualistic experience, not a private affair between each person and God. Our time in Nicaragua helped make this lesson incarnate. As Kirsten says, "I see now better than before that conversion happens in the context of relationship. It means turning around to see your sisters and brothers surrounding you."

> *Being converted means facing all people as whole persons whose patterns of living may be entirely different from ours. Actually meeting these people, whose lives are as valid as our own, we were able to move from manipulative prejudgments into active dialogue.*
>
> —PAT

While we were in Nicaragua we were moved by the vitality of the people's faith in God and one another. There we caught a glimpse of the spirituality for which we had been searching. The Nicaraguan people we met in the Christian base communities displayed a powerful and profound faith and commitment to God and one another. Their faith was alive and full of passion, giving testimony to a personal and powerful God among them. This was a faith firmly rooted in the social dimension of struggle for justice and liberation. This was where Gutiérrez's understanding of conversion radically differed from the highly individualized spiritualities that most of us had known best. Conversion calls for a new way of living in the world, not merely a new way of seeing and feeling, but also a new way of acting.

When the earth had trembled, when we had swum in the haunted waters of Tiscapa Lake, and when we had witnessed our actions toward a dying animal while surrounded by humans' deaths wrought by our country, we had begun to understand more deeply ourselves and that complex of values and attitudes that is tearing apart the fabric of life in the United States. When we were present with the people of Nicaragua in the Christian base community, at the funeral in Estelí, at the Well of Death, and throughout that country under siege, we saw ways of living and acting and witnessing that can heal us as a death-bearing nation and as broken people.

Mural in Managua

Children at a wake in Estelí

Farming cooperative outside Estelí

The center of Managua was devastated by the 1972 earthquake. The new Managua is being constructed around the ruins of the old.

Intergenerational survivors of the massacre at the Well of Death

Memorial constructed over the Well of Death

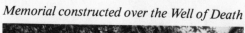

Jane Van Zandt and children at orphanage in Estelí

Children in Estelí

3

Revolution

"But you in the United States can be revolutionary. And the progressive—revolutionary—Christians there, just as here in Nicaragua, *know* you can. It is the same in the church throughout the world. There are those who work for, and those who work against, basic social change. Each of us must decide which side we are on, mustn't we?"[1]

—ERNESTO CARDENAL

Conversion is not the interiorized result of a magical zap by God. We are not spiritual renegades one day and saints the next. Our lives and our faith are more complicated. Conversion is a difficult process of spiritual transformation which involves the turning around of our commitments and priorities as sisters and brothers in the human family. Conversion has to do with where we put our money, our time, our energy.

Each of us in Amanecida had begun the process of conversion before we visited Nicaragua. As an educational arena, Nicaragua provided time and space for us to reflect upon the conversion process that had taken us to Nicaragua and had been clarified and strengthened for us by what we were learning while we were there. It was in this process of conversion that we began to perceive more clearly, while we were in Nicaragua, certain deeply engrained and pernicious elements of U.S. culture and how those forces—for example, the distortion of faith and love, racism, sexism, classism, homophobia, and institutionalized violence—affect our lives. Thus we wanted to know in greater detail precisely what the Nicaraguan revolutionary process had to say about those issues. To do that we had to gain greater understanding of revolution in general and of the Nicaraguan Revolution in particular.

This chapter is about the Nicaraguan revolutionary process and how—on specific issues—it relates to our lives in the United States; furthermore, this chapter explores how what we learned from the Nicaraguan Revolution can help us work to overcome oppressive structures in the United States. As we studied and evaluated the Nicaraguan Revolution, we asked ourselves how what we were learning related to our faith—a question close to the faith and politics of many Nicaraguans. We found that we needed to examine more deeply than we had prior to our trip the relationship between faith and politics in the United States and in Nicaragua. As we delved into that relationship we came to understand clearly that the U.S.-backed war against Nicaragua is being waged not only on military and economic levels, but also on a theological level. The relationship of politics and faith becomes a key to understanding the Nicaraguan Revolution and forces of oppression at work in Nicaragua, the United States, and our lives.

PREREQUISITES TO UNDERSTANDING REVOLUTION: AN OPEN MIND AND SELF-UNDERSTANDING

Tonight in Estelí Kirsten and I had a two-and-a-half hour meeting with the Mothers of Heroes and Martyrs, women whose children have died either fighting in the insurrection against Somoza or since then defending the revolution. Eight mothers got together with us to talk about their dead children.

One mother said that her son was seventeen years old when he started working with the Sandinista Front. He entered the National University and worked organizing student demonstrations against Somoza. After the Triumph he went to the northern border of Nicaragua to work with security forces. He died in November 1983 in combat. The contras gouged his eyes out and tortured and mangled him.

Another mother said that during the war for liberation her sons left to take up armed struggle. Her sons returned, but the National Guard had cut off the entrance to Estelí. It was being attacked by land and air. They were with fourteen other men. Her twenty-one-year-old son stayed to cover their retreat. "That's when they killed him. He was the only one left to face the fire of a whole squadron and three bombers. He knew he would be killed. They tortured him and burned him alive. We couldn't retrieve his body, but the retreat was successful."

The third woman to speak to us said: "After the Triumph, my son was in the reserve battalion because he didn't want to see the people exploited by contras. In 1982, in the mountains, at the age of eighteen, he fell in combat. They brought my son to me dead. We're still suffering the same way. My son grew up having a gun in his hands."[2]

—ANNE

What do *we* know about revolution—we who are North Americans, U.S. citizens? What in our lives prepares us for meeting the people and hearing the stories of revolution in Nicaragua? Many, or most, people in the United States view revolutions and their causes in abstract and monolithic terms: for instance, believing that all revolutions have as their roots communism or atheism and that all are somehow caused by the Soviet Union. This abstract, generalized, and simplistic view of revolution prevents people from coming to grips with the reality of revolution. As we saw in Chapter 1, revolutions—such as that in Nicaragua—are caused by oppression.

I should never even have been able to speak the word: revolution. *White southern ladies do not give a damn about revolution. Debutantes do not speak of revolution unless we are deranged. Randolph-Macon Women's College girls have seen "revolution" only as a ten-letter word in textbooks that we hurry on through. Christians don't approve of revolution unless it refers to the spiritual war in heaven between, in the racist imagery we know so well, "the children of light" and "the children of darkness." Patriotic U.S. citizens do not believe in the virtues of any revolution, except our own little fracas some two hundred years ago against England, a bloody battle we've cleaned up in our historical memory out of respect for those nice white English gentry who are, after all, our right-cultured ancestors.*

I should never have even come upon the word, certainly not to linger. But I lucked out. My tenth-grade world history teacher understood that the history of the world cannot be comprehended apart from students' willingness to study revolution. Thus, in 1960, at age fifteen, I became a student of revolution—specifically, of the turbulence in the Congo, which my teacher, in her wisdom, would not allow us to dismiss as part of a communist plot.

Since then I have always assumed that behind every revolutionary lurks a teacher, parent, friend, someone who knew how to teach people how to think. Not what to think, but how. Rule number one: You must begin with an open mind.

I am clear, as a teacher, that an open mind is the most precious gift I can offer, and certainly the most valuable offering I can receive, in relation to those who go with me into unexplored terrain and who discover there, with me, something we have not known before—and something we would not know today had we begun our travel with a closed set of assumptions.

A revolutionary is a participant in the historical process of social transformation in which basic institutions—that is, government, church, family—become something other than what they were. A revolutionary teacher knows that we are apt to find something new, an image we have not seen before in quite this way. A revolutionary teacher knows the revolutionary meaning, hence the social value, of what she teaches. She knows that knowledge is never neutral and that all we say, write, or read—and all we do not say, write, or read—does some service or disservice to the well-being of the creation in which we live.

—CARTER

Before beginning to look at the revolutionary process in Nicaragua, we must begin the process of letting go of the idolatry-making structures that would keep our minds closed and keep us from finding something new in this journey. Thus the second step in understanding and learning from revolution is that we need to look carefully at *our own lives*—the faces and places that have brought us to this point. Our study of revolution would be only an academic appraisal if we remained unconscious of the movements in our own lives. Anne has written of this process:

> *Once upon a time I believed that my "ideal" revolutionary self should not hesitate to become a defender of the revolution living in the mountains. But to be honest, I just couldn't jump into that. To jump into what many North Americans see as a romantic revolutionary lifestyle with no understanding of or accountability to the movements that lie beyond the guise of romanticism would be to trivialize the lives of the Nicaraguan people as well as my own life. If I jumped into someone else's revolution expecting to be an "instant revolutionary," that jump would be but a shallow jump because I wouldn't have paused long enough to see the connections between our lives and deaths, our movements for liberation. To move into solidarity with the Nicaraguan people is to be in touch with what lies under the romantic guise of revolution. This requires, too, that I be in touch with the lives and deaths and the movements for liberation in my own life. If I am to jump, I must do so with the ever-evolving knowledge that I do so from a position of privilege as a white, middle-class, educated U.S. citizen and from the position of oppression as a woman and a lesbian. Then, and only then, does a jump into someone else's revolution become a collective leap into our own lives.*
>
> —ANNE

So we move, sometimes slowly, sometimes quickly, into an understanding of revolution that digs beneath the surface of what we have been so carefully taught. And we are moved to ponder in our hearts the implications for our own lives of all that we are seeing, hearing, feeling, and living. What has been a first step in this work for many of us, before we even contemplated going to Nicaragua, is coming to know the relation between our faith and our politics, a relation we came to understand more profoundly after our encounters with Christians in Nicaragua.

THE RELATION OF FAITH AND POLITICS

In the Nicaraguan Revolution

Towards the beginning of the group's stay in Estelí we met with a dynamic woman who, along with her husband and others, had been instrumental in the organization of the Christian base communities in Estelí. Josefa Rodríguez is a grade school teacher and church worker. She recounted the involvement of church people in the revolutionary struggle since 1977. Her description of the Nicaraguan insurrection and revolution reveals how faith and politics can be united to overcome oppressive situations:

> The fundamental role of the people was our own liberation. The people of the church looked for ways to meet the oppression of the National Guard head on. We organized in each block to confront the repression in an organized way. Solidarity with each other meant that we were committed to dying or changing the situation. Up until 1979, we were organizing without the FSLN and without substantial arms. After the September 9-22, 1978 massacre in Estelí, ours became an armed struggle, fought with homemade arms. Our role was to help in any way possible. We supplied food, safehouses, refugee centers. Many Christians took up arms. Our grassroots work in the churches was to try to understand our political role in a situation that was violent and destructive. At that time the FSLN was mostly underground. Christians were able to speak more freely—right from the altar in small groups. The National Guard was an overwhelming force over the people. There were massive arrests. We were looking for ways to head off that kind of oppression. We organized to confront this oppression.
>
> In April of 1979 [the second insurrection in Estelí], the open and public organizing by the Christian communities joined with the underground military organizing of this FSLN, and in July we won our liberation—running out Somoza and his people.
>
> After the July 1979 Triumph, we Christians helped with the reconstruction of the whole nation. As a result, we have suffered pain, death, and hunger as well as freedom and liberty. Our task has become that of enlightening people about their role in the reconstruction—all taking place at grassroots levels. As Christians, we consider it our role to work *with* political people. The Sandinistas show that working with religious people is *their* agenda. As Christians, we believe that the mission of Christians is to side with the poor. Christian-based community organizations are an attempt to give a response to a historical event in a living context—the life of Jesus Christ as it relates to our lives. The church is not a political power—our participation is not parallel with revolution, but directly integrated within it.
>
> We, as Christians, are in accord with the FSLN. We don't believe in any other platform because none has been shown to be effective in paying attention to the poor majority. Christian people here have decided to live, guard, and defend their freedom.

In February of 1984 during their preliminary visit to Nicaragua, Kirsten and Anne spent some time talking with Christian base community members in Estelí about how they understood this connection between faith and revolutionary commitment, between Christianity and praxis. A young woman named

Elena spoke without hesitation, emphasizing the work of Christians with the Sandinistas since the Triumph:

> In the Bible of Latin America, for us faith is the connection between practice and belief. And there's a passage from St. Paul in which he discusses this. For us it's not simply praying, it's not simply *thinking* about faith. We *feel* our faith. We feel that in order to make it mean something we have to join it together with practice.
>
> Faith without deeds is worthless. Just as deeds without faith are no good either. You have to join both of them together, simultaneously. The connection between faith and practice in such areas as education and health is seen as an aspect of the revolution. Education is first of all being given to the people, which is in itself an expression of faith and commitment to the poor.
>
> Jesus was a person who sided with the poor and the oppressed. And so we see our task as being to educate people in the spirit of Jesus' example. When we go into the reserve battalions and learn how to carry guns and backpacks filled with ammunition, we don't do it with the aim of killing someone. We're only doing this to defend our country. Because if someone comes and knocks on our door at night with the intention of hurting us, we're not going to allow that. Our faith calls for the integration of theory with practice. The need for defending ourselves and protecting the new-found liberation of the poor is very much in line with what people's idea of Christianity is.

Central to the Nicaraguan intersection of faith and politics are the various images of Jesus. In Latin America liberation theology Jesus has often been portrayed as the Liberator:[3] Jesus as one who walks among us and awakens the marginalized of society to throw off the yoke of oppression; Jesus as the Liberator who drove the money-changers out of the temple, fed, clothed, healed, and listened to the poor, and bade us to seek justice.

The Central American Historical Institute (IHCA), initiated by Jesuits in sympathy with the revolution, illustrates on the cover of one of its publications the concept of Jesus as Revolutionary.[4] The illustration is of a revolutionary soldier standing with outstretched arms, one hand grasping a rifle. Superimposed on the soldier is the figure of the crucified Jesus. The connection is clear. In Managua's Barrio El Riguero, the church of Santa María de Los Angeles, a focal point of community organizing before, during, and since the revolution, has murals painted on the walls. One of these murals depicts an unmistakably peasant Jesus carrying a cross. Jesus is one of the people and one *with* the people.

In Estelí Kirsten and Anne encountered a person who explained his conception of the interlinking of the peasants, faith, the revolution, and the sacred:

> *Joaquin Rodríquez is a Salvadoran musician and teacher who lives in Estelí. He found Anne and me sitting on the doorstep of the House of*

Culture (CPC) four or five hours early for our meeting with the NICA coordinators who were going to introduce us to the family with whom we would live for the next week. With our heavy suitcase and backpack, there was little for us to do but wait. Joaquin lives in the CPC where he writes songs and teaches music to young children and to others in the community. He invited us into his music room where he showed us his piano-organ and guitar. He then proceeded to entertain us with his music—songs of the people, of the revolution, love songs, and children's songs. We clapped with delight, pleased to be sharing his music and hospitality.

Anne had her tape recorder and we taped the songs. We asked if he would give us a testimony, which he did. He told us, "The revolution is love; it is more Christian than we are ourselves because the land is given and divided among poor people." One thought which he shared with us impressed me deeply—he said, "Here, the peasant is a sacred person; for us he is someone very great because he harvests the food." Joaquin's statement is no romantic abstraction about "the poor"; he makes the very real connections between the peasants and the food we eat, and he affirms the sacredness of the people and the Earth, conveying through his words a sense of gratitude and humility. That is a lesson to me, encouraging me to look at the poor people in my own country, to understand the ways our lives do intersect, and the very tangible as well as spiritual ways that we are connected.

—Kirsten

La Chavalita is the young girl-child who represents the Nicaraguan Revolution. As each year passes since the Triumph, she ages. Jesus also is imaged as *La Chavalita*, symbolizing the revolution, as well as the revolutionary, and the peasant. The image of Jesus as revolutionary is a powerful and important symbol with Nicaragua, showing yet again the uniqueness of the Nicaraguan Revolution that has so deeply involved Christians in the revolutionary struggle. In Nicaraguan Christian base communities, Jesus is within the reach of the people—definitely not put off on a pedestal somewhere. Jesus is present, in this moment, in the faith of the revolutionary and the peasant—the girl-child. Jesus *is* La Chavalita. For those of us in Amanecida who have had difficulty accepting traditional christological formulations, this very concrete encounter with the Jesus who is present and *with* the people, who *is* the people, helped us to see ourselves and our roles in the United States in a new way:

One evening in Estelí Virginia, Kirsten, and I decided to go to a worship service. I was sure it began at 5:00 P.M., but when we arrived no one else was around and the sanctuary was empty. We sat down for awhile anyway and soon all three of us were appreciating the time of silence. There was no reason why I should have been surprised by this, but the pews, too, were "empty": there were no bulletins, Bibles, hymnals, or little visitors cards to fill out. The only visible thing in the church to focus on was the cross and crucified Jesus hanging in front. I was drawn into the "holiness" of the place, not because of the physical beauty of the building—it was a large, open, cold space with stone walls and floors and bare wooden pews—but because the emptiness of the space was filled with our thoughts. I felt each of us in contemplation and prayer. Kirsten knelt for a long time and Virginia bowed her head. I was imaging faces and stories we had seen and heard, and imagining all the events, the pain, struggle, and celebrations this church had witnessed over the years. We spoke to each other now and then, softly sharing our thoughts. My eyes were stuck on that crucifix up front—something that one rarely sees in a Moravian church, and which is a symbol that I personally had been unable to relate to in my own religious experience. This moment was different, however, for some reason. At one point Virginia said, "That Jesus [on the cross in front] looks more real than any I have ever seen; he looks so young, and so Latin." It was true, and with that I heard again the words one Nicaraguan mother had spoken to us: "When I saw my dead son, I knew in my heart the pain that Mary must've felt when she looked at Jesus on the cross."

It is these kinds of connections—among the three of us North Americans; between an individual and her faith; between people of the North and South—which must be made if there is to be any hope of realizing a just future for this world. And for me it is and was fully appropriate that these connections were and are made in a church.

—CAROL

When Carter was in Nicaragua in November of 1983, her group met with the Christian base community in Estelí. The group of U.S. women and Nicaraguans met in the newly-built cement church. One of the Nicaraguans emphasized the strong bonds among all people throughout the world who struggle for justice and thus linked our work in the United States to the revolutionary process in Nicaragua:

God is always on the side of the oppressed, the victims, comforting them, strengthening them to resist their oppression—always, it doesn't matter which victims. For us, it is us, and our people now. But we are aware there are victims throughout the world. And wherever and whoever they are, God is with them. And will never depart from them. And even if bombs drop or the torturers come and cut us into pieces, we will rise, like Christ, and we will win—whoever we are, we and you who are victims who struggle for justice, or who are *not* victims, but who struggle on behalf of justice for others. You and we are daughters and sons of God. And it is up to us to fight for God even if they kill us. We will never die. We will be *¡presente!* just as Jesus lives today.

This vision and growing reality of the oppressed and those who work with them, uniting their faith with political action for liberation throughout the world, is an inspiration to those of us in the United States who struggle for justice; however, that same vision and reality frightens and infuriates leaders of government and of most churches in the United States because it is a direct challenge to their power.

The Prevalent Views in the United States

In the United States the predominate ideas about the relation between faith and politics function to uphold the status quo. One of the frequently touted principles is that of the separation of church and state; many of us in Amanecida come from an environment saturated with the myth that faith and politics are separate realms. In order to be "effective" seminarians, preachers, ministers, and teachers, we have been told in no uncertain terms that we should be politicaly neutral, eschewing all advocacy. We have until recently been heavily influenced by the assumption that we must fit into the slots which the institutions of our U.S. society and church have proscribed: we must be religious *or* political.

A second prevalent concept in the United States—and one that is mutually supportive of the notion of separation of faith and politics—is that faith is a personal matter. In most U.S. churches, one of the fundamental concepts is of Jesus as a personal savior—a concept diametrically opposed to that of Jesus as the Liberator working in solidarity with the poor. The notions of Jesus as a personal savior and of faith as a personal asset prevent people from using their faith as a basis of solidarity with those in their own communities or elsewhere in the world. These notions keep persons separated and therefore work to uphold and solidify the status quo.

A third view of the relation between politics and faith in the United States is one now being promulgated by religious-political neoconservatives. They have essentially created a mix of politics and faith that is used to support oppression. The neoconservative movement has organized to justify the eradication of various liberation movements—for example those of the elderly, Blacks, Native Americans, lesbians, and gay men in the United States; the peace movements in the United States and other countries; and movements for liberation in Central America, South Africa, and elsewhere. The rise of religious-political neoconservatives has increased the determination of some of us to conquer the separation of faith and politics, as they have, but we are determined to use our faith as a basis to stand with the oppressed.

In Trust or Fear? Two Spiritual Paths

When the Nicaraguan Christian base communities' conception of the relation between faith and politics is set alongside that held by religious-political neoconservatives in the United States, we see two spiritualities in opposition.

The spirituality of the revolutionary Christians of Nicaragua is based on a concrete love of neighbor: to love one's neighbor as oneself demands an act of political solidarity on the basis of trusting that the neighbor is worth loving simply because the neighbor is human. The spirituality that predominates in the United States, by contrast, is one of fear—the fear of losing control. Losing control means risking the unknown. Losing control means admission that one is not always a superpower, not always superior. The fear of losing control is a spiritual disease that functions to diminish our capacity of love. *We have learned to fear our neighbors as ourselves.*

This spirituality of fear has a political dimension because it ultimately works to strengthen the existing economic and political structures that are built on individualism not community. The Nicaraguan spirituality of trust challenges age-old, oppressive political and economic structures and demands systems that benefit the common good.

In the United States many leaders in the churches and government give their blessings to those conceptions of faith that uphold individual rights (largely belonging to white, propertied males) and prevent solidarity among oppressed people. Those leaders work to deny full rights to Blacks, women, gay men and lesbians, and other marginalized people. They work to destroy the Nicaraguan Revolution because they understand the connection between the revolutionary potential in the United States and the Nicaraguan Revolution's linking of faith and politics. They understand that the link between faith and justice-making generates a powerful force that can root out oppressive structures and overthrow governments that practice injustice. This is why they and others, such as the Roman Catholic hierarchy in Nicaragua and in the Vatican, with high stakes in the capitalist-order, attack liberation theology and the government of Nicaragua with vicious rhetoric, dollars, and bullets. The Roman Catholic church hierarchy *and* the U.S. government fear the loss of control in relation to the people of the world. They fear the collapse of systems at once economic and theological. They fear losing their role as "god" in relation to the world.

THEOLOGICAL TENSIONS IN THE ROMAN CATHOLIC CHURCH IN NICARAGUA

What is happening among Christians in Nicaragua is no different than what has always happened among Christians and still happens today throughout the world. There is always tension between those who believe that the church must help lead in the work of justice and those who do not. There is always a struggle between social radicals and reactionaries.[5]
—ERNESTO CARDENAL

The members of Amanecida have been aware for some time of the repressive atmosphere growing in the United States and among the right-wing allies of the United States. We know, for instance, that the tension in the Nicaraguan Catholic church between the church hierarchy and the Christian base communities is manipulated enthusiastically by U.S.-based agencies such as the Institute for Religion and Democracy (IRD).

Before we left the United States for Nicaragua, several of us had been studying in detail the role of the neoconservative think tanks—in particular, the IRD. The IRD was formed as a network of neoconservatives who support the goals of the Reagan Administration. Its particular focus is the theological justification of anticommunist, procapitalist policy.

> What IRD has done in its arena is essentially twofold: it has conducted a disinformation campaign and it has created a Madison Avenue-like media blitz that has succeeded in pinning labels on mainline churches and ecumenical bodies. For its effectiveness in this effort, it has been rewarded well with conservative foundation support and with ready access to the Reagan Administration, including participation in the inner workings of the United States Information Agency's "Project Democracy." It has thus been guaranteed ongoing foundation support as well as probable access to funds available through "Project Democracy" or through other branches of USIA administration. In short, IRD has succeeded brilliantly in positioning itself as a patriotic critic of dangerous anti-democratic, anti-capitalist, and anti-popular tendencies within the churches. It has a long-term lease on its mission and can be counted on to keep up the conservative and neoconservative ideological drumbeat for a few years to come.[6]

The disinformation campaign of the IRD was well underway in the months before we left for Nicaragua. The National Council of Churches, the World Council of Churches, in addition to mainline denominations, had all been under attack for stances on human rights and alleged support of pro-Marxist groups. A full-scale attempt was underway to sabotage the solidarity work of U.S. churches on behalf of Central America. And so it was with details of the attempts to undermine U.S. church support of the Sandinistas in particular that we went to Nicaragua, determined to ask questions of both pro- and antigovernment church people regarding the accusations of the IRD.

Liberation theology, rooted in the empowering, converting, revolutionary faith of the people, is naturally a threat to the keepers at the gates of advanced capitalism. The repression of popular movements for economic change is a hallmark of both Central American reactionaries and the church-state coalition in the United States. The struggle in Nicaragua is the same battle for economic justice that eludes us in the United States. Long after the Nicaraguan situation has been resolved, the U.S. situation will be begging attention.

A primary effect of U. S.-sponsored disinformation campaigns, as well as of the economic and military war being waged against Nicaragua, is the division of Nicaraguan from Nicaraguan. One of the major divisions is between the Roman Catholic hierarchy and the Christian base communites. This conflict reflects several distinct, but related, political dynamics: (1) a stand-off between different loci of ecclesial authority: clergy and laity; (2) a tension between men and women, because it is no mere coincidence that all Roman Catholic bishops and priests are men and many lay leaders are women; and (3) mutually supportive interactions between reactionary civil and religious institutions and between radical civil and religious forces. John Paul II's active resistance to the Christian base communities and liberation theology, together with his contempt for both women and the Sandinista regime, exemplifies these various dynamics. The pope's key role is to maintain authority over church people, most of whom are women and/or laity. The civil forces that can support his ecclesial grip most effectively are themselves authoritarian politicians and principles that can benefit from religious legitimation. Thus, the "best interests" of church and state tend to coincide in the subjugation of popular, egalitarian movements, whether in the United States, the Vatican, or the Roman Catholic church hierarchy in Nicaragua.

In Managua we met with Mary Hartman, a U.S. nun who works with the Human Rights Commission. She told us, in answer to our questions about the conflict between the church hierarchy and the Christian base communities, that the Archbishop of Managua (now Cardinal), Obando y Bravo, has refused to talk with people in *any* Christian base community, accusing them of atheism. Hartman added that the archbishop has even gone so far as to refuse to donate a guitar and songbooks for religious services at the prisons. In detailing the support of IRD and the Agency for International Development (AID) for the church hierarchy, Hartman reported to us that Obando y Bravo received $600,000 from AID to continue work with anti-Sandinista groups and $40,000 from the IRD. She also informed us that Obando y Bravo had expelled eighteen priests from the archdiocese for their political activities in support of the revolution.

South of Managua we visited the village of San Marcos. We were especially interested in meeting the Roman Catholic priest there because in July 1984 another San Marcos priest allegedly had been ousted from his work by the Sandinistas. The priest with whom we spoke asked us not to tape record the interview or to refer to him by name. He told us that the priest who had been ousted from San Marcos was not Nicaraguan. Several other priests the Sandinistas have expelled have been Canadian. Their rationale has been to expel the so-called First-World influence. We asked the San Marcos priest about the politics of the expelled priests, and his reply was that the political position of these priests had been a vow of obedience to Archbishop Obando y Bravo. When asked about the priest the Sandinistas had charged with giving aid to the contras, he replied that due to the confusion around the issue he could not give an opinion.

When asked if he thought that Obando y Bravo understood the revolution, his answer was, "Yes, I think he does because the church played an important part in bringing about the Triumph of the Revolution." The refrain heard over and over again from the Catholic church hierarchy and its supporters regarding the revolution was that they had worked for the overthrow of Somoza and then had been betrayed by the Sandinistas.[7]

Less than a week later in Managua we went to see Father Bismark Carballo, Archbishop Obando y Bravo's right-hand man. He began the interview by saying, at some length, that he hoped we would be open to hearing the *truth* from *his* perspective and that we would not ask belligerent questions. When asked about the tensions between the hierarchical church and the Christian base communities, Carballo voiced several complaints. He reported to us the disrespectful treatment accorded Pope John Paul II during his visit to Nicaragua, primarily consisting of the disruption of his speech.[8] Further complaints took the form of alleged Sandinista violations of the freedom of religion: that the government prohibited Mass from being celebrated on TV (July 1981) and requested that Mass broadcast on radio be prerecorded and censored (March 1983); that the government had expelled sixteen priests; and that the government had formed a popular church. Obando y Bravo accused the Nicaraguan government of trying to "eliminate the Catholic church and implant the so-called popular church."[9] The term *popular* or *people's* church is commonly used by the hierarchy and their U.S. allies in an effort to discredit the movement of liberation theology taking place in the Roman Catholic Christian base communities. They would like nothing better than to separate the people's, or popular, church from what they view as the real church—that which has the hierarchy as its foundation.

To the question of whether one could be both a Christian and a Marxist, Carballo replied:

> It is not possible, according to the teachings of the Catholic church. Deep down in Marxism is an ideology of materialism which negates a God and it would be difficult to be a Marxist without following that ideology. Furthermore, the ideology of Marxism involves itself in a class struggle which means a hatred between classes which runs counter to Christianity and the commandments to love one another. The Christians have turned into Marxists. But almost never do Marxists turn into Christians.[10]

We then asked about the major role of Mary, the mother of Jesus, and the revolutionary character of Jesus in Nicaragua's "popular" theology. The response was:

> The popular church is losing its Catholic characteristics. The popular church has expressed more support for the Marxists than the ideology of the Catholic church. The popular church's purpose is to justify Marxism in Latin America. Mary has been politicized. The objective of the government seems to be to weaken the Catholic church.[11]

The Catholic church hierarchy has been linked with both Nicaraguan and U.S. political forces that oppose the Nicaraguan government. The Consejo Superiór de la Empresa Privada (COSEP—the private enterprise organization in Nicaragua)[12] and *La Prensa*, the opposition daily paper, are the archbishop's staunch allies. The Reagan Administration and, particularly, the Institute for Religion and Democracy provide financial support for Nicaragua's official church. Not surprisingly, the Vatican is right there too—as evidenced by the increasing opposition to Latin American liberation theology.[13] We believe this coming together of superpowers has everything in the world to do with faith and politics.

What is at stake here for the church hierarchy, the U.S. government, COSEP, and other counterrevolutionary forces is *power*—or control over. These forces are afraid of losing their power, their god, and their investment in the status quo. They will do anything to keep that power from being threatened. The church hierarchy has power to lose with the spread of the theology of liberation. As the laity organize themselves and come into their own power, the orthodoxy of the church is challenged. Whenever Marxists and Christians share the faith in the people and commitment to justice for all, the God-ordained sanctity of capitalism is called into question. This is the case not only in Nicaragua, but in the Philippines and in South Africa—wherever liberation movements are growing strong.

Carballo's response to the images of Jesus as revolutionary—that the popular church is losing its Catholic and Christian characteristics—is a response that presumes to define the nature of faith. It is no surprise that Carballo says that the popular church is outside the faith. How many times have challengers of the status quo been cast out and crucified, branded, and burned as heretics? Anathematized, cast under the feet of those in power? How many times have U.S. citizens who question and protest government policy been called un-American, a threat to democracy?

Those of us in Amanecida who have experienced marginalization in the church and society as Latina, as women, or as lesbians are no strangers to being told that we do not fit the one, true, acceptable mold. It is when the historically marginalized come into a recognition of our own power and insist on claiming our places in church and society that the institutional forces of church and state band together to attack the revolution. When we documented that the United States is financing a war against Nicaragua, we came more clearly to understand the dynamics and structures within U.S. culture that generate oppression in Nicaragua and the United States. The Nicaraguan Revolution in many ways is a counterforce to those structures and values that are major causes of oppression in the United States and elsewhere. Carol has written of the interrelatedness of these forces:

> *I went to Nicaragua firmly convinced that it is and was possible to prioritize the issues—that the revolution, and the preference for the poor is somehow more important than other issues (especially sexism). My thoughts have changed to the point where I now see that racism, sexism, and homophobia must be dealt with and understood as forces integrated in opposition to the revolutionary process.*
>
> —CAROL

We found that if we were to learn something from the Nicaraguan Revolution about how to combat the forces of oppression, and if we were to discover the connections between ourselves and the revolution, then we had to turn a critical eye on the revolutionary process. We had to understand its failures and its successes. It became important during and after our time in Nicaragua to raise issues of racism, sexism, homophobia and violence *because* of our connection with the people of Nicaragua.

RACISM IN THE NICARAGUAN REVOLUTION

One of the most frequent charges against the revolution is the racism of the Sandinista government in relation to Miskito, Suma, and Rama Indians. The Sandinista government has admitted the mistakes of some of its past policies toward the Indians. Milú Vargas (at the Council of State), Justiniano Leibl of the Center for Rural Education and Development (CEPA), Benjamin Cortéz of the Evangelical Committee for Aid and Development (CEPAD), Pastor Norman Bent of the East Coast–based Moravian church, and Bishop Sturdie Downs of the Episcopal church helped us begin to understand the problems facing the Sandinistas and the Indians.

A long history of distrust exists between the Spanish-speaking people of the West Coast and the Suma, Rama, and Miskito Indians of the East Coast. The East Coast, historically, has been dominated by Great Britain, the West Coast by Spain. Thus, the two coasts differ in language, culture, and religion. The West Coast is mainly Roman Catholic, and the East Coast is Anglican and Moravian. Those on the East Coast regard those on the West Coast as their enemies; those on the West Coast refer to the East Coast peoples as *los hermanitos de la costa*, "the little brothers of the coast," thereby withholding full, adult Nicaraguan status from the Indians.[14]

The current problems between the Sandinista government and the Indians developed in 1979 in an attempt to integrate the East Coast into the revolutionary process. The government attempted to make the East a part of the national system of reconstruction without regard for cultural differences. This triggered a spiral of misunderstanding in which the Sandinista representatives failed to work constructively with Indian liberation leaders, leading to the subsequent jailing of Indian people. In addition, the forced removal of Indian people for military and economic reasons from the Rio Coco area (bordering Honduras) heightened the tensions.

East Coast church leaders have been working with the Sandinista government to improve the situation.

On December 5, 1984, Nicaragua's newly elected government announced its recognition of the historic claim of the Atlantic Coast for greater autonomy and inaugurated a national commission to study and implement this process. . . . At the same time, regional commissions for reflection on the autonomy question were formalized in Northern and Southern Zelaya. Following broad consultations with the coastal peoples to be carried out by these regional Committees, the national commission will be mandated to draft a special statute for incorporation into the country's new constitution. For the first time in Nicaragua's history, the word *autonomy* is making headlines in a positive way.[15]

What the agreement means for those on the East Coast is 1) a guarantee of special cultural rights and 2) the opportunity for the development of local self-management. Popularly elected governments will be formed in Zelaya North and Zelaya South provinces.

Moravian pastor Norman Bent notes that the East Coast situation is made more difficult because of CIA involvement in the area. With the counterrevolutionaries, the CIA recruits Indian people in its campaign to "destabilize" further the Nicaraguan government.[16]

As long as the United States is involved in "covert" assaults on Nicaragua, the situation between East and West Coast Nicaraguans is likely to remain stalemated. U.S. citizens need to be clear about the fact that our nation is attempting to exacerbate, and capitalize on, the racism of the dominant (majority) group of Nicaraguans (Hispanics on the West Coast). The United States works to fuel racism and then points an accusatory finger at the Hispanics (including most of the Sandinistas) charging them with racism; in this way U.S. leaders attempt to bolster the credibility of their efforts to "remove" the Sandinistas.

It is ironic that the government of the United States and the administration of Ronald Reagan in particular have the audacity to accuse another government of being racist. The Reagan Administration has systematically assaulted the rights of Blacks and other minorities in the United States. Moreover, while charges of racism are leveled by Washington against Nicaragua almost daily, we seldom hear any significant condemnation of the genocide against Indian people that has been implemented by the U.S.-allied government of Guatemala; nor do we see many forceful and concrete actions initiated by the Reagan Administration against South Africa's blatant and murderous system of apartheid. The U.S. administration accuses and condemns other governments of racism but is rarely willing to listen or negotiate when it comes to its own racist policies. By contrast, the government of Nicaragua has begun to negotiate with the Indians of the East Coast, and has granted greater autonomy to the Indian groups.

SEXISM IN NICARAGUA

At a meeting one night in a poor barrio outside Estelí, the face of one woman, Josefina, caught and held my attention throughout the meeting. She sat on the other side of the fire from me, with a young child in her arms. Her face was rather gaunt with pronounced cheekbones, and the firelight etched the shadows deeper into her face. Her eyes caught the light of the flames, and they communicated a dignity and a depth of experience. Hers was a face older than her years. I was captivated by her spirit which shone through her eyes, and when we returned that night to our hotel, I took out my drawing pad and sketched for a long time trying to feel her expression and her spirit through my pencil.

A few days later we went back to that neighborhood to help the people plant trees for firewood. Josefina was there laughing and smiling a toothless smile. She was playful as she handed us the baby trees and helped us over the fence. I asked to take her picture, and she became very serious as she looked directly into my lens. We talked some and she explained to me how her husband had abandoned her and the children years before, and she was left alone with the responsibility of raising and providing for her family. The situation is typical of many women in Latin American countries. She told me about her life, not in such a way that she was complaining, but simply describing her situation as it is. She had at least four children. (In Nicaragua it is often difficult to determine how many children a woman has since they all take care of each other's children.)

A day or so later we saw Josefina, with her youngest child in her arms, at the rally for Daniel Ortega. I had my tape recorder with me, and she asked if she could recite a poem. I could not understand the words but listened to the tone of her voice, which rose and fell in a passionate lament.

When I returned to Boston, I again sketched her face one night from one of the photographs I had taken of her. I did not get to know Josefina well or learn a lot about her personal history, but her spirit indeed touched my own and I felt her as a sister to me. My sense of responsibility and commitment to the people of Nicaragua is inspired by my sense of connection to such a one.

—KIRSTEN

Amanecida was interested in the status of women in Nicaragua since the revolution. Those of us who identify ourselves as feminists were particularly insistent on raising questions about the treatment of women. We first had to consider the relationship between our perspective and that of Nicaraguan women:

I am very conscious as a white, North American feminist that it would be presumptuous of me to impose a white, North American feminist agenda on women in Nicaragua. For instance, abortion is illegal in Nicaragua. It would be wrong for me to focus on that issue without acknowledging the different context of women in Nicaragua. The infant mortality rate has been so high that the issue for Nicaraguan women is

*keeping their babies alive. The health clinics are encouraging women to
breast feed and are engaged in teaching women sanitary health practices
in the care of themselves and their children. How can I say that women's
issues in Nicaragua are the same as in the United States? The primary
goals of Nicaraguan women are to stop the killing, to feed people so they
have the energy to think about what they want to do with their lives, to
eradicate illiteracy, and to make certain that all persons have access to
health care. Since the Triumph significant improvements have been made
in each of these areas and they are changing women's lives.*

—SUSAN

In Nicaragua we met with many women—mothers, factory workers, women
in the militias, lawyers, girl-children, members of AMNLAE (the umbrella
organization of Nicaraguan women), social workers, campesinas, day-care
workers, and women from the Christian base communities. We found that
there have been magnificent strides in working against institutional sexism in
Nicaragua since 1979. Advertising that exploits women's bodies is now illegal.
An enforced paternity law demands that a man be responsible for sharing
economically in the care of his children. Women in volunteer militias make up
60 percent of the personnel, although women are *not* drafted. Rape statistics
have gone down because of block committees that guard neighborhoods at
night. Women are extensively involved in the work of the revolution—
particularly through organizations such as AMNLAE and the Mothers of
Heroes and Martyrs.

In Estelí Berta Zelidon, who works with AMNLAE, told us about the work
of the organization:

After the Triumph, we formed ourselves into Civil Defense Brigades, and
AMNLAE helps to organize the brigades. There are representatives of
AMNLAE in all of the barrios. We organize health brigades and the
cleaning of the barrios—we check the sanitation conditions: cleanliness
of latrines, number of pigs around. . . . We also organize nutrition
brigades. During the war against Somocismo we organized brigades.
When houses were bombed, we went and cleaned up the dead. Women
have been changing their position in society to one of increased participation and a refusal to be discriminated against.

The day after the Triumph, July 20, 1979, the Sandinista government
declared that women have value and are equal citizens in the country and
should be treated that way. Women's work is being recognized as having
value and, for the women who are working outside of the home, day-care
centers are being made available so that their children will be taken care
of. Of course this in itself shows that it's still women's responsibility to
arrange child care. We are trying to increase our academic level and, after
all the tasks of the day, many of us attend night school. Women are
organizing to participate in all of the different tasks of the revolution—

battalions, brigades, food production, health care. Before the Triumph we stayed in the house. Boy-children were valued more than girl-children. You might notice that people ask if you have any brothers, not if you have any sisters? . . . . Now, even though we have twice as much work, we work (in the house and voluntarily in the tasks of the revolution) because we want to participate.

AMNLAE also works with battered women to work out solutions to their problems and to let women know they have a right not to be battered. The individual woman will decide what she wants to do and whether or not she wants our help. What happens if the man leaves? Who's going to help feed the kids? These are common questions. There's a line between meddling with a relationship and respecting the marriage. We advise the women on what their options are and the decision is up to the woman. We also give a report to the police and they then deal with the husband. But, if it continues to happen, then the woman has to decide whether to leave the relationship. And, if she does that, she is confronted with a whole new set of problems. If the woman does decide to leave the relationship, AMNLAE will help her find work and a placement for the children in day care.

A big help to this work is the fact that there are now women lawyers who take our cases. Before the Triumph there were only male lawyers who always sided with the men. In Managua, women now win the majority of cases against men who abandon children. Now there is a law requiring men to pay a part of their salaries for child support, and it is taken out before they even get their paycheck. AMNLAE does many things, as you can see. We also work with the Mothers of Heroes and Martyrs, with vaccination campaigns, and we visit women in barrios who can't make our meetings. We have made a decision that with our spirit and our energy we will continue to fight against the aggression of the United States, so that we might be free to continue the tasks of the revolution.[17]

It is clear that the Nicaraguan government is working to counteract many of the effects of sexism; however, there are still many problems caused by deeply rooted machismo, which is still very much of a problem. We were keenly aware of all the posters and newscasts we saw featuring the leaders of the country— the nine-*man* ruling junta. Male faces all the time. Not all that different from home. Many of the Nicaraguan women with whom we spoke agreed wholeheartedly with us on the subject of sexism in Nicaragua. As Milú Vargas, a member of the Council of State, told us: "To call yourself a revolutionary you really have to accept equality. But in practicality, it's hard. Now we're trying to convince compañeros that it's better to be equal." Berta Zelidon summed up the current situation of women in Nicaragua:

The men have a fear of AMNLAE because they feel women's eyes are being opened and the men are afraid of that. This means that the men are very threatened by change. The men have always had the opportunity to leave the house, and women have had to stay in the house and take care of children, cook, sew, and clean. Women have an equal right not to be forced to stay in the home.

One of the big problems we're dealing with is machismo. We women in Nicaragua have twice the fight because we're fighting against the military and economic aggression of the United States and the aggression of having a machismo husband in the house.

The situation of women in a cooperative we visited near Estelí bore out Berta's words:

The day we visited a self-defense cooperative farm was somewhat unusual. Only half of our group went, and those of us who did go were very low in energy. Moreover, our spirits were tempered by the fact that there had been more *gunfire than usual closer to Estelí, and rumors of a possible contra attack on the city. We were told that, although the threat had to be taken seriously, the contras often announce attacks and then never follow through on them. When one realizes the toll this takes on the people—to continually prepare for attack—one can see it is clearly a war tactic, for this kind of pressure whittles away at their emotional stamina. We spent only one weekend immersed in that feeling and canceled only a swimming trip because of it. What must it be like to live with this feeling daily?*

Appropriately, the farm we visited was organized for self-defense. That is, members of the co-op work and patrol the farm keeping a twenty-four-hour guard against contra attacks. These have been organized more recently in response to increased fighting deeper into the country (not simply along the borders) and the fact that contra targets are most often farms, schools, and day-care centers. On this particular farm, nearly one hundred people—men, women, and children—work together to plant and harvest potatoes. We were told that just the week before a contingent of contras was seen marching along the top of one of the surrounding hills.

Even though we were told time and again that the change in status of Nicaraguan women since the revolution has been to full inclusion and equality, it certainly wasn't obvious in the workings of this farm! Our guide's attitude toward women (he asked a few of us to stay and have children and didn't believe women should be "allowed" to carry guns on patrol or participate in decision-making) was one reminder that the revolution is still in process, but so too was what we observed in terms of women's participation as being very "traditional"—tending to household chores, raising children, cooking as well as working in the fields. At one point Kirsten disappeared into a living area to talk with a young woman who was making tortillas (a daily ritual) and watching an infant asleep in a hammock. The woman told Kirsten that she would like to be able to go to the city and have a job away from her house. It was sad to realize that, for all its gains, the revolution has had little effect on the deeply rooted sexism of Latino culture, and here at this cooperative the discrepancy was so obvious. We were impressed with the farm itself and glad to see the successful harvest, but we were somewhat disheartened by the lack of completeness of revolutionary change, and some of us said a prayer for the women of that farm in particular and for women in general before we left.

—CAROL

As all the women we spoke to made clear, sexism continues to be a powerful force and problem within Nicaragua. However, it is also clear from what these women said and from what we saw and heard that the government has taken concrete measures to begin to overcome the problem. Pornography has been banned. Day-care centers have been established so that women may work and act outside the home. Through AMNLAE and other organizations, women have become involved in virtually every level of the revolutionary process. Thus, the record of the Sandinista government on the problem of sexism is vastly different from that of the Reagan Administration, which has taken concrete actions against women's rights. The U.S. administration, for example, is reducing the number of day-care centers; making certain that women will not be paid wages equal to those of men performing similar tasks; and giving tax breaks to families in which the woman does not work. In short, the Reagan Administration is working to drive women back into the home. This is the very situation that the Nicaraguan government has taken steps to overcome.

HOMOPHOBIA/HETEROSEXISM IN NICARAGUA

It is an indication of some degree of tolerance that there are no laws against homosexuality in Nicaragua. When asked what the difference before and after the revolution was for lesbians and gay men, Milú Vargas responded: "We haven't paid attention before or now. It is a personal decision. Perhaps now there is a more generous feeling. There is no official policy and no organizational pressure group."

We continued to raise questions about gays and lesbians. And we were repeatedly told that this was a nonissue. "The revolution is more important than these things" was the message from a representative of AMNLAE. Other responses we received from the Nicaraguans with whom we spoke included: "Homosexuality doesn't exist in Nicaragua." "There are more important things to worry about." "Homosexual behavior is being eradicated." "Homosexuals are child abusers." Confusion over the issue results in the linking of homosexuality with prostitution and coercion, because that was a common male homosexual experience under Somoza's National Guard. The Sandinistas are trying to recreate the image of the army as a highly moral organization that does not permit coercion, prostitution, *or* open homosexuality. For many, homosexuality is equated with immorality.[18]

It was not surprising that we encountered such uninformed responses about homosexuality, for homophobia has deep-seated and complex roots in Nicaragua and elsewhere throughout the world. However, because we knew that homophobia, like misogyny, causes blatant and subtle forms of oppression that spread throughout a society, we chose not to refrain from raising the issues of homophobia and heterosexism. Too many revolutionary movements have excluded or denounced gay men and lesbians. These are issues over which many revolutionary movements have become mired in moral inconsistency.

Although the crisis in Nicaragua demands that energy be focused on defense, until sexism, racism, and homophobia are recognized as issues and dealt with, the revolutionary process will be far from complete.

I am what I am and I am a North American. I still have problems with it. It causes pain to my other self, my Cuban self, my Hispanic self, that part of me that hears Sara González and Oscar de León—those hot latin rhythms, the drums, the vivacity. I love Silvio Rodriguez's voice and Ernesto Lecuona's piano. I feel them in my blood. They are part of me. They grab me and threaten me with life, life denied to me for years, years of whiteness, of anglicization, of pastels. I want red and purple, royal blue and turquoise, orange and black. Those are my colors. Tell me of life, Popi, why were you always so silent? Why was our language kept hidden from me? Why was white so important? You saw that I had the rhythms—we danced together. Were you afraid for me? Did you think my blood would cause me pain? Red blood running in the streets, the cries of the mothers and sisters, the babies wailing, "Moma, dondeestás?" I live in a nightmare that I have barely seen. I hardly know it and yet there it is in my dreams: "Cuidado, la guardia está afuera. Where is Alicia, my baby? Do they know? Will they find out?" Yes . . . they always find out . . . the ears . . . the eyes . . . are all around us . . . Listening . . . Watching . . . Reporting back . . . .

Aye Dios . . . The white nuns taught me that you listen to your people. Are my people your people? Do you hear the screams of the children who run and hide for their lives, the children who have no food or clothing or medicines or education? But you are not there! Fidel knew that.

But Fidel doesn't know me. I am different. I am a lesbian Latina. That is not revolutionary, he says. But I am a revolutionary. I am sexual. Did you see that, Popi, were you afraid that I had Cuban sexuality? I do, you know. I am like you. I love women . . . all women . . . and one special woman. Could you see that? Is that why you hid yourself from me? Did you want me to be like sister Susan or Momi . . . Sweet . . . Little girl . . . Cooperative . . . Compromising . . . NO! I will not be. I refuse.

I am what I am una lesbiana norteamericana, una mujer cubana, la hija de los dos padres.

*How do I embrace this brokenness? Is it madness that I feel? Is it
passion, the passions of thousands like me who know no other life? How
do I convince Fidel? or Daniel? or Tomás? or Ernesto? Why won't they
see our struggles as connected? Why are they frightened? I am not the
enemy. The white man is our enemy.* Mis hermanas y mis hermanos—mis
compañeros: *part of our path is to free all people. To do this we must
work together. We must find a different God. A God beyond Father,
beyond the jealous patriarchal role model we have been subjected to. We
who have no power have nothing to lose. The white man will never give us
power, we must find our own. We must take our power. The revolution is
for all who believe that the world can be a better place . . . not just for a
wealthy few but for those who have had the scraps from the table.*

—MARGARITA

Margarita's very personal statement protests against the heterosexism and
homophobia that are rampant in Latin and North American cultures. While
many in the government and churches of the United States openly and aggres-
sively attack the rights and lifestyles of lesbians and gay men, the Nicaraguan
government has seemingly decided that homophobia is an unimportant issue.
In its favor, it has not promoted policies that further oppress homosexuals.
However, we believe that those who lead the revolutionary struggles for
liberation must understand that, as Margarita makes clear, all causes of
oppression are interrelated.

THE ISSUE OF VIOLENCE

*There are civil defense ditches in every yard—in preparation for
invasion. They look like graves . . . . Met four-month-old daughter of
a woman killed defending the revolution . . . . Meeting with Sandinista Civil Defense yesterday. Are preparing for an expected invasion this
year. . . . Reports of contra attacks . . . report of United States slaying
of fisherfolk on the coast . . . 70 percent of the people of Nicaragua
would die defending the revolution. . . .*

—ANNE

As stated in Chapter 1, the Nicaraguan Revolution had its roots in the
repressive conditions under the Somozas. Not long after the Triumph, the
contras began their terrorist campaign against Nicaragua. The Sandinistas
struck back. Beyond Nicaragua's borders, the other nations of Central
America—especially El Salvador and Honduras—are being flooded with
arms, most of them coming from the United States. Nicaragua and the rest of
Central America are awash in violence.

A number of people in the United States—especially those in certain factions
of the church—argue that nonviolence and pacifism are the only means to

break the rising spiral of violence in Central America. Many of us in Amanecida have been influenced by pacifism. We all have different interpretations and experiences of how we relate to that in our present lives. Carol's denomination (Moravian) is a traditional peace church, and many of our denominations have taken strong stands on peace. Laurie and Laura have done extensive work on issues of violence and nonviolence.. Many of us have been involved in feminist work on the subject. All of us have been involved in nonviolent resistance movements in the U.S.

The violence in Nicaragua and the United States are interrelated. The United States is the primary source of the violence in Nicaragua, which night and day threatens the Nicaraguan people. From the day we landed, we were aware that we were in a country at war. The violence of the war was at times terrifying, at times surreal, at times unbelievable. One of the things that impressed us was the courage of the Nicaraguans who affirm life in the midst of death wrought by our country. Flo and Jane have written of the pervasive environment of violence and war in Nicaragua and of the Nicaraguans' and our varied responses to it:

It was our first day in Managua. We had arrived the evening before. We were standing outside a building waiting to meet. I don't remember all the details of the moment. Only that I saw two young boys, one a foot shorter than the other, walking down the street with a large box of cereal in their hands. They were holding the box with one hand each, while each had his free hand in the box. . . . I remember smiling at the sight of this box between them, a box that was bulging with two hands digging for cereal. It was apparent they were enjoying themselves.

I arrived in Nicaragua with a head full of ideas and preconceptions about war, about living life surrounded by the many threats that war brings—only to find evidence that love and life prevail during such conflicts. Two ideas came from this experience that reflected changes in my attitude before and after the trip to Nicaragua. The first was a deeper understanding that the instinct toward life is greater than that of death. The Nicaraguans often talk about the fact that they could all be destroyed, but what they have accomplished to this point cannot: it will always live on in those who know and remember. Yet simultaneously I gained a deeper understanding of the evil and tragedy of war and the damage it inflicts—it attacks people in their states of life and love, when they are vulnerable, where they are most vulnerable. War destroys their homes and possessions, divides their friendships and forces death onto their loved ones. There it was in real people, like the two boys, life being lived under the constant threat of it being destroyed, taken away.

I recall two other images that expressed the same idea.

On the morning we visited the Christian base community in Estelí to join the people in a service, it was raining. The streets were muddy.

People were slow to arrive at the service. One woman caught my attention. She was wearing a white, polyester print dress, nylons, and high heels. Her mood reflected the spirit of her dress despite the splatterings of mud on her legs and shoes. What amazed me was that despite the daily threats to the life of the people in Estelí, so close to the fighting, despite the poverty, this woman could retain a frame of mind, an outlook, that prevented her from looking upon such things as dressing up as futile.

On the evening of Ortega's visit to Estelí. I was roaming among the crowd taking pictures of the people. At one point I felt someone poking at my back. I turned and a woman pointed to her two little children and to my camera. There stood two little girls, no more than four or five years of age, in matching dresses that were stained and ragged but neatly "pressed." Their hair was combed and they wore matching ribbons. Each held a bright red flower in her hands. It was clear this was a festive occasion for them. This woman was asking me to take a picture of her children. . . .

During our time in Estelí, it always seemed that the roosters would act up much more on evenings when there was constant mortar fire. Some nights I would lie in bed and listen, not being able to sleep. I remember how often the sounds they made would sound like human moaning.

—FLO

We had fun despite the seriousness surrounding us. One of the things I enjoyed the most was our trip to a waterfall. Scott, our translator, took us in the back of a truck up into the hills outside Estelí to a pool beneath a beautiful high waterfall. It was a fairly long, hot walk down a dirt road and then through the woods after we parked the truck. Quiet except for the occasional gunfire. The water was brown and very cold. It was hard to wade because of the rocky ground, but it was worth it to swim in the deep water behind the falls. It felt so good to play and we felt perfectly safe. I don't know why. When we tired of swimming, we sat around on the ground with the ants that bite, and talked, read, and wrote in our journals. At the waterfall, a new experience for us was finding bullet shells. There were lots of them. Anne and I made a game of it. She'd hide them under rocks and fallen tree limbs, in the shallow pools of water, and among the leaves on the ground. All I could think of was writing a letter home: "Dear Mom, Today we went swimming and I collected shells." Sounds like a Club Med vacation. Two small boys were watching us and I felt kind of foolish, but we didn't stop. I could have played at that all afternoon, but it was starting to rain. The thunder sounded like gunfire or vice versa; it was hard to distinguish. The walk back to the truck was uphill most of the way, and I was worn out by the time we got there, hot and happy. For me, as I looked at my handful of spent bullet shells, the war was not real. I don't know why the shells were there. Who had been shooting at what or whom? Why? Playing a game with something as

*serious and final as bullets, I felt a little ashamed. The next Sunday we
couldn't go swimming again because it was too dangerous. Contras.*

—JANE

The war in Nicaragua impinges upon festivity and play, upon the lives of
children, visitors, everyone. One is forced to think deeply of its causes and how
it can be stopped. During and after our trip we spoke among ourselves about
violence and our response to it. As we dialogued, we saw more clearly the
interconnectedness of the violence and oppression within the United States and
the violence being waged by our country against the people of Nicaragua.
What follows is an edited transcript of a conversation we had about violence,
nonviolence, and pacifism:

Carol: When pacifists criticize the Nicaraguan Revolution because of the
Sandinistas' violence in defense of the country, I am perplexed.

Carter: The pure pacifism that I hear from some of the Catholic left bespeaks a
detachment from life in the world as it is actually lived by the vast majority
of people. To condemn all revolutionary struggle as violent and, therefore, wrong is, I believe, arrogant. It also reflects often a classist, racist,
sexist perception of our life together. This idealization of how the world
ought to be is promulgated largely by white, highly-educated, class-
privileged people who can advocate nonviolence while not having to think
about how to protect themselves from death squads, rapists, or starva-
tion.

Kirsten: Learning about the horrors of the Somoza dictatorship, as well as
those currently perpetrated by the contras—acts of terror, torture, the
murdering of children, women, and men, doctors, nurses, teachers; the
bombings of day-care centers, hospitals, schools, farms, food storage
centers—I can understand why people are carrying guns and defending their
lives in Nicaragua.

Susan: Jesus was executed on a cross very violently by the state and religious
leaders. Jesus chose to be totally unprotected by choosing that kind of
death. Here we are as a First World—exploitative—country, getting so
wrapped up in wanting to secure and defend ourselves with more weapons
and more barriers so people can stay away from us.

The image of Jesus that we have is a Jesus who did not have these barriers,
did *not* defend, and chose to live unprotected. Nonviolence for us as U.S.
citizens is something very different than it is for those who are the victims of
our defense system. We can't advocate nonviolence for everyone.

Anne: Last February one of the young women in a Christian base community
said to Kirsten and me that if people were going to come into their houses
and kill them, then they weren't just going to stay on their knees and pray.
They were going to *do* something about it. You see, for too long those who
hold power have brainwashed the powerless into believing that pacifism,
passivity, and nonviolence are all the same and constitute the greatest ideal
for which to strive. When the powerless resist the violence being done to

them in their home or country, those in power are quick to name that "violent."

Laurie: I agree. I think that the line drawn between what is a violent act and what is not is often very fuzzy. Violence can be anything from *thinking* vengeful thoughts to *speaking* (psychological abuse, manipulation, character assassination) to *touching* another person in an objectifying way (pornography, rape, stabbing, shooting, beating) to *treating* any groups or peoples as objects (as in race, class, sex, or sexual preference oppression).

Elaine: But you're defining violence in strictly *negative* terms! "Violence" is sometimes a means of liberation for people who are suffering.

Laurie: I know that, but I think that the goals of our struggle are nonviolent goals. And I agree with Gandhi who said, "It is better to resist oppression by violent means than to submit, but it is best of all to resist by nonviolent means." I also think that we can only understand violence within particular, concrete, historical situations, and that sometimes nonviolence may not be the best solution to an oppressive situation.

Elaine: "Nonviolence" is a negative term. I prefer something like "peace"—by whatever means necessary, even if the means are violent. Plus, I think that we need to make a distinction between "violence" used to exploit people in an oppressive situation and "violence" used to defend and liberate oneself from a destructive and dehumanizing situation. In my opinion, these two types of violence are not the same thing and using the word *violence* for both situations obscures this. The violence versus nonviolence issue is not an issue for me.

Margarita: I think I can see what you're saying, Elaine. Peace is a complicated matter for all of us—those of us who are pacifists and those of us who are not. But it is imperative to see the issues of peace as intricately connected with justice. It is very difficult to explain the need for armed struggle to people who are pacifists. I have many friends who are pacifists and who see any and all violence as perpetuating the cycle of violence. Some of these folks make the necessary connections between peace and justice and some do not. Some understand the parallels between imperialism, militarism, and capitalism on one hand and sexism, classism, racism, and heterosexism on the other. Some do not. I believe that it is imperative for us to help make these connections if there is ever to be a true and lasting peace—a peace where the rich do not have all the power to exploit labor for profits, a peace where the marginalized and exploited can be empowered and self-determining about the direction their lives will take.

Kirsten: Back in the United States, although my eyes have been opened to the violence that our country directs against other nations as well as at the poor, the elderly, the people of color, the women, and the gay men and lesbians of this nation, I have no intention of "learning how to handle a gun." Though our struggles are intimately linked with the people of Nicaragua (and elsewhere), our struggle is a different one.

Flo: Yet, although our struggle is a different one, at base is the common desire to resist injustice. Even while the masses of people cannot use violence against those in power, violence is being used against them. U.S. violence, both foreign and domestic, is perpetrated on the most vulnerable—Blacks, Hispanics, Native people, women, children, the poor.

A number of themes and attitudes ran through our discussions about violence. First, we are critical of certain aspects of the nonviolent movement in the United States. What many of us see as missing in the nonviolence movement of the predominantly white, male, radical Roman Catholic left is a liberation perspective that *includes* an analysis of the connections among, as Margarita pointed out, imperialism, militarism, and capitalism on the one hand and classism, racism, sexism, and heterosexism on the other. Those of us who work from an explicitly feminist perspective find we cannot accept an analysis that does not take into account the effect its pronouncements have on the oppressed—particularly on women of all colors and children. Many of us came to see pacifism as a class privilege not open to the poor and besieged of Estelí, Roxbury, and Harlem.

Second, we began to analyze the various types of violence. For us, the most salient of these are violence used to oppress and violence employed to liberate. The violence of Somoza, the National Guard, and the contras was and is oppressive. The violence used by the FSLN to overthrow Somoza's tyranny was liberative, and the violence used by Nicaraguans to defend their families, communities, and farms from the contras is simply necessary.

Third, most of the violence raging in Nicaragua is the result of U.S. policy toward Nicaragua and Central America. As the United States supplied the money and arms for the oppressive violence of Somoza's National Guard, so too does our government supply money and arms for the contras, the principle figures of which are ex-National Guardsmen. To defend themselves, Nicaraguans must strike back against the contras as they did against Somoza's National Guard.

The prevalence of the violence of oppression being used against Nicaragua presents complex problems for the government. Nicaraguan leaders acknowledge the validity of the goal of nonviolence, but civilians are being kidnapped, tortured, raped, and murdered by the contras, and the people of Nicaragua must be defended. Benjamin Cortez of the Evangelical Committee for Aid and Development (CEPAD)[19] explained to us that the Sandinistas have not acknowledged conscientious objectors. The churches have proposed that those who are conscientious objectors could work on civil service projects or on harvesting brigades instead of serving in the military. The FSLN agrees with this proposal in theory, but fears that large numbers of Protestant and Catholic youth would choose that option, thus seriously diminishing Nicaragua's defense resources.

The Nicaraguan government has taken steps to break the spiraling cycle of violence. For instance, one of the reasons for abolishing the death penalty in Nicaragua was that its abolition is a symbol that the government does not seek revenge against the National Guard. It seeks reconciliation, rehabilitation, and healing. To have executed the National Guardsmen for their brutal acts would have been to further up the ante of violence. Thus the government is attempting, as much as possible, to begin to eradicate the roots of violence in Nicaragua. Its efforts are severely limited by the U.S. government, which has for decades continuously planted the seeds of violence in Nicaragua, has turned Central America into a cauldron of violence, and has so brutally attacked the people of Nicaragua that they have no choice but to fight back to defend themselves and their revolution.

U. S. REVOLUTIONARIES?

When I think about the possibility of a revolution in the United States, I think of it in three ways: (1) That it will take place as a result of a transformation of values and priorities rather than in response to overt oppression or violence. That is, this revolution would emerge from consciousness of the changes which need to be made. (2) That this revolution will be a nonviolent one. Unless things in the United States degenerate to the point where violence is absolutely necessary, I think that our revolution can and should be nonviolent in character. Perhaps Martin Luther King's spirit can become the Sandino of the United States. (3) That this revolution will be spiritually based. I personally would like to see it emerge from understanding religion in new ways but it need not emerge from religious institutions.

—CAROL

The goal of revolution, fundamentally, is peace with justice, systemically and individually. A revolution in the life of a people is a response to oppression, injustice, and violence on economic, social, military, and other levels. A revolution seeks to eliminate the sources of those oppressions as perceived. A revolution in the life of an individual may involve a conversion experience, an awakening to and throwing off of the yoke of oppression with, again, a determination to eliminate the injustice and violence being done to one's self or by one's self.

—LAURIE

The revolutionary faith of the Nicaraguan people has helped them work with their government to build structures that have as their goal justice for all, and especially for the poor. As part of the revolutionary process, the Nicaraguan government is sincerely and actively attempting to uproot the racism that has caused misunderstanding and confrontation among the various peoples of Nicaragua. Although it has much work to do, the government has taken numerous concrete steps to begin lessening the insufferable effects of sexism. Evidently, the government is unaware of the deep-seated problems of homophobia and heterosexism. The level of violence in Nicaragua is a problem of utmost importance, but because the United States is waging war against the people of Nicaragua, the Nicaraguan government has few opportunities to decrease the violence. The government seems to be pursuing those opportunities open to it.

The evils of race, class, gender, and sexual preference oppression continue to flourish in the United States. The power and the wealth in our land is held in the hands of a few—a situation that the Nicaraguan people know well from their own history. Our leaders are obsessed with maintaining and extending our nation's power over other peoples. Ours is a government composed almost entirely of white, propertied males who wish to continue their dominance over racial/ethnic minorities, women, and others who are marginalized. Ours is a government that, rather than working to eliminate racism, classism, sexism, homophobia, and violence, seems to be working in fact to promote those elements in North American culture.

Helder Camara, former Archbishop of Recife, Brazil, has written of the "spiral of violence."[20] His analysis is threefold: (1) the systemic violence of militarism and capitalism results in the violence of poverty; (2) the oppressed revolt, using what is labeled "violent" means; and (3) repressive police violence is used in response to the revolt of oppressed people.

Through our study of the Nicaraguan revolutionary process and of the government and dominant culture of the United States, we came to understand more clearly that many of the foundations of violence in Nicaragua lie in the United States. For instance, male gender supremacy and white racial superiority in the United States generates violence in our country against our citizens. They also generate the oppression of Nicaraguans by forces armed and funded by the United States forces steeped in sexism, racism, and ethnocentrism. The people of Nicaragua respond violently and counter these forces.

Those who strive to build justice in the United States and people involved in the revolutionary process in Nicaragua long to eradicate the bases of the spiral of oppression. Our solidarity is grounded in that longing. More than once in Nicaragua, the people expressed their solidarity with the people of the United States: *"Estamos en solidaridad con el pueblo de los Estados Unidos."* The concrete discovery that solidarity is not a one-way street amazed and empowered us. The Mothers of Heroes and Martyrs in Estelí expressed their sympathy with mothers in the United States.[21] Time and time again the Nicaraguans stressed to us that it was our *government* which was their enemy, not the people of the United States. They never doubted the human connectedness between us, but prayed that the struggle for liberation in the United States might succeed.

We saw that the wellspring of the Nicaraguans' determination is their faith and the powerful link between their faith and their political acts. While in Nicaragua we encountered many people from all walks of life who embodied the melding of faith and political action for justice. Carter has written of a meeting we had with Ernesto Cardenal in which the poet's faith and political vision empowered us to act upon our understanding that our faith is the basis of revolutionary and liberative work.

Ernesto Cardenal is a faith-keeper, a Christian revolutionary. Outside the Ministry of Culture building, formerly one of Somoza's homes, our group mills, chatting, waiting for Ernesto to join us.

He arrives rapidly, wasting no time, accompanied by a handful of younger men, presumably compañeros who are at once his comrades, friends, and bodyguards. All of the men greet us with a warmth that suggests they are pleased we are there, and with a reserve that signals a certain respect for themselves and for us. Ernesto Cardenal smiles and asks what he may do to help us.

We tell him that we are eager to befriend the Nicaraguan Revolution in concrete, tangible ways, and that we have come to Nicaragua in order to see best how we can work most responsibly in relation to the struggle for justice waged so courageously by the people of Nicaragua. Ernesto asks what questions we may have about the revolution.

We ask about the church. What is going on in the church in Nicaragua?

Ernesto Cardenal nods, "The church here is like the church everywhere. It is divided into reactionaries and progressives. The progressives believe that the love of God is inseparable from the love of one's neighbor and that, therefore, we must help create a society in which all people are cared for if we are to love God. The reactionaries believe that to love God is more important than to love one's neighbor and that these two loves are really separate issues."

"Yes," we concur, "this is like the church we know in the United States. The same division . . . . But how have you progressive Christians managed to become a movement and also to demonstrate that working for justice strengthens, rather than weakens, the church's various related ministries such as pastoral care and evangelizing?"

Ernesto Cardenal smiles, "When the conditions are what they have been in our country, it is very clear to many people that the survival of the people, the actual feeding of the hungry and clothing of the naked, is the most basic form of pastoral care . . . . This revolution has happened because there are so many faithful people."

"But," we press on, wondering if Ernesto Cardenal is aware of how frustrated and ashamed we are about the apathy that trickles down from North American Christianity, our situation in the United States seems so remarkably different. Christians in the United States, most Christians of all colors, do not believe that we can be revolutionary.

Ernesto Cardenal is quiet for a moment, and he nods, "But you in the United States can be revolutionary. And the progressive—revolutionary—Christians there, just as here in Nicaragua know you can. It is the same in the church throughout the world. There are those who work for, and those who work against, basic social change. Each of us must decide which side we are on, mustn't we?"

Here, in the person of Ernesto Cardenal, we are met by a Christian revolutionary whose politics are his faith and whose faith is his politics.

Ernesto Cardenal is a revolutionary because he is a Christian; and he is able to remain a Christian-in-good-faith because he is a revolutionary. We are met here by an incarnation of Christian faith and revolutionary fervor as a single commitment in a person's life. There is no split between divine imperative and human love or between the gospel and our passion for justice.

—CARTER

"We Support a
Free Nicaragua!"

The peasant Christ in a
Managua church

La Chavalita, symbol of the revolution

Mother and child in Managua

Christian base community meeting in Estelí

Children at a Sandinista rally in Estelí

Nicaraguan youth en route to the front

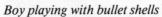

Pat Michaels with orphan

4

Forgiveness

I learned in Nicaragua that forgiveness is a revolutionary virtue. It is revolutionary not because everyone is forgiven, or because forgiveness is all in God's hands. God is part of the revolution. Forgiveness is revolutionary because the former victims of an unjust system—such as that of Somoza—are able to see the systemic character of victimization and recognize thereby their former oppressors also as victims. Those who forgive are prepared to blame the way society was structured rather than simply the individuals who participated in it. The individuals are held responsible primarily for the future, not the past. They are given a chance to change rather than being cast away.

—LAURA

We could hardly bear the hospitality extended to us in Nicaragua. At first we did not trust it. We assumed that the kindnesses shown us were part of a strategy to "win us over," a manipulative ploy by which we were being seduced to stand with the Nicaraguan Revolution against the United States. The longer we were there the more fully we enjoyed (because the more honestly we trusted) this splendid welcome. In a journal entry Laura writes of a chance meeting with a woman who embodied the gracious, welcoming presence of many Nicaraguans we met who are proud of their country.

I separated from the larger group today for a while and walked through some of the buildings ruined in the earthquake of 1972. People live in those buildings, which look a little like some of the buildings in Roxbury and Dorchester that have been boarded up and are waiting to be torn down so some big business can move in. These buildings in Managua were not boarded up, and the government has no intention of renovating this city for big business. No, the government is renovating buildings in Managua so that the homeless will have homes. I spoke with one woman today whom I found in the street washing her clothes in the rain water running through the gutter. Of course my Spanish is about three days old—so any communicating was done through sign language and a few words. This woman spoke with me, helped me understand her, and brought me into her "home"—the ruined building (an old cinema). She seemed proud to show me what she had done with the little resources she had. I remained shocked by her ability to trust me—a North American— so quickly. She told me that she had been living in the building for two years. She was warm and welcoming throughout our conversation. I was amazed—I expected hostility. As we talked and signed about her life, she spoke with pride—in spite of her apparent poverty. I wanted to know and understand more. Finally, because of my inability to speak the language, I returned to our group and asked Scott, our translator, to join me and ask this woman more about where she came from, where her food came from, and if she was a campesina, a refugee, a mother. . . .

She was a twenty-six year-old Nicaraguan with three children. Up until two years ago she rented an apartment from a private owner. After the revolution, the owner was afraid of losing his property (to the poor), so he stopped renting. She moved out and the government put her on a list of people who needed safe, free housing as soon as possible. Meanwhile, she has been living in the ruined building. She receives food from the government; her children live in a public day-care center and will remain there until she moves and can afford to take care of them—she has been told that will happen in about four months. She trusts what the government is doing with her children. She is not worried. She sees her children every day and is proud to be who she is and where she is. It's not easy, but she believes that the government cares about her and especially about her children. She trusts the government. Everyone understands that children are the priority here. I felt sad for her, living in such desperate conditions, but also I understood and championed her pride, strength, and courage to endure and to work for the future in her own way.

As I reflected on this visit, I realized very clearly that the cause of this woman's having to wait as long as two years for her housing is the violent, hateful involvement of my country in Nicaragua. If we would let the Sandinista government continue on with its reconstruction plans, people's lives would be more comfortable and safer, and they would have strength to participate in the reconstruction for the sake of their children. The civilian women and children are suffering most from U.S. policies. I can't help but contrast our greed in the United States with this woman's hospitality, warmth, and generosity. She invited me, a North American gringa, into the building. I could have been CIA, but she offered her story to me—free and without hesitation.

This was not a woman in the Frente or the underground or even a Christian base community. She was simply a mother, a twenty-six-year-old woman with three children. She was proud to be a Nicaraguan and trusts that her life is important to the government—important enough that the government feeds her, clothes her, is working to help to house her, and takes full responsibility for her children while she is unable to do so. The Nicaraguan government is able to recognize that poor people are victims of an old, unjust, violent system. The welfare system is not something people have to beg to get access to or feel embarrassed about—as is the case in the United States. In Nicaragua welfare is precisely that—well fare for all people. This is a right, not a privilege. The poor and the government are able to see that the primary cause of oppression is the old system instituted by the United States and Somoza, and that understanding is a first step toward forgiving the oppressors.

—LAURA

We in the United States are not accustomed to being accepted by strangers because we have not learned to welcome those who are unlike us, or unknown to us, into our midst—especially if we have reason to believe they might do us harm. On the basis of many decades of history, the people of Nicaragua have good reason to be suspicious of U.S. citizens. Yet they welcomed us.

In our attempts to comprehend this graciousness, many in Amanecida referred to how amazed we were by the Nicaraguans' "forgiveness" of us. But, as Flo suggests, "We are giving the Nicaraguans' behavior toward us a meaning that we needed to give it. We called it 'forgiveness' possibly because we felt trapped by our guilt, embarrassment, pain, and helplessness in recognizing what our government is doing to these people."

Do we need to experience ourselves as forgiven in relation to Nicaraguan people? What would real forgiveness involve? This is what we are attempting to explore in this book and especially in this chapter: What is revolutionary forgiveness? When we attempted to answer that question we found our focus directed to three contexts of forgiveness: Nicaragua, our personal lives, and U.S. culture. Examining these three contexts, we discovered that there is much we in the United States can learn from the fullness and complexity of the Nicaraguan embodiment of forgiveness.

FORGIVENESS IN NICARAGUA

We recognized forgiveness in Nicaragua among the Sandinista leaders, within the prison system, among Salvadoran refugees who have fled to Nicaragua away from a U.S.-backed government and army, and among those who have suffered greatly under Somoza and from the contras.

The story of Comandante Tomas Borge and his torturer has become for our times a parable of forgiveness no less revealing than holy scriptures.[1] After the Triumph in 1979, the new Minister of the Interior, Tomas Borge, was visiting the prisons which house members of Somoza's National Guard, visiting the leaders of those who had tortured and murdered up to fifty thousand Nicaraguan women, men, and children during the insurrection. It is reported that on one of his visits to the prisons Comandante Borge came upon the guardsman who had tortured him. When the guardsman realized that Borge recognized him, he asked, "What are you going to do to me? What is your revenge?" Borge responded by extending his hand, "I forgive you. That is my revenge."

The savage brutality of Somoza's Guard and of the contras have generated innumerable opportunities for acts of radical forgiveness by the people and government of Nicaragua. For instance, many children were trained by Somoza's National Guard in the 1970s to torture captured revolutionaries. These ten- and twelve-year-olds were taken, often from peasant families, and given puppies. After some time, they were told they must torture their puppies—poke their eyes out, cut their tongues off, flail their skin—and finally kill them. If the children refused, they themselves were denied food and drink. In this way, the *Somocistas* created dozens of juvenile criminals. At the time of the Triumph in 1979, the victorious Sandinista revolutionaries were faced with a decision—what to do with these vicious young people. The Sandinistas were advised by both capitalist and socialist bloc leaders to destroy the children whose very consciences, it would seem, had been obliterated. But the Sandinistas decided to forgive them.

Tomas Borge referred to this decision:

> Perhaps the worst crime of Somoza and his son was not to have killed Nicaraguans, was not to have converted the guards into criminals, but to have converted our children into criminals. Those children that are now detained were trained to take out the eyes of prisoners with a spoon. This was one of the techniques used by these monstrously deformed children. The revolution has made the political decision to rehabilitate rather than send them before the courts. Unfortunately, some of them are now in facilities for adults; but while the revolution creates adequate centers for them, they are separated from adult prisoners. We are going to transfer them as soon as we can. Right now, we cannot afford to leave them in the streets because we would transform them into delinquents; without work and with all the deformities they have suffered, these little kids would become murderers and thieves and would come back to prison to pay for their new crimes. Thus, we would not do them any favor. We will transfer them to proper establishments to rehabilitate them.[2]

We all spoke with women whose children had been killed—and often tortured—at random or in battle by the contras. Kirsten reflects upon a meeting with one such woman:

> *It is incredible to fathom the spirit of a people who can forgive such horrors and atrocities as those committed during Somoza's rule and now by the contras, both with U.S. backing. In my visits to Nicaragua, I talked with mothers of heroes and martyrs. One woman described how the National Guard killed young people and wouldn't let others near*

them before the animals got to them. When asked how she carries on without hatred, she responded: "I don't hate, but I won't hug them [the counterrevolutionaries] either. When I think of my dead son, then I feel hate. What are we going to do with the old people if all the young people are being killed? We don't hate but we have to defend ourselves. . . . We want to live, to work in peace. We are poor; we are humble. . . . They are killing entire families, assassinating innocent people, unarmed people, nurses, doctors, those who are helping the farmers—this has no forgiveness."

This woman contradicted herself by saying, "I don't hate. I feel hate. We don't hate. . . . This has no forgiveness." I think this is the nature of the process of forgiveness. It is not a one-time act but a daily practice. To be forgiving we need to forgive ourselves and others every day, perhaps several times a day. To say I hate and I don't hate is a contradiction which is healed through the process of forgiveness.

—KIRSTEN

When National Guardsmen were captured after the Triumph and when they—as contras—are captured now, the Sandinista government is faced with the problem of how to deal with those men, many of whom have spent years of their lives torturing and murdering civilians. The government is faced with a choice of retribution or forgiveness, and it has taken the difficult step of building a prison system whose goal is rehabilitation. To determine if and how this systemic forgiveness is carried out, we visited various types of prisons in Nicaragua. Laura and Virginia went to a "C" (minimum security) unit in Estelí, and most of us visited a "B" (medium security) prison in Managua. Laura writes of her experiences in the prisons in Estelí and Managua:

The most profound experience for me in Nicaragua was to recognize the compassionate relationship between prisoners and the community. The trust between them allowed for prisoners' growth and rehabilitation and the whole community's creative reintegration. This trust is, in part, a product of the government's belief that all human life is sacred. Forgiveness has to do with this recognition. When the decision was being made as to whether capital punishment, for example, was consistent with or a contradiction of the new system, the government decided it was a contradiction.

Forgiveness is much grander than our individuality. From my visit to the "C" prison in Estelí I learned that systemic change is not based on a unilateral decision made by the government or the hierarchy of a prison system and then forced upon the people. Systemic change is a process rooted in the lives of all the people. The lives of prisoners are as important as those of priests, business people, Sandinista leaders, and soldiers. Real forgiveness requires the mutual participation of all human life: the whole society.

The "B" prison [La Granja] in Managua was even more striking in its forgiving character. The fifty inmates of this unguarded, unfenced prison cooperative were members of Somoza's National Guard and/or the CIA-backed contras. The prisoner who spoke with us was one of Somoza's bodyguards. This man's violent past was beyond question. But there he stood, speaking with love about his country, his family, his fellow prisoners, and his future.

I was screaming inside. How can he be forgiven? How can the poor of this country, of any country, forgive? I began to question my own work with prisoners. I began to question my ability to forgive myself—an upper-middle-class white woman—and I began to ask myself: What is prison ministry? What is forgiveness? If we incarcerated all the wealthy, greedy business people, all the members of the Reagan Administration, and Mr. Reagan himself, would I still be interested in prison ministry? Would I care if these people lived or died?

My answer, after our experience in Nicaragua and after a lot of thought, is yes. Because I now recognize that ministry with the oppressor is also part of the process of systemic change. Ministry, in this sense, participates in the process of radical change.

—LAURA

We not only witnessed the Nicaraguan implementation of a vision of systemic forgiveness and conversion; at times we were directly challenged by and invited into that vision. One festive night in Estelí, members of a Salvadoran refugee collective invited us to a party in one of their homes. Like the Nicaraguans who had shown us similar hospitality, these people, who had fled neighboring El Salvador for their lives, greeted us with gratitude for our presence and offered us coffee and small squares of cake. We sat together, small children playing in our midst, and discussed the current political situation in El Salvador as well as the refugees' experiences of Nicaragua.

They told us that, of the few countries that are offering refuge to Salvadoran peasants and other targets of the right-wing death squads and military forces in El Salvador, Nicaragua is the only country in which the refugees can live and work freely. In Honduras and Costa Rica, they are confined in camps. In the United States, if detected, they face immediate deportation because the Reagan Administration categorizes them as economic, not political, refugees. Workers in an agricultural collective reported that the Sandinista government had given them sixteen acres of fertile land to farm as their own. They can keep the crops they need and sell the rest, and the land belongs to them as long as they need to stay. All of the Salvadorans spoke, moreover, of how good it is to be accorded the same respect and privileges that are given to Nicaraguan citizens. All people in Nicaragua—Salvadorans, U.S. citizens, Nicaraguans, or others—have access to the same schools and medical resources. The only right denied non-Nicaraguans is voting.

The extension of basic human rights to everyone in the country had become apparent to our group. After the death of Terremoto, who may have been rabid, it seemed that Elaine, who had spent much time with the dog, would have to undergo a series of rabies shots. We assumed that she would have to return to the United States because we had been told by U.S. citizens in Nicaragua that the vaccine, much in demand in Nicaragua, is scarce. To our surprise, we were informed by Nicaraguan medical authorities that Elaine could stay and receive the series of fourteen shots in the Estelí health clinic. We were astonished when we prepared to pay for the expensive treatment and were told that in Nicaragua the shots are free—to everyone. This, we were told by the medical staff in the clinic, is because everyone has a right to live—and rabies kills people. People do not have to pay in order to live, which is why Nicaragua (like most nations in the world) has socialized its entire health care program.

The Salvadoran refugees confirmed our experience. People who are seeking refuge from death do not have to pay—for land, shelter, food, or survival resources. Later in the evening, the Salvadoran children entertained us with song, dance, and skits. In one of the skits, most of the children portrayed campesinos working the land. One boy played the role of the landowner who, with loud voice and the tip of his pointed boot, was forcing the peasants to work for him. Soon the peasants began whispering among themselves— organizing. When the landowner returned, they wrestled him to the ground and finally cast him out of their midst. In the final act of the skit, the children returned into our midst wearing the red masks of the Farabundo Martí Liberación de Naciónal movement (FMLN). They demanded that we gringos raise our hands and do as we were told. They then told us to dance and enjoy ourselves! After a few minutes of cavorting, our group was told to stop dancing and to commit ourselves *to solidarity work with the people of El Salvador*. These children had managed to transform entertainment into con- scientization, and to do so in the most life-affirming, celebrative spirit.

> *The people did not approach us with suspicion. Rather, they received us with an openness and love that was very difficult for me to understand or even completely believe: Why should they trust us? But this is one expression of their ability to forgive. Persons are not guilty until their actions prove them so. There were no assumptions about us; that is to say we were not guilty "by association" (for being U.S. citizens). This was reiterated repeatedly; person after person said, "It's not you or the American people we don't like; it's your government.*
>
> —CAROL

What did these Nicaraguans and Salvadorans assume about us, our group? Surely they know, some of them in any case, that we pay taxes which provide guns for the contras and mines for the Nicaraguan harbors. Did it not occur to them that we might be just one more group of bleeding-heart liberals who hate to see dying babies but who have no intention of standing with revolutionaries—not at the expense of our own privilege? In truth, we did not know yet the extent of our own solidarity with the people of Nicaragua and El Salvador. What did they know about us that we did not yet know?

The skit by the Salvadoran children was an invitation into their understanding of forgiveness grounded in solidarity with the victims, with the oppressed. Our nation is funding and arming forces that are slaughtering the people of Nicaragua and El Salvador, and yet the Salvadorans and Nicaraguans were absolutely open to us—it became clear to us that their openness is based on great self-confidence and trust. Against this backdrop of self-confidence, of trust, and of a holistic understanding of forgiveness, we began to examine the quality of forgiveness in our own lives and in our nation.

FORGIVENESS IN OUR LIVES

When confronted with the examples of Tomas Borge, the Nicaraguan prison system, the Salvadorans, and people throughout Nicaragua, our initial reaction was disbelief. We found their forgiveness incredible because it did not fit into our understanding of forgiveness. In Nicaragua, forgiveness was a particular way of loving one's neighbor that was not within the realm of what we had experienced in our lives. For some of us, the Nicaraguan embodiment of forgiveness did not seem entirely just or responsible. We found ourselves confused, asking what our experiences of forgiveness had been.

As a priest in the Episcopal church, I am called upon "to declare God's forgiveness to penitent sinners." It is a very powerful feeling for me to say to someone, " . . . By Christ's authority committed to me, I absolve you from all your sins, . . . " or "Our Lord Jesus Christ . . . absolves you through my ministry by the grace of the Holy Spirit."

I have never dwelt on what forgiveness means. My only recollection in childhood is that punishment canceled a wrongdoing. But I don't remember, in either childhood or adulthood, hearing those words, "I forgive you." I don't even know what they mean anymore.

I think there is a danger in the "turn the other cheek" kind of thinking. I lose respect for someone, myself included, who forgives again and again without making any demands. That begins to look like avoidance and an inability to confront. I am learning more and more toward saying, "These are the ground rules. We both understand and accept them. If either of us breaks them, there will be these consequences."

I cannot "forgive and forget." I resent and remember. I discovered this in my most important relationship. I had decided, at the beginning, that no matter what I would be honest with him. I would not lie. I would not be deceitful. I am convinced that a relationship will begin to break down as soon as either person is dishonest. It never occurred to me to discuss that with him, to propose a covenant which we both could accept, or at the very least to tell him what my expectations were. The fact is, he did not bring the same assumptions to our relationship. He did not assume that he must be entirely candid with me. Because of subtle changes in his behavior toward me, or things he'd say inadvertently, I discovered that he was pursuing or trying to pursue other relationships while remaining in what I had assumed was our monogamous one. Even though we were able to talk about these things when I found out, I discovered that I could not forget and that I could not forgive him, not entirely.

I am angry that I no longer feel that I can trust him at some level, and I am afraid this may always be true. Forgiveness is not such a simple matter. Saying the words, "I forgive you," does not insure that, as of that moment, forgiveness has occurred. And it certainly does not mean that the deed is forgiven.

The key to me in forgiving and forgetting is the letting go. Whether it is by means of a ritual, dialoguing with the person I feel has done me wrong, or a conviction that the incident is resolved to my satisfaction, until I am able to let go, I shall dwell on it and harbor resentment. If, however, I really am able to let go of the anger, and forgive, there is a part of me that feels self-righteous. Either way, I don't seem to be able to feel good about myself.

How the Nicaraguans do it, how those who've been tortured and still today are fighting for their lives are able to forgive their enemies, let go of their resentments, I can't imagine. To have no capital punishment and a maximum sentence of thirty years no matter how vicious the crime, to provide education and rehabilitation for all, no matter how reprehensible their behavior has been, is to me unbelievable. I can't make sense of it, and it makes me feel very, very guilty. I can see why U.S. leaders don't trust this. It seems to me that no one person, much less an entire nation, can live responsibly on the basis of such trust. Still, it is a powerful vision.

—Jane

When we returned from Nicaragua and began laying our plans for class discussion, my stomach knotted when it became evident that everyone, myself included, believed we needed to spend a good bit of time probing the meaning of the forgiveness we had witnessed in Nicaragua. In fact, I do not even remember very well what was discussed during the class meetings on forgiveness. . . . It was as if the word forgiveness *was in a language I could not comprehend. . . . The palms of my hands grew sweaty. It felt like something had been shaken loose. . . . Ever since that damned earthquake in Managua I had been remembering well-buried scenes from my marriage.*

"Forgive . . . forgive me. . . . " my former husband would plead with me. Six months married. An argument, yelling, a slap across the face, a shove against the wall, a slam of the door, the sound of tires squealing, and gone for another night. "What is wrong with me?" I wondered. "What have I done wrong?" Next morning I awoke from a

*restless sleep to the sound of the apartment door opening. He is back. He
pleads. "Forgive . . . forgive me. . . . " And all is well . . . until the
next time . . . and the next . . . and the next . . . until finally I leave.
Forgive? Forgive him? What does forgiveness mean? To me it has meant
broken promises and pain. Have I ever forgiven? Have I ever been
forgiven? I don't know what it means.*

—ANNE

Can forgiveness mean anything except naiveté, broken promises, and finally
stupidity when those who perpetuate violence and harm do not change their
behavior? Can forgiveness be nothing more than limp acquiesence to reigns of
relational terror, whether in personal relationships or international affairs?

*I think my difficulty, maybe ours, in accepting the genuine character of
the forgiveness we met in Nicaragua has to do with a difficulty in
accepting—or forgiving—ourselves. To forgive someone, including oneself, is to release that person from any debt or payment you think is due
you. I have learned really to accept myself. By that I mean that in order to
truly like and respect myself I have to give up all those expectations of
what I "should" do. I have to stop trying to prove or shape myself
according to what others define as an "acceptable" person.*

*For me, this lesson has come primarily through my struggle about
whether to pursue ordained ministry. Originally, the very notion seemed
outlandish, incomprehensible to me. After all, I was at the time a forty-
year-old woman married to a medically retired man; the mother of two
children, with no undergraduate degree. I was employed full-time in a
job that provided my family with the money it needed.*

*As real as these obstacles were, I can admit now the true source of
tension in me. More of a stumbling block than anything else was a deep-
seated sense of my unworthiness—as a woman—to be a priest. In this
way, I was not entirely unlike the poor of Nicaragua or any nation who
must be converted to their own worthiness and value before they are able
to claim their right to justice. Whether we are U.S. women or Nicaraguan
campesinos, our capacity to forgive anyone—the men in our lives or the
people of the United States—has a lot to do with whether we believe we
have a right to justice because we are human and not because we do, or do
not, play by the rules society has given us. I honestly believe that the
trouble I, and we, have had in knowing what to make of the way the
Nicaraguans live in relation to one another and us is fastened in our
failures to believe in anyone, including ourselves, as people who are
worthy.*

—VIRGINIA

If, as Virginia suggests, forgiveness has as much to do with how we regard
ourselves—whether or not we respect ourselves—as with how we experience

others' treatment of us, what are we to make of our common resistance to experiencing ourselves as a forgiven and forgiving people? In Nicaragua we witnessed examples of forgiveness grounded in trust and self-confidence. We began to wonder if it could be true that we had traveled all the way to the towns and hills of Nicaragua in order to begin to imagine that, at the center of our government's contempt for Nicaragua, may reside a *lack of genuine self-respect among many U.S. persons.*

FORGIVENESS IN THE UNITED STATES

Jane's, Anne's, and Virginia's stories provide an opportunity for some analysis of the conception of forgiveness prevalent in the United States. Their reflections help sharpen and clarify the significance of a social malady (with profound psychological and spiritual symptoms) that besets our life together in the United States and, as such, threatens to destroy the beginnings of a better way being attempted by Nicaragua.

In the first place, Jane, Anne, and Virginia speak as white U.S. women from different socioeconomic locations. Their individual journeys are distinct, but they voice a common theme: self-deprecation—a sense of being unworthy; of having no right to be in affirming relationships, to live in a marriage free of violence, to be a priest; of being unable to make claims for themselves. Virginia connects this experience explicitly with the sense of powerlessness embodied by all persons who have been led to believe that they are worthless relative to others in the society.

Self-loathing—irrespective of one's race, class, or gender—is a mighty form of powerlessness. When the experience of being worthless is structured into the social order as one's "natural place," an individual's feelings of powerlessness are not simply her or his "personal problem." They are symptomatic of injustice, an experience representative of many people: a woman's inability to feel good about herself, regardless of whether she is able to forgive, cannot be relegated, for example, simply into the realm of private therapeutic, or spiritual, neediness. Jane, Anne, and Virginia give voice to *all* marginalized people who fail to perceive, in their personal feelings of guilt and inadequacy, the extent to which structures of injustice, such as sexism, are wreaking havoc in their own "private" lives.

These stories must be told. They are not private tales. They provide important glimpses into the roots and effects of public policy such as that being hammered out today by our government against women of all colors, the poor of all racial and ethnic roots, gay men and lesbians, children and elderly citizens, differently-abled people, and most assuredly against the vast majority of people (the poor) in Nicaragua, El Salvador, South Africa, the Philippines, and elsewhere in the world where people are struggling for justice. The stories of these three women, each trying to survive the forces of male gender domination in U.S. society, have helped teach us something about how we misunderstand forgiveness: we understand it primarily in individualistic, psychological terms. There are religious and economic roots of this misunderstanding; these roots are interrelated and function to uphold the status quo; they are both grounded in the principle that sin and forgiveness are individual matters.

Wrong Relation: The Price of Individualism

One of the fundamental tenets of Western Christianity is that human beings are sin-ridden. We are, as Augustine put it, a *massa damnata*, a corrupt and damned species. In this vintage Christian schema, God's response to our confession that we are worthless is that it is only through the merits of Jesus Christ that we have been accorded voice with which we may confess our worthlessness to God.[3] Our understandings of forgiveness have been shaped, like all theology, by our experiences in relation to another. In the United States, the dominant understanding of forgiveness has been shaped, like all theology, by our experiences in relation to one another. In the United States, the dominant understanding of forgiveness is rooted in the formative capitalist experience of the need to earn our rewards and to pursue them on our own, expecially if we are white propertied males. All others receive "benefits"—food, shelter, pleasure, forgiveness of our sins—at the will and mercy of those who hold social and spiritual power over them.

Like wealth and power, forgiveness is handed down from the top. It is given to individuals on the basis of merit. This "trickle-down" theology has become a cornerstone of our faith in economic and spiritual salvation. Reflecting troubling elements of traditional Protestantism (individualism) and Catholicism (working towards salvation), this understanding of forgiveness takes the shape of a debilitating theory of redemption, in which our faithful and corporate possibility of living and working on behalf of one another is lost.

This notion of the forgiveness of sin as something given to us without attendant social responsibility works as a paradigm of forgiveness in our culture and affects relations among us. Thus Anne's ex-husband, for example, believed that by merely saying "forgive me, forgive me" he would be forgiven. This individualized understanding of sin and forgiveness is—it becomes clear—very useful for the oppressors. If the oppressed and others can be convinced that sin and forgiveness are individual matters, then they will not see that sin and forgiveness have systemic and structural roots. They will not see that in order to root out sin and promote real forgiveness, the structures of oppression have to be changed. Furthermore, the oppressors often preach to the oppressed that their condition is the result of their sin. Battered women are frequently counseled by priests or ministers to try to understand their battering spouse—worse yet, to examine their own attitudes and behavior for clues as to why their husbands may be abusing them.[4] Similarly, Blacks and other racial and ethnic minorities in our society have been told historically that they invite violence, that they ask for what they get by refusing to submit to majority rule by law and order.[5] A typical Christian response to victims of social injustice is to counsel such people to be patient, forebearing, and "forgiving" of the wrongs done to them.[6] As such, "good Negroes," "good girls," and "good peasants" harbor no grudges. They "forgive" the harm done to them by acting as if nothing were the matter.

This dangerously sweet, transparently individualized understanding of forgiveness, with roots deep in the history of Christian interpretation, is pervasive today among the people of the United States. It has become increasingly instrumental to the "good ordering" of our nation as we have more and more become the paradigm of the advanced capitalist society.[7] Today more than ever, human relationships in the United States are structured according to how they might best serve the accumulation of wealth in the hands of a very tiny number of white males. The actual realization of forgiveness would necessitate changes in those structures. In the United States it literally does not pay for the dominant groups to live as a forgiven and forgiving people. Those who hold financial and political power cannot afford to love their neighbors as much as they love themselves. It would be too costly for them to respect their sisters and brothers. As Elaine reflects,

My father is a rubbish collector. He's been working on the trash and garbage detail in the town of Arlington, Massachusetts, for over thirty years. In the last five or so years, he's become a working foreman, supervising trash crews, making sure that the rubbish gets to its destination, the Arlington town yard, on time. Among many other things, he drives out ahead of the trash trucks to see if the roads are clear and to determine where there might be any unusually large loads for the crews to pick up during the day.

What is it like to have picked up trash for over thirty years? My father never discusses this topic. To most people trash collection has no prestige and is not conducive to bestowing upon anyone a sense of dignity. But I think my father feels a connection with trash. He knows what to do with it. He's an expert at disposing of that which no one wants. He picks up rubbish, jokes about it with his trash-collecting friends, and disposes of it because it's not needed. It's his job to get rid of what other people don't want.

Now, what does this have to do with forgiveness? What especially does this have to do with Nicaragua and the United States? The United States has a lot of trash: racism, sexism, imperialism, an arrogant sense of nationalism, and so forth. That's a pile of rubbish.

If you can't eliminate waste, you die. If you don't dispose of trash, you'll be buried in it. The United States has to get rid of the excesses of its hazardous materials, so it dumps them all over the world. For well over a century the United States has dumped its trash all over Latin America. The United States needs Nicaragua's and Latin America's forgiveness, but the United States is not a forgiving nation and so does not know much about forgiveness. We don't know how to forgive. We don't know that we need to be forgiven. We don't know how to receive forgiveness because forgiveness involves a desire to relate mutually. Forgiveness does not mean just saying, "I forgive you." It's a process. The first step in forgiveness is for both parties to be willing to admit to and dispose of the injury that has been done.

For Nicaragua to forgive the United States would require that the United States do something with its trash besides financing contras with it. The only way Nicaragua could forgive the United States for its treatment of Nicaraguans would be for the United States to admit to its wrong-doing and ask Nicaragua's help in disposing properly, safely, and well, of the death-bearing rubbish we have spread all over Central America and the Caribbean in the shape of such "doctrines" as "national security," "free enterprise," and "manifest destiny."

—ELAINE

Those in North America who monopolize our economic resources by drawing them into the military-industrial arena of big business cannot afford genuine forgiveness, for they cannot afford systemic changes that would result in racial, gender, or economic justice in this country or in any place that the United States has defined as within its sphere of influence (e.g., Nicaragua, Chile, the Philippines, South Africa). Just as insurance companies in the United States could not afford the passage of ERA, the Pentagon-Wall Street alliance cannot afford a revolutionary economic movement in Nicaragua. In the former case, the demands of gender justice would prove costly in policies constructed on gender inequities. In the latter, a successful mixed socialist-capitalist economy (such as that being attempted in Nicaragua) would threaten the credibility of the so-called American Way as the only way for small nations in the Western hemisphere to order their economies.

In the United States true forgiveness and equality have been subordinated to profit-making: By contrast, the vast majority of Nicaraguans—including their Sandinista leadership—have put into practice an ethic of forgiveness based on justice. Therein is the strength of their revolution. This ethic is grounded in the realization of embattled, oppressed people that the creative power of a revolution is in looking forward while remembering the past. The process of revolution depends on an ability to organize as a network of participants shaped around a common dream and commitment: to live as one Body, in which every person is not only a vital member but is also deserving of respect.

There is no forgiveness apart from justice. To grant pardon, those on the receiving end must recognize their actions as being wrong, in need of pardon. The complete act of forgiveness is a two-way street, involving both the forgiver and the one being forgiven. The act is not complete unless it is both given and received. It requires the acquisition on both ends of a sense of self as forgiver and as one needing forgiveness. It requires on both sides the exercise of judgment—located in a holistic sense of self—to determine injustice and to act together (forgiving, being forgiven) on behalf of justice.

—LAURIE

The members of Amanecida have begun to realize that we went to Nicaragua unaware of how deeply individualized, privatized, and sentimental our images of forgiveness were. Only as we have probed our incapacity to believe in the forgiveness we saw with our own eyes have we become aware of how fully our experiences of forgiveness have been shaped by an unholy and unhealthy alliance between faulty Christian interpretation and the demands of our economic system.

We have been raised in environments dominated by individualism. The "best" individual has specific characteristics: maleness, whiteness, affluence, and self-possession.[8] Women and other marginalized people live as appendages, servants, helpers, wives, accomplices, companions of the true individuals who represent the ideal of what it is to be human—fully human (and, therefore, in proximate correspondence, fully divine). All women and all nonruling-class men live to various degrees in the shadows of what it means to be either a whole person or a holy person: a self-possessed individual. Such an individual is set apart from all others. Intimacy is inappropriate. Love can be only patronization. And all visions of a cooperative human network are suspect. As goals, "socialism," "egalitariansim," even "social justice" are denigrated as "unrealistic" (individuals are too greedy) or "dehumanizing" (contrary to the interest of white, affluent males).

Individualism has its price in the lives of all U.S. citizens and in the nation's domestic and foreign policy. It fosters fear and distrust of other human beings, because they are viewed as threats and competitors. Those who do not match the characteristics of the ideal individual are marginalized and feared. At an individual level, Virginia viewed herself as unworthy of the priesthood because she had been indoctrinated with the belief that she did not fulfill the ideal of being male and affluent. In the United States, domestic policies that would benefit Blacks, women, and other marginalized groups are scorned because they would not secure the special privileges of white propertied males. At home and abroad, those who struggle for collective responsibility and the common good are, thus, enemies of "the American way."

If we are to move beyond the theopolitics of despair toward a vision of a world based on cooperation, equality, and justice, we must move beyond individualism and its attendant assumptions. We in the United States must let go of the assumption that our country must be the best, the strongest, the most technologically advanced. We must let go of the American dream that it is possible to defend half of the world, attempt to convert the entire world to "democracy," save it from "communism," and lay claims to whatever we want because of our status as a superpower. We must let go of the lie with which many of us grew up—that if we do not win, we lose.

We must let go of the lies we have been told that peace is "permanent prehostility,"[9] that nuclear warheads are peacekeepers, and that marines are defenders of democracy. We must let go of the lies that would convince us that the United States is "preserving a way of life" when, in the course of CIA masterminding of military coups around the world, tens of thousands of people die. We must let go of the myth of a constantly improving lifestyle, an ever-upward socioeconomic trajectory. We must let go of the belief that our ultimate salvation is technology, resulting in the avoidance and devaluation of human passion. We must give up the lie of the theories of economics and salvation that ravish the most powerless in every social situation. We must let go of the illusion that we are not connected, that your loss is not my loss too. We must abandon the lies that tell us that some human beings are more worthy of living than other human beings, that some people are more human than others. We must end our complicity in structural violence by changing structures.

Working for international economic and social justice means also that we must live lives reflective of our values, working to overcome the tremendous power that our socialization to individualism has over us. We must move out of the isolated perspectives which keep us locked in the fear and illusion that we are alone. In the struggle for justice, we must work for a world in which all can live as *embodied* people—with enough to eat, health care, clothes to wear, adequate shelter, and freedom from being tortured and murdered. The root of liberation movements throughout the world is the flesh and blood reality of the demands of people for justice. Upon our return from Nicaragua, we saw more clearly the price of worshipping individual rights.

We returned at last to the United States, to the land that proclaims "liberty and justice for all." The following week I started a class at seminary entitled "The Genealogy of Race, Class, and Sex Oppression."[10] It connected with what I had been learning in Nicaragua. Blacks, Native Americans, Hispanics, women, the poor, lesbians/gays are the voices of revolution in this country. My fear is that the rulers of the United States are showing no more skill at hearing criticism than the ones in Nicaragua before the revolution. Because of the immense wealth of the United States, the leaders have come up with very sophisticated methods to numb the pain and the fear that comes with hearing the voices of anguish in this country and around the world.

Instead of working to insure that everyone has a place to sleep, enough to eat, health care, and education, we build death-dealing nuclear arsenals. Justice is measured by the plumb line of the "vital interest of the United States." But our "interest" is insatiable. Our country represents 5 to 7 percent of the world population, yet we consume 60 to 70 percent of the world's resources. We disguise this greed by calling it "good" by calling the United States the "promised land." The demands of Black America for justice are muffled by name-calling and racist backlash. Women's demands for justice are met with physical rape and exploita-

tion. The demands of the poor for justice are met with the destruction of domestic social welfare programs and the injunction to "pull yourselves up by your own bootstraps." The demands of lesbians and gays for justice are met by taking away access to children, jobs, and churches.

—VIRGINIA

Nicaragua has begun to create justice, in which the needs and desires of individuals are taken seriously in the context of community. It is the opposite of what we have learned to value, or even to believe is possible, as a way of life together. The effects of our disbelief are harsh and cruel.

The Criminal Justice System

The Nicaraguan prison system not only inspired us to reassess forgiveness in our lives but to examine the role forgiveness plays in the institutions of the United States. When the U.S. and Nicaragua criminal justice systems are juxtaposed, startling contrasts leap forth. Kirsten states the essential characteristics and goals of the Nicaraguan system:

Forgiveness allows for and encourages personal and social change. From accounts I have read about the Nicaraguan prison system and from what I experienced and saw in the prison we toured near Managua, it seems to be a system based on forgiveness. There was a sign in one prison that read: "We do not look to the past, but move forward into the future." In visiting the prison, we were asked not to question any of the prisoners about their past. We were told by our guide that the men had been members of Somoza's corp of bodyguards; in other words, they had been responsible for murder and torture. Yet from what we saw, they were treated with dignity, allowed to move and work around the farm without armed guards, allowed visits with their families on a regular basis, and charged with a maximum sentence of thirty years. There was an understanding that these men could change.

—KIRSTEN

When we returned from Nicaragua, Laura began working in a state prison in Massachusetts. Her description and analysis of the U.S. criminal justice system stands in sharp contrast to the Nicaraguan system. In a newsletter to her network of friends, Laura writes of the U.S. system:

The poor who are incarcerated in our prison systems and then released to an uncaring, unforgiving community are like war veterans or political refugees who are fleeing from an oppressive system and hoping to find compassion, support, freedom, dignity, and the material needs to survive comfortably. Our prison system willingly marginalizes and reincarcerates ex-prisoners who cannot make it on the outside. As if it is completely their fault. Making it on the outside takes more than walking out from behind the prison walls.

I believe that we as Christians need to reconsider a theology of forgiveness and see how terribly unforgiving our justice system is. We need to put our spirituality into action on behalf of ex-prisoners who are products of our economic, political, and social structures. The war against the poor here in the United States is as insane as the war against the poor in Central America and South Africa. We in the United States are more institutionalized than people in the Third World, so the suffering here is harder to see and comprehend. But by not seeing, we perpetuate racism, poverty, sexism, and dehumanization. Ex-prisoners are political refugees who need support, guidance, counseling, and compassionate people who will take action to help. We must create an alternative to recidivism and incarceration. One of the difficult realities of the criminal justice system is that it locks people away for a certain time but it does not follow through with support when they come out. . . .

As I think about the cold months coming upon us, and recognize the faces of homeless people from last year—waiting at the shelter gates, hovering in the subways, and sleeping in the bus stops—I wonder about the lies we've all been living, the lies that allow us to forget the poverty and the despair, the lies that attempt to make everything simpler than it really is. And I think about my own lies: I live in fear of losing control, paralyzed and indifferent because of my fear, convinced that somebody will help those dying people. But the time is now, and the lies that I create or buy into, to keep myself blind, are deadly lies.

I sometimes place myself in the position of one of many persons I have worked with as they are circulated and recirculated through the prison system. That person's story goes something like this: "I just got out of prison. I was in for two years because I stole food and clothes in order to keep my five children and myself alive. I actually don't regret the crime because it was a matter of life or death for me and my kids, but I do regret two years of lock-up in prison. When I got out, my kids were unavailable to me because the state took them and put them in foster homes. I need a job and a house or apartment before I can get them back. But no one wants to hire an ex-prisoner; plus, I'm losing the energy I need to look for jobs because it's cold and I don't have a safe, comfortable home to return to at night. I'm lacking the incentive to get out there—not the need, just the enthusiasm. My stomach is growling now—I'll have to wait for the church soup kitchen to open at noon in order to get some food. Then maybe I'll have enough energy to go search for some temporary employment. In all honesty, I wouldn't hire someone who looks like me. I'm not sure why I think I'll get a job—my kids, I guess. I want them to live with me. I want to be their mother again. I want to get them back. They are my whole world. If I only had a friend or some people I could turn to for help. . . . "

We have grown up believing a curious lie that if we really want to be successful we can be, that if we think "success," we'll be successful. As long as we continue to live with this lie, and hold fast to our isolated individualized lives, we won't be vulnerable to other people, and we won't be able to hear the gospel message to love our neighbors as ourselves, to take seriously the life that Jesus led and sacrifice some of our individualized success for the empowerment of others—to help each other, to live in community and not expect anyone to make it alone.

—LAURA

As Laura points out, people are simply released from the U.S. prison system. While in prison they are not rehabilitated. They are simply released to make it on their own, if they can—"forgiven," U.S. style. They are not reintegrated into a community. Their forgiveness begins and ends with their release. Most of us in the United States do not want to assume any responsibility with or for them. We refuse to genuinely forgive them. We deprive them of the possibility of repentance, understood as a *social act*, not simply a change of heart. We set up prisoners in our society to become increasingly antisocial, unrepentant, unforgiving. We set in motion a cycle of violence in which all of us play some role.

The final and most telling aspect of the criminal justice system in the United States is capital punishment. Since 1976, when the U.S. Supreme Court decided that executions could begin again in this country after a fourteen-year hiatus, fifty persons have been executed. As of February 1986, over 1,600 people are on death-row in the United States. The vast majority of these men and women are poor.[11] Capital punishment constitutes legalized murder of oppressed people. It is the denial of human potentiality. It is the denial that persons can be rehabilitated. It is the denial of forgiveness. It is the epitome of an individualized vision of life, for it says that if a culture is ridden with crime, then individuals—the oppressed—should be executed. It signals our collective refusal to search for the systemic and structural roots of crime and sin.

FORGING RIGHT-RELATION: REVOLUTIONARY FORGIVENESS

In this book we have been examining right, or just, relation and wrong, oppressive relation. We have analyzed personal relation, relation between individual and community (as between prisoners and communities), and relation between nations—Nicaragua and the United States. We have seen that human social relations have been frequently distorted by oppression and inequality, and we have demonstrated that all relations are interconnected.

The prevailing reality of our lives is wrong-relation. Our goal is right-relation. The reason we have placed this chapter after those on conversion and revolution, and the reason our book bears its title, is that we have come to believe that an essential key for moving beyond wrong-relation to right-relation is forgiveness. Individuals, communities, and nations are locked within cycles of oppression, violence, and wrong-relation. We in Amanecida have struggled to determine where we must begin if we are to participate in breaking these cycles. In Nicaragua we saw a way to begin to forge revolutionary forgiveness and just relations. We caught sight of some of the characteristics of forgiveness that—if embodied in our lives, in our nation, and in Nicaragua—can help create justice.

Right-Relation: The Praxis of Community

A sacred relationship exists between all living things. The world is held together by the power of positive, mutually-beneficial relationship. Without it there is no world.

> *Right-relation and forgiveness can be cultivated only in those situations in which we know ourselves to be basically good because we are essentially social—connected, related to one another. Our relatedness is holy ground. The power that connects us is love, God; hence, we are "by nature" bound in love, members of a good and holy order—creation itself.*
>
> *Far from romantic, this view of human nature and of our power to forgive our enemies seems to me laden with theological radicalism and pragmatic social implications. To begin with, this affirmation of human goodness presupposes our social nature and, hence, our social responsibility. No one is left out of either the benefits or the responsibilities of living in a relation of love toward the neighbor. We share a moral imperative to insure that neither we nor others live outside or at the margins of a common pool of resources. From a moral perspective we must socialize our economic gains and losses because, from a theological perspective, we are a common folk.*
>
> —CARTER

In Nicaragua we saw many times and in many contexts the embodiment of the community-based relationships of which Carter writes. We saw that they were rooted in an enormously potent faith in humankind. And that is what impressed us most in Nicaragua—a dogged belief of the people in the people, which is the spiritual prerequisite for forgiveness. Only in such strong belief—that women and men are able to do good and want to do it—could a nation forgive those who raped, maimed, and killed so many thousands of its own people. The Nicaraguan people believe in the capacity of Somoza's former bodyguards to become creative participants in the new society. They have faith in the masses of people to understand themselves as shapers of a new world in which there is food and comfort enough for all. We saw this faith and trust embodied in the Salvadoran children who, though they had every reason to fear and hate U.S. citizens, opened themselves to us. We witnessed it over and over again in the Christian base communities where the poor opened their doors and lives to us. Kirsten has described one base community which manifested many of the characteristics of right-relation:

> *The Nicaraguans seem to understand better than we do that God's power is made manifest in community. During my first trip to Nicaragua, Anne and I went to a church service of one of the base communities, on the outskirts of Estelí. The service was in a large, unadorned building made of cement, wood, and corrugated metal. The scripture passage that day was from Matthew:*

>> *But if the salt loses its taste,*
>> *how can it be salted again?*
>> *It is now no good for anything except to*
>> *be thrown out and trampled by the people.*
>> *You are the light of the world.*
>> *A city that is on a hilltop cannot be hidden.*

> *To our surprise and delight, the congregation turned the pews around, forming small groups, to discuss the meaning of the scripture. A microphone was then passed around to each group, and a spokesperson shared what each discussion had revealed. The gospel took on a whole new life and meaning in the context of this community. Most inspiring to me was that the words were interpreted communally, not simply in method, but in the meaning discovered through the method. My North American ears had generally heard this passage as guidance to the individual: let your light shine. This time it was interpreted differently. One of the community members stated:*

>> *If we are the salt of the earth, then we are meant to give flavor to life, through our lives. If we are the light of the world, we are meant to illuminate ourselves and each other, to illuminate our communities. We illuminate through actions in the revolution. We cannot turn our backs on those who are organizing collectives. We need to join them, allowing their light to shine.*

> *Our presence in the Mass was not as observers but as participants. We too were called into relationship with the Word, with the people, with the community, and we responded by saying, "We North Americans cannot turn our backs on our sisters and brothers in Nicaragua. We need to illuminate the truth to our people in the United States." Everyone present participated in the process of finding meaning in the gospel, in their lives together. Through their reflections on the gospel, the people were calling each other to act, to be agents of the Word, through transforming their lives in their communities.*

The biblical reflections in the base community meetings reveal a faith that is grounded in experience, as well as expressed through concrete actions. They reveal an understanding of the kingdom of God as something which is tangible, embodied, of the Earth. And they convey an understanding of God as that Power experienced and expressed in relation, in community and communion.

—KIRSTEN

As we emphasized in Chapter 3, we believe that there are serious shortcomings in the Nicaraguan Revolution, especially in the areas of sexism, racism, and homophobia. However, we believe that what Kirsten and Anne witnessed during the Christian base community meeting in Estelí was an example of a justice that is established and growing in the Nicaraguan revolutionary process—a way of relation that is in opposition to dominant U.S. culture. As Kirsten states, in the United States, the passage from Matthew is usually interpreted as an endorsement of individualism. In Nicaragua, it is interpreted as an endorsement of community and revolution; of persons who wish to be equal rather than best; who within their communities cooperate for the common good rather than compete; who combine faith and political action into a praxis that is primarily devoted to improving the lives of the poor; who can admit wrong-doing and shortcomings and forgive and be forgiven.

We cannot creatively acknowledge an individual's wrong-doing, much less know how best to respond to this person, unless we recognize that the "sinner" is not a monad. He or she *becomes* whatever he or she becomes always in relation to others in the world. This does not mean we are not morally bound to hold one another accountable. We *are*—and liberal Christians fail too often to understand this.[12] It *does* mean that we cannot appreciate to any constructive extent the significance of what any one of us does, or fails to do, or what should be done about it, unless we see that the sin is social: a breaking of love *with* one another, a violation of a God who is love, the creative power in our life together as family, friends, colleagues, races, genders, nations. . . .

In Nicaragua, there is at work an assumption that most women and men will *want* to help create their neighbors' well-being *if* they themselves are provided with the essential creature-comforts—such as shelter and food—and if they have been shown that their neighbors care about them. Nicaraguan society, as envisioned by the Sandinista leadership, is predicated upon an active faith in the neighbor and in oneself in relation to others. This is a cooperative image of human society rather than a competitive, individualistic notion of society in which each person is, first and foremost, "for himself."

In regard to forgiveness, the Nicaraguan leadership—in agreement with liberation theologians—have made the important distinction between *persons* and oppressive *systems*. Liberation ethics recognize that supporters of an oppressive system have been adversaries because of their relation to the system and might cease to be adversaries under new social structures. It recognizes that most oppressive structures extend over a period of years and involve many persons.[13] The revolutionaries want liberation not revenge. As embodied in the Nicaraguan prison system, both secular and Christian revolutionaries have deemed it good to say that those who supported the suppressive system are to be respected as sisters and brothers while the unjust system is being dismantled.

In creating right-relation, revolutionary forgiveness is necessary as a basis for change. Revolutionary forgiveness has as one of its corequisites that systems and structures be changed so that their primary goal is to build communities in which justice and material benefits are for all. If we are to engender communities of justice, then we must understand the qualities of revolutionary forgiveness.

Conscientization: Learning About Power

Revolutionary forgiveness cannot take place unless both victim and victimizer acknowledge that wrong-doing has occurred. When the Salvadoran refugee children performed their skit, a powerful idea was clarified for us. They were telling us that they understood that they and their people have been exploited and that we and our people have much to do with that exploitation. "Do solidarity work with the people of El Salvador," they told us. We understood: If we acknowledge the wrong-relation between ourselves and them and between our nation and theirs, and if we act to change that oppressive relation, we could be forgiven by them and could begin to forgive ourselves.

Reflecting on our experience in Nicaragua we have come to understand that forgiveness is based in part on the conscientization of victim and victimizer: We have come to understand clearly that all of us share a common predicament: we recognize that we participate in a broken world in which sometimes we are the violators and oppressors, and sometimes the victims and oppressed. We realize also that new attitudes, our own and those of others, most often follow new behavior. We are beginning to see that forgiveness is not basically an attitude or feeling. It is, rather, an act, which, after it has been accepted, sometimes becomes an attitude. In this way we may learn gradually to feel better about our enemies. But this usually happens only after an extended period of learning to forgive. We must be re-educated in order to know how to forgive our enemies and to accept the forgiveness of those we have hurt. From a liberation pedagogical perspective, this re-education is called "conscientization," a political education in which we help each other see the ways in which our lives are connected by power relations. Amanecida believes that all good theological education is basically conscientization.[14]

One of the deep spiritual and psychological failures of the leaders and members of dominant groups in the United States is that bound by our arrogance we fail to see ourselves in equal relations with others. We fear conscientization. Our failure thwarts the possibility of forgiveness between the United States and other nations and breeds wrong-relation. The Nicaraguan government is founded on the faith that oppressors can change. We fervently hope so.

Re-membering: On Behalf of the Future

An accurate and creative remembering goes hand in hand with conscientization. Carter has written of an experience that helped her see the difference between merely reviewing memories and coming to understand the past in such a way that it can be used creatively to shape the present and future. In 1980, at the Detroit Conference of Theology in the Americas, Carter heard an address by Father Edicio de la Torre (a Filipino priest who had been imprisoned for five years under Marcos and is again, at the outset of this writing, incarcerated in the Philippines). Father de la Torre's words enable us to comprehend the urgency in not forgetting, but, to the contrary, in *re-membering*:

We had Mass [in prison]. And this was a problem because we had a wide range of participants, from Marxists to traditional Christians. And we could not have Mass pretending that we were doing something that we did not really believe in. We had to celebrate it in some way that we all really accepted. . . .

And this is what we all agreed on . . . . We reflected on the Last Supper and the first Mass, as Christ and his disciples met in that upper room. There was an arresting team about to come, a military force about to strike at them. Their group, their community, was going to experience an external crisis. And the military had pinpointed and were going to hit them because their group had internal weakness. They had an informer who turned traitor. And the second in line of leadership was going to vacillate—Peter! It was a very familiar experience to us, to look at the Mass and the Eucharist as a gathering of people who have been trying to form one body, an organization, committed to each other and to liberation, but who are going to be subjected to external pressures. And that body will break up because it still has internal weaknesses; it is still too weak; it is still on the strategic defensive.

What was the meaning of this for us? We focused on one word. We played on the word "remember." . . . Why "remember"? *Remember* is the opposite of *forgetting*. We played on the word "re-member," to put together again something that has been dismembered. . . .

To re-member is to resume gathering with people who have shown weakness, with a group that has already made mistakes, especially under repression. But to be able to work together again, to renew commitments, we have to criticize ourselves and to sum up our mistakes. This is the only way we can form a strong body. . . . We need to forge forward steadily, from mistake to mistake, failure to failure; . . . it is victory enough at least to be able to identify our mistakes and analyze them, and to learn lessons and move forward. . . . [15]

Forgiveness occurs at the intersection of past, present, and future. In the United States those convicted of crimes are cut off from the community, locked away; some are executed. The past in this scheme is not viewed as bearing the seeds of rehabilitation or healing but rather is seen only as a basis for retribution and revenge. In Nicaragua structures have been erected that encourage people to examine the past in order to reconstruct in the present the systems that caused wrong-doing. As with their treatment of ex-National Guardsmen and the children trained as torturers, the Nicaraguans look to the past with the purpose of re-membering the present and future so that the systemic causes of victimization and wrong-relation can be eliminated.

"To forgive is not to forget, but rather to re-member whatever has been dis-membered."[16] Tomas Borge's forgiveness of his torturer was by no means a sign that he was able or willing "to forget." His act of forgiveness was an *invitation*—in spite of what had happened—in which Borge was signaling his desire that this man come into right-relation with him and with the Nicaraguan revolutionary movement. To try to forget acts of violence which have been done to us is foolish, probably impossible. It can lead us only to lies and denial. To base forgiveness on re-membering what happened is to move toward the future in the belief that we will be stronger together than we would be apart. Borge may have determined also that after persons are forgiven they are at least as likely to join those who forgave them as to repeat their violent behavior. Forgiveness can also be a pragmatic political act.

Confessing: Acknowledging Wrong-Relation

Conscientization and analysis of the past are often preludes to confessing. We have said much about the Nicaraguan government's establishment of a prison system based on rehabilitation and forgiveness. It has offered forgiveness. The Sandinista government is also in need of forgiveness. It has shown that it is capable of being forgiven because it is able to confess.

For instance, many Sandinistas have admitted the racism of the Spanish-speaking majority's treatment of Black (Creole) and Indian (Miskito, Rama, and Suma) peoples of the East Coast. These Sandinistas, notably Tomas Borge (who is part Indian), have begun to see that racism plagues the revolution and, according to Episcopal bishop Sturdie Downs, a Black Nicaraguan, have taken positive steps toward addressing the problem.[17] The Sandinista leadership meets regularly, weekly we were told, with Black and Indian leaders to work on ways of eliminating the racism that had rendered the East Coast people invisible to Somoza and, more recently, to the Sandinistas. When the contras began soliciting and kidnapping Blacks and Indians to function as counter-revolutionaries, the Sandinistas became alert to a problem they had helped perpetuate by their own cultural and racial arrogance. They admitted they were wrong and have acted to redress their wrong-doing so as to open a process by which they and the Hispanic majority can be forgiven. The Indian peoples have responded—many are moving back onto their homeland. The situation, however, is not yet resolved. As Carol writes,

I wonder what forgiveness means to the Miskito population. What can it mean? How can forgiveness fit into what those people have gone through and suffered since the Triumph? My questions are not only, Will they be able to forgive? but also, Should they be expected to forgive? What are the circumstances under which they will forgive the government for the dislocation and imprisonment of so many people or the racism and insensitivity undergirding those actions?

The situation is an important one, for it represents the most well-publicized internal conflict of the nation. It is also a very complicated problem given the diversity of the region, the extent of the people's suffering, and the involvement and effects of other outside influences (such as the U.S. interest in exacerbating the problem). There is no question that the government of Nicaragua acted wrongly toward the Miskito population soon after the Triumph. The damage is done. Still, there have been definitive changes in the government's behavior since that time—including the release of nearly all the political prisoners and a decidedly different approach to interaction with the East Coast— through dialogue, not force.

In other words, the government of Nicaragua is doing something that may be unique: It has recognized its mistakes and is attempting to make amends for its actions. The Sandinistas have a long way to go, and there is much work to be done to clear up the differences and establish trust (of which there was so little to begin with) in order to build a workable relationship. The rift between the Sandinistas and the Indians is great: anger is justified; the people of the East Coast can neither be expected to forgive nor forced to do so. And yet the rift will only grow deeper if there is no openness for change.

Another important factor to consider when looking at the situation of the East and West Coasts is that outside influences are purposefully capitalizing on the tense relationship. The U.S.-backed contra forces are making reconciliation nearly impossible because they are focusing on the northeast area of the country as a major incursion point. The contras are taking advantage of the people's hostility and fear, not only to recruit and force people to join them but also to perpetuate the differences, thereby destabilizing the situation further. The trust, which is so critical to forgiveness, will be impossible to establish fully as long as this continues.

—CAROL

Not until the Sandinistas began to confess their racism was there any realistic reason to believe that their treatment of the racial minorities in the nation might change. And not until it has changed significantly—a process that the United States and its contras are determined to impede—can any mutually beneficial, forgiving relation actually come into being between the Hispanic majority and the Creole, Miskito, and other Nicaraguan people.

Other serious flaws in the Nicaraguan revolution are sexism and heterosexism. Sexism and heterosexism cannot be tolerated in any truly just social order, because as interlocking structures of domination, they continue to insure the socio-economic subjugation of women and of all people who do not conform publicly to patterns of mating and family that have been sanctified as "normal" and "good" by Euro-American (both Anglo and Spanish) colonizers.

While we were troubled by misogyny and homophobia in Nicaragua, we understand that these twin evils have their roots in our common—Anglo/ Hispanic European—cultures. We realize also that neither the United States nor the Roman Catholic church is interested in promoting the well-being of women or sexual minorities. Consequently, to the extent that Nicaragua might attempt to create gender or sexual justice, the resulting turmoil would only be exacerbated by the Vatican and the White House. This is, in part, why the revolutionary possibility of a society in which women, gay men, and lesbians live as self-defined contributors to the common good is not likely to be actualized as long as Nicaragua is under attack. The uprooting of sexism and heterosexism would constitute social disruption and would be feared as a threat to the national security of Nicaragua. We deplore the injustices that break the lives and bodies of lesbians, gay men, and all women. This concern leads us not to a denunciation of Nicaragua; rather it leads to a condemnation of the injustice to all women, especially poor women, and to gay men and lesbians in the United States.

Like confused carnivores who criticize their prey for eating meat, citizens of the United States exercise arrogance when we dwell upon the same flaws in the Nicaraguan Revolution that our nation has failed historically to correct in itself. It is our business to name these systemic evils wherever they exist—in Nicaragua or elsewhere—and to help fight them. But it will always be our fundamental responsibility to recognize, name, and struggle to break the stranglehold that such evils as racism, sexism, and heterosexism have on our own nation and our own people—and, partly as a consequence, on the people of Nicaragua. "Let those who have not sinned cast the first stone."

What disturbs us most about our government's treatment of Nicaragua (and so many smaller nations throughout the world) is the hypocrisy of our national attitude toward the violence we are reaping. As Laurie says, "What the Nicaraguan people have been met with in the actions of the U.S. government is an immoral, cynical, hell-bent-on-destruction-and-death, high- and low-intensity warfare calculated to undermine all Nicaraguan efforts towards justice and peace."

As Flo notes, "The Reagan Administration won't admit that it is acting in violent ways toward nations like Nicaragua that are struggling for justice and peace." Our nation calls those who feed the hungry "terrorists" and those who murder coffee harvesters "freedom fighters." Good is called evil, and evil is called good. It is the essence of perversion.

It is also the unforgivable sin: to call good evil and evil good. The unforgivable sin is that the Reagan Administration lies. It doesn't admit the atrocities it is committing against the people of Nicaragua. It contin-ues to deny involvement while, simultaneously, increasing its violent aggression. Even today, there is talk of private businessmen further financing the "freedom-fighters." How can Nicaragua forgive? Is for-giveness even a possibility when the United States is so rooted in narcis-sism, arrogance, and self-interest that we perceive ourselves as beyond the need for forgiveness?

—FLO

Forgiveness is a process in which, we have come to believe, there is room for us to experience all the contradictions: "I don't hate and yet I do hate." These are real, daily feelings in all of us. Those who forgive invest all their feelings, including the contradictions, in the future. This means that forgiveness does not negate, but rather includes, all of what we have experienced, which is why re-membering is so important. We cannot forgive if we attempt to block out or erase hostile feelings. We cannot be forgiven if we do not see that we are in wrong-relation to persons whom we are, thereby, injuring.

The willingness to forgive or be forgiven is rooted in genuine humility. None of us, and none of the people to whom we believe ourselves responsible, lives without feeling hatred and hostility toward someone at sometime, maybe toward many people much of the time. To confess this, not necessarily as wrong but as real, can empower us to forgive the very people we hate. As the Nicaraguan people testify, forgiveness is an invitation into a future in which hatred does not have the last word.

Forgiveness is an act of love, allowing others to be fully who they are, acknowledging the power we all carry for transforming ourselves and the world around us. In forgiving, we allow ourselves to see the best in others. Forgiving and accepting forgiveness are acts of letting go of our false pride and inflated egos. They involve allowing ourselves to be mutually vulnerable. So much of the process of forgiveness has to do with self-forgiveness—of looking to the future and not the past for a sense of what we can be. Though the men in the Nicaraguan prisons are encouraged to let go of the past and see themselves as new persons, though they may be forgiven by the government and the people, do they accept that forgiveness? In my understanding of the process of transfor-mation, self-forgiveness is essential. Unless I can forgive myself, I can neither fully accept forgiveness from another nor give it to others.

—KIRSTEN

Repenting: Stopping the Violence

Call to mind two scenes—one interpersonal, one international—described earlier in this book: Anne's ex-husband, after having struck her and driven away, has returned asking for forgiveness. He acknowledges his wrong-doing; he confesses to it. On the level of international relations, remember the women of Nicaragua who have lost their children and friends to the U.S.-backed contras: the contras have recently been in the women's village and have tortured, murdered, and kidnapped children, husbands, friends. And the contras, the women know, will be back. How can forgiveness begin in these situations? Must it be initiated by victim or victimizer? As we discussed this, many of us came to the conclusion that if revolutionary forgiveness is to occur the victimizer must not only confess. The victmizer must repent, cease the violence.

Many women who are survivors of abuse and violence in their lives—rape, incest, and battering—have a great deal of difficulty even discussing the subject of forgiveness. As a survivor of a battering marriage, I have felt battered by the very word "forgiveness." I was forced to forgive; the alternative was a fist in my face.

Survivors of violence have been counseled that the violence perpetrated against us is our fault or that, in order to be acceptable Christians, unconditional forgiveness must be forthcoming. This is more often than not the experience of oppressed people everywhere who complain about their suffering. Any responsible theological treatment of forgiveness cannot ignore the ways in which the concept has been perverted at the expense of those who have been abused. Forgiveness can never be forced. Sometimes forgiveness will never take place. Sometimes the person who has been wronged cannot forgive.

*—*Anne

Those who forgive must be wise as serpents, and the act of forgiving must be as strategically potent as it is spiritually potent. Which is why, at this time, the Sandinistas cannot forgive the contras. People cannot simply "forgive"—invite back into their lives on a mutual basis—those who continue to do harm to them and their people. We do not believe that any of us can forgive those who continue to violate us. Otherwise "forgiveness" is an empty word. Forgiveness is possible only when the violence stops. Only then can those who have been violated even consider the possibility of actually loving those who once brutalized and battered them. Only then can the former victims empower the victimizers by helping them to realize their own power to live as liberated liberators, people able to see in themselves and others a corporate capacity to shape the future.

*—*Carter and Pat

What is the difference between a comandante forgiving a prisoner who, when the tables had been turned, had tortured him, and the comandante forgiving the contra who would cut out his heart if given a chance? In the first instance, the killing has stopped; in the second, it has not. "For that reason,"

Carter suggests, "the comandante has the power to forgive in the former case and does not in the latter. We can forgive only those who have begun to repent, those who no longer stand with their feet on our necks."

In this spirit, many of us assert that until the violation of a battered woman has irrevocably ceased she cannot even begin to forgive, and most of us believe that the contras *cannot* be forgiven as long as they continue to attack the people of Nicaragua. The Sandinistas *cannot* signal the possibility of forgiveness to the counterrevolutionary leaders by inviting them into dialogue (which is what Cardinal Obando y Bravo and other critics of the Nicaraguan government would have them do) *until the contras stop murdering Nicaraguans.* Women and Blacks and others against whom violence is being waged can forgive those who attack them only when the violence ceases.

These were the conclusions of most of us. Some dissented and argued that the victim, like Jesus, can indeed begin the process of forgiveness even while the persecution goes on. When Jesus prayed, "Forgive them, for they know not what they do," was he asking God to have mercy on us, a people unrepentant, starved for forgiveness, bent upon harrowing, bludgeoning, and bombing the Power of Love right out of this world? When Jesus asked God to forgive those who were crucifying him, was he imploring God to touch the lives of his oppressors *in spite of* their refusal to repent? Did Jesus pray unspoken words, silent prayers for this executioners' repentance so that, someday, all people could at last come home together? Carol has implied that a commitment to nonviolence may be rooted in the latter understanding of forgiveness: to pardon those who persecute *regardless* of the hardness of their hearts.

We understand the power of Jesus' words of forgiveness, but many of us who have suffered violence in our personal lives or as the result of policies of those who rule our country, or who witnessed the violence loosed by our nation upon the people of Nicaragua, do not believe that the process of forgiveness in our lives or in the lives of the Nicaraguans can begin until the violence ceases. There can be no praxis of repentance until the oppressors cease their violations of the oppressed.

Solidarity: Standing with the Victim

The solidarity of oppressors with the oppressed, of victimizer with victim, is another element of the process of forgiveness, and it is a theme that has sounded throughout our consideration of forgiveness. Recall two of the central images of this chapter. In Estelí, in the base Christian community, all turned their pews to face one another and participated in the discussion of the verses from Matthew. Those who participated had worked in concrete ways to create structures that would assure food, shelter, and medicine for all. In community they participated in building a system based on justice. If their vision is to be realized, they must act in community and solidarity with others—and they openly invited us into their vision and praxis. On the other hand, remember the image of the unrepentant, dominant-class male who can neither forgive nor be forgiven because he is always in competition with the other. His vision is of a culture composed of individuals who are merely mirrors of himself. He conceives of forgiveness as involving only a few words: "I am sorry . . . That's okay."

In Nicaragua, we began to see that forgiveness cannot happen unless people give up images of themselves as alone, set apart, or different and join in the struggle to build a social order in which every person and living creature is respected.

Typical street in Estelí

Amanecida eucharist with milk (wine was unavailable), other symbols of life in the United States, and elements from Nicaragua such as bullet shells, malaria pills, and Solentiname paintings.

Rally for Daniel Ortega in Estelí

Opposition political grafitti on a street in Estelí

Children's library in Managua

Anne Gilson at a day-care center in Estelí

Marketplace in Masaya

Washing clothes in Estelí

Mother and child

Kirsten and Laura at rally in Nicaragua: "Listen, we are with you in struggle," signed by friends from Boston, U.S. in solidarity with the people of Nicaragua

Laura at U.S. rally

A typical roadside memorial in honor of the Nicaraguan dead

5

We, The People

Is there a role for converted oppressors and, if so, what? We turn to our own nation in the knowledge that our survival—the survival of the Nicaraguan and the U.S. people and others elsewhere in the world—is at stake. The road is long, the questions are many. Where and how to begin? And how do we keep from being paralyzed by despair?

Who are "we, the people?" Argentinian liberation theologian José Míguez-Bonino insists that a revolutionary agenda cannot be separated from the particular context of the people involved.[1] We are the people of the United States of America. We have in this book frequently turned our attention to an analysis of our context, our nation. In the course of our analysis some of us in Amanecida have concluded that the United States is being methodically transformed into a fascist state; others of us believe the transformation has already occurred. Throughout our description and analysis of our lives in the United States, we have shown that the principal characteristics of fascism are coming more and more to dominate U.S. culture. Militarism, belligerent nationalism, sexism and heterosexim; white supremacy, anti-Semitism and other forms of racism; obsession with order and appearance at the expense of compassion and morality; incorporation of a nationalistic, chauvinistic segment of the church into the "national religion"; marginalization and brutalization of the poor and minorities; addiction to dominance, power, and property; fear and oppression of any persons different from the carefully manipulated "ideal" personality; substitution of idols and lies for truth—these are many of the qualities of a classic fascism and of the United States today.

As with fascism under Mussolini, Hitler, and Franco, so too in the United States fascism's roots lie in fear, insecurity, and an inability to cope with demands of the oppressed for justice and structural changes. As in the fascism of the 1930s and 1940s, so in the United States what is offered to the people is a myth of a glorious national history and future constructed by persons who possess certain racial, religious, ethnic, gender, and economic characteristics.

Our nation is in need of conversion. It needs revolutionary change. It needs forgiveness. In this concluding chapter we shall suggest ways for bringing about this social and spiritual transformation. In our study of Nicaragua, we saw an example of how a people can resist and overturn oppressive situations, and we saw a people at work to embody a vision of a new social order. If we are to forge a just nation and world, we need to work to build communities and coalitions that will act on at least three fronts: resistance to present structures in the United States, solidarity with the oppressed, and conversion of the oppressors.

WORKING TOGETHER

The people of Nicaragua told us to return to the United States to build collectives, communities, and coalitions that would resist oppressive structures and build those that are just. The women and men of Estelí told us how the members of the Christian communities had risked their lives working in coalition with the Sandinistas to overthrow the tyranny of the Somozas. During the funeral of the young soldiers of Estelí, we witnessed a village unified to resist the terrorism of the contras. During meetings of Christian base communities, we saw people shaping a way of life that will insure food, medicine, clothing, housing, and political power for the poor. When we returned to the United States we kept this image of the praxis of communities before us as we began to shape this book and as we began acting within a variety of groups.

Coming together in community is not only necessary as a means of engaging in the work of our revolution in the United States; it will also keep us from falling into despair. I have experienced this in my own life. For several months I have been meeting with an affinity group, a group of students and a professor from Harvard Divinity School who are planning to do civil disobedience in Washington, D.C., to protest U.S. military involvement in Central America. Recently it came to our attention that Penthouse *magazine was featuring an article on the sexual torture of women in Latin America. The article was being advertised on the local top-forty radio station as a way of enticing men to buy the edition. We were outraged. Rather than sinking in despair, turning our rage inward, being left with a sense of powerlessness and frustration, we brought the issue to our affinity group where immediately we began making plans for voicing our protest locally, holding actions at local newsstands and corner stores. I was so grateful to be a part of an affinity group, where immediately we were able to address the issue—as a group—and to take action.*

—KIRSTEN

It is in affinity groups and other communities and collectives that our hope lies. As Kirsten's description and the Nicaraguans' examples suggest, God as the Power of Transformation is experienced and made manifest in community.

We experience God's power as we meet and work with one another, empowering one another to act, to transform ourselves, and to transform the world around us.

There are many tasks to be addressed in transforming the values and institutions of our country. The forming of community groups enables us to take action. How do we form these groups? Richard Shaull has discussed the necessity for those of us who are white middle/upper strata people to form groups to discuss how *we* are dehumanized by systems of oppression, and how we experience and understand oppression in our own lives.[2] We cannot be effective agents of transformation if we assume that we are acting only for the liberation of "others"—people unlike ourselves. Another approach is to form Bible study groups, using the methodology of the base communities, reflecting on scripture through our own experience in community and commitment to justice. It is vital that Christians who are privileged and are participating in systems of oppression begin to hear the Bible interpreted through the lives of the poor and oppressed. The process of forging communities and collectives involves both conscientization and action. Just as during the insurrection in Nicaraguan Christian communities, student groups, middle-class organizations, and guerrillas united to oust Somoza, so in our conscientization and resistance work in the United States it is crucial to form coalitions of groups. Efforts such as Jesse Jackson's Rainbow Coalition and political economist Manning Marable's outline of the Common Program[3] are two examples of how coalition-building can take root. If we are to avoid the pitfalls of over-extension, burn-out, and inefficacy, we must strategize with other similarly committed people. The ideology of individualism that dominates U.S. culture is a convenient and effective means to keep people and groups isolated. In the United States the glorification of voting—an individual act—as the means of participating in politics is another way of keeping persons and groups apart. The Nicaraguans who overthrew Somoza and are building a revolution did not merely vote and talk: they came together in communities and coalitions and fought. We must do the same and thus must determine what concrete forms our acts of resistance and solidarity will take.

RESISTING OPPRESSION

Jane's struggle to resist U.S. policy reflects a dilema shared by people in the United States:

> *I have certain choices in deciding how much responsibility I shall take in response to injustice. I can ignore the unjust situation though I know it exists—I don't have time; I'm not that interested. I can become informed—go to lectures, read, discuss with and ask questions of those who know more than I, or watch documentaries. One needs to know what is truth and what is not: that is, know the sources and how well they can be trusted. It is imperative to know both sides in order to decide what*

to accept and what to reject. Moving into an active role, I can offer programs or classes in schools, churches, or for independent groups. I shall begin to effect change either on the more subtle end of the spectrum or I shall make an effort to be more persuasive. Taking a more active role, I can go to Nicaragua in a fact-finding capacity or I can work (physically or administratively) with and for the people of Nicaragua—nonviolently, within the limits of the law. A more radical step would be to protest in some way (join a picket line, a boycott, or protest in front of the U.S. embassy), do civil disobedience and get arrested, or be violent. I personally am willing to go no further than to protest.

The discussion of the level of participation also ties in with the level of responsibility. Does one's distance from the site or the event diminish one's responsibility? Is there a difference between working for AVCO or any company which designs or manufactures parts for something that will kill or destroy and carrying a weapon and shooting someone? As long as I pay taxes, I participate in preventing Nicaragua from rebuilding after the Triumph. But what shall I gain by refusing? The government will eventually get its money in addition to a fine or interest. If I do nothing, I feel responsible; if I try to participate, I feel self-righteous. In any case I feel helpless. But I know I can't call myself a Christian if I don't participate.

—JANE

Pat reminds us that conscientization—making one another conscious—is an important part of our resistance to U.S. policy in Central America.

We citizens of the United States need to educate ourselves like the Nicaraguans have done and are doing. We need to ask, What rights (as opposed to privileges) does our self-determination include? The right to own a home? The right to health care? To employment? To own land? To walk the streets without fear of rape? To paid vacations? To a good education? To a nutritional diet? To consume large quantities of imported goods? To use military force to insure the availability of scarce resources for our use? To use as much of the world's resources as we can secure? To invade other countries to determine their form of government? To define issues in Central America, Africa, Asia, and Europe in terms of a Cold War between the Soviet Union and the United States? Which are our rights and which are privileges gained through abuse of power? What are the rights of responsible citizens of a world community?

Answering these questions, in community, is revolution.

—PAT

Conscientization is a necessary element of resistance. Upon returning to the United States, we began working to raise the consciousness of others about the situation in Central America. Many of us began delivering lectures, giving slideshows, and working in general to inform others about Nicaragua and what we had experienced and learned there. But our discussions kept returning to how best to go about acting directly against U.S. policy toward Nicaragua and toward the oppressed in our country. While in Nicaragua we had questioned Nicaraguans about the use of violence and nonviolence within their revolutionary process. In the United States we took up the discussion again in relation to acts of resistance against the growing fascistic policies of this country. What follows is a transcript of one of our discussions on this theme. We had been discussing whether or not we would take up arms to defend Nicaragua against the United States (many of us declared that, if we were in Nicaragua, we would), and we had been debating whether or not nonviolence and pacifism are elitist positions, luxuries available to those whose lives are not being threatened by oppressors. We had begun to discuss our options for responding to oppressive structures in the United States.

Carol: What I wanted to ask is how are we to respond as U.S. citizens? In the United States I don't have the option to pick up a gun and go out to fight against something concrete and tangible. Or *is* that an option in our country?

Laura: I don't think that is an option in our country. I think that we live in such an institutionalized society that to do anything violent from underneath would mean that those in power would stamp us out immediately. We have to organize a nonviolent protest movement with numbers of people and use constant networking.

Carol: But that's going on and doesn't seem to be working. I go to protests all the time. You go one day, you're thrown in jail overnight, and then that's it. What good does *that* do?

Laura: Perhaps the problem is that the organizing that's been going on has stayed pretty much at a certain economic level and in certain areas. Justice organizing is certainly not going into big business and it's not reaching into the very poor communities. The kind of literacy campaign that goes on in Nicaragua—that is the kind of thing that needs to be going on within the poor communities. And inside the prison system. I think that picking up guns won't be an option for us in the United States.

Elaine: What does everyone mean by picking up a gun? We're using the action of picking up a gun as *the* symbol of violence. Why the hell do we have to pick up a gun? Why can't it be in lots of other ways?

Carter: Strategically, in terms of community organizing within institutions, I think it's possible to work on how to *disrupt* institutions. Those in power in institutions consider that quite violent. It's quite ironic because violence in the United States can be defined as upsetting someone's xerox machine or breaking a window. Damaging property *is* considered violent. I can't think of the numbers of marches I've been on where the instructions have been not only "Don't touch anybody," but also "Don't touch anything." The sacred value that has been attached to private property has to be challenged.

Anne: It is important for me to be clear about what I mean by being within an institution and also clear about when I am no longer effective within an institution. As a feminist liberation theologian, I often wonder, on the one hand, how long I can be effective within the patriarchal institutional church without sacrificing my well-being. On the other hand, I hear the voices of many feminist sisters and a few feminist brothers, both in and outside of the church, and question where I can best work strategically for institutional change. It is a process of constant evaluation and re-evaluation. And, of course, as you say Carter, many consider violent what I am about in even challenging church authority. But the church isn't the only place to be working. We need to be working within the prison systems, the military-industrial complex, and big business.

Carol: Okay. Then what about nonviolence? How does that fit in? I don't think we should just write off the whole movement!

Carter: I see non-violence as a means of resistance and pacifism as an ideology. In the United States, at this time, non-violence and pacifism seem to me frequently steeped in class and race privilege. Some folks on the Catholic Left, for example, frustrate me with their blanket condemnations of all violence—as if "non-violence" were really an option for most Nicaraguan peasants or South African Blacks.

Carol: Yes, but many of these same workers for non-violence have a wonderful sense of what is really valuable. For example, they understand the difference between violence to human beings and damage to private property.

Margarita: Right, like damaging the Trident—that's quite a wonderful act I think. To attack a nuclear warhead. . . . I think there are important distinctions to be made and some things we can learn, that I can learn, from the peace movement. And, in fact, I consider myself part of the peace movement. It's just that I'm not a pacifist.

Laura: Well, I don't believe in nonviolence being the only way either. But I *do* believe that in the United States our use of violent resistance would just be squelched.

Flo: But I can see a violent movement organizing. In fact, I have a friend who's writing a novel about our country becoming a fascist state. One of the dramas in the book is the equation of our government with the Somoza regime. The National Guard is used as a "strong arm" to control the people and instill terror. In the book there is an armed underground that develops in resistance. I could imagine such a thing. When all nonviolent means are exhausted and injustice continues, violent actions become the only means to counter oppression. Maybe in the United States a revolutionary movement of such a kind wouldn't be as well organized, but people can only be pushed so far.

Laura: I think that we've already got fascism in the United States, Flo, and I think that the spread of capital punishment is supporting that fascism. All poor people are susceptible to being arrested and jailed. Once they're arrested, they're stuck in the whole prison cycle. By the time they're thirty-five, they're on death row. Our revolution, if there is one, is within institutions and organizations.

Carol: Your talk about prisons and poor people, Laura, brings us back to the class issue. The fact that we can sit around and talk like this is a mark of class privilege. We are in comfortable positions in universities where we have the leisure to talk. Very often a conversation like this ends up in people not talking to one another because people are so sure their position is the right one. I get angry when people say that pacifism is simply elitist, sexist, and racist. Those kinds of comments write off the kind of pacifist resistance that is definitely going on in protesting. It is written off as if it's not even a possibility. Isn't there any way we can incorporate nonviolence into our movements of resistance?

Carter: Doesn't it depend on *who* we are and what situation we're in? Doesn't it depend on whether our children are being tortured, our sisters raped?

Anne: In the United States it's time for me to be willing to begin on the terms of people that I need most to listen to—people of other races. I have a hard time right now putting a lot of my energy into a movement that is being led primarily by white men. There are enough white men at the front of the peace movement and I don't intend to be following them around.

Carter: I have experienced the peace movement as classist and racist. Poor kids are drafted and sent off to war. When I was in college during the Vietnam War, men of my class stratum got college deferments. Poor people of all colors were, as Holly Near phrases it, "the cheap cannon fodder." How does a non-violent movement get envisioned and on whose terms? I don't think we can discuss that without taking into account our skin color, class, gender, sexuality, and all kinds of things.

We had reached no consensus about the viability of non-violence as a means of revolutionary change. We agreed, however, that much has to do with context. Are not pacifism and nonviolence most often means of resistance advocated by middle- and upper-class persons? How might the positions of those who advocate pacifism and nonviolence be different had they lived in a country battered by U.S. imperialism or in Harlem or Roxbury battered by U.S. domestic, capitalist policy? Latin American liberation theologians have shown oppressive structures to be the root cause of violence in their nations. Their analysis is relevant to the situation in the United States because in our nation violence is being done to women, persons of color, ethnic minorities, and the poor. How are they and we to respond to that violence? In our discussion of forgiveness it became clear that before revolutionary forgiveness can occur, the oppressors and victimizers must reject their violence and repent. We disagreed on how to bring about that rejection, but we concurred that a variety of means—and for some of us that includes violence—are necessary in our struggles of resistance.

*Even before you can forgive me, I must repent: turn away from whatever
I have done to violate you and/or others. And why would I stop this
violence? Because either I have been forced to stop or I have been
inspired to turn around.*

—CARTER

BUILDING SOLIDARITY

Like the people and government of Nicaragua, we in Amanecida have come
to understand that along with resistance to oppressive governments like those
of Somoza and Reagan, we must carry out a reconstruction of our nation.
Resistance to destructive international and domestic policy and to structures
that foster sexism, racism, and homophobia must be integrated with working
to embody our vision of a new society by building new structures. One basis of
that process of rebuilding is solidarity with the poor and oppressed.

In the Introduction to this book we made the distinction between charity
toward and solidarity with the poor and oppressed. We reject the principle of
charity, for it perpetuates inequality—the haves offer the have-nots just
enough to keep them from death or revolution. There is no changing of the
sinful systems and structures that cause the poverty and suffering. There is,
thus, no real opportunity for true forgiveness because the relationship between
oppressor and oppressed remains unchallenged and unchanged. We deplore
especially the notion of "private-sector" charity heralded by the Reagan Administration. It is an abnegation of the state's responsibility to the poor; it
furthers the deadly ethos of individualism; it perpetuates structures of inequality.

With other liberation theologians, we advocate solidarity with the oppressed. The meeting of the basic Christian community in Estelí is a symbol of
this process. Kirsten and Anne were not invited into the meeting in order to give
money to the poor in the community. They did not go to give advice. They were
invited in as equal partners with the poor. From that relationship of equality
and solidarity the citizens of a victimized nation were empowered to begin
building from the grassroots a new society.

It is important that middle- and upper-class citizens of the United States
form groups devoted to fighting for justice. It is even more important that
those who are privileged enter solidarity with the poor and oppressed and form
collectives, communities, and coalitions with them.

*In recent years many books have been written emphasizing the dra-
matic need for global caring and sharing on this small, fragile earth, "our
global village." I would fantasize what conditions would need to exist to
create such a global reality. I had visions of Eastern and Western leaders
shaking hands and disarming the world. Or perhaps the United Nations
would live up to its potential role of fostering dialogue and equality. Or
maybe a great church leader gifted with appealing charisma would lead*

all to repent and be saved! In these fantasies I made the same mistakes that have been made untold times before me. I looked in the wrong direction for justice.

The most powerful and profound hope for a global transformation is the oppressed and those who stand in solidarity with them. Our hope lies in ourselves.

—Virginia

CONVERTING THE OPPRESSOR

The bonding of the poor and others into a community willing to struggle to overthrow an oppressive regime reveals the power that comes from solidarity. What prevents the community from eventually becoming the oppressor is the community's acceptance of the responsibility to liberate the oppressor as part of its own self-liberation. Therefore, liberation spirituality adheres to a conversion, revolution, forgiveness process. From a liberation theological perspective, the people's forgiveness of their oppressors is based on their trust in the relational, communal fabric of both divine and human life well-lived. God's greatness is in the fact that God—the Power of love—draws us into right-relation with one another. To forgive is to invite back into right-relation. It is a supreme act of love. It is an act of God, and God is the heart-beat of the Nicaraguan Revolution.

We have in many ways come full circle. We went to Nicaragua not fully understanding the relationship between oppressor and oppressed or the oppressive and fascistic tendencies exploding in our nation. But in Nicaragua, we began letting go of many of the distortions and lies that predominate in U.S. culture and that have bound us to roles in a nation that oppresses its citizens and many throughout the world. We began to be converted to a revolutionary vision, and we began slowly to forgive ourselves and be forgiven.

Liberation theology speaks of something we experienced in Nicaragua and have seen in our country: oppression ravages the oppressor. The victimizer is also victim. Liberation theology teaches forgiveness of the victimizer. The oppressor, as sinner, stands in need of forgiveness by the oppressed. In Nicaragua, we came to understand that one of our responsibilities in the struggle in the United States is to continue a process begun in us—we must work from our positions of solidarity with the oppressed to convert the oppressor.

There is much to be gained by those who are converted. As victimizers we live in that web of lies we have repeatedly named in this book. As we resist the destructive policies of the United States, convert to solidarity with the oppressed, and give up some of those illusions and lies, we shall become more fully present members of a world community. We stand to gain peace and opportunities for cross-cultural enrichment as we listen, believe, and respond to others' perspectives. We stand to gain an abundant life—not an over-consumptive life—for all. We shall gain hope.

As United States citizens, we shall gain the ability to see ourselves as *in need* of forgiveness and to allow ourselves to be forgiven, to forgive, and to move toward justice among ourselves; between ourselves and those we have oppressed; and between ourselves and those who have oppressed us. We shall move in love, giving up the illusion of control over the lives of others and over the world. We shall gain the ability to *feel* as we claim our common humanity. We are coming to a realization that we who are in a privileged position have a responsibility to liberate those who oppress as a part of our self-liberation, moving toward the empowerment of all people. We shall gain the ability to remember—to put together again—to name, and to refuse to project evil onto that which is "other." In taking the responsibility for the brokenness in us we begin to break the stranglehold of fascism. We shall gain the power that comes from working collectively as responsible moral agents; and we shall gain the power of positive relation, personally and systemically, as we gain wisdom about our common life and struggle together.

CONFLICT AND THE DEMANDS OF REVOLUTIONARY LOVE

When Ernesto Cardenal, standing in front of one of Somoza's former homes told us that we in the United States can be in a revolutionary situation, he was suggesting that we are in a situation of oppression, in which we must decide which side we are on. To make such a decision puts us, inescapably, into conflict. Those who wish to construct a just society in the United States are in conflict with the leaders of our nation. But there is also conflict among those of us who share a vision of new structures—just as during the insurrection and reconstruction there has been and is conflict among the Sandinistas and among the people of Nicaragua.

> *If we are communicating with the enemy, we must be willing to accept conflict as part of the process. This is not only true with "the enemy," but also with those who we may consider our allies: those people who are also struggling for justice, but with different ideas, priorities, issues, or experiences than ourselves.*
>
> —KIRSTEN

The Amanecida Collective is one example of people working together. As this book demonstrates, there has been conflict among us. There have been long editorial meetings, hurt feelings, angry words, and sharp disagreement. We do not envision the end of this book as an end to a process of transformation taking place in our lives, and we realize that changing lives is a process that engenders conflict.

Flo has written of a situation that arose in Nicaragua which reveals how difficult the transformation is from an individualistic view of life—one of the hallmarks of which is consumerism—to one of solidarity and community. Consumerism, a denial of the needs of others in order to satisfy our individual desires, is woven into the very fabric of life and aspiration in the United States.

Flo reflects not only on the seductive character of consumerist values, but also on the critical conflict that arises among those who, like us, live with one foot in the realm of justice and the other in the mystified empire of capitalist values and behavior:

Two women from our group were leaving early to go to the United States. They left Estelí a day early to go to the market in Managua. We arrived in Managua the next day and met them at lunch. They were excited about their day at the market, the bus ride, and seeing us. They told us about some of their experiences in the market. I asked if they had found rugs and wall hangings; they said that they had and that they would tell us all about the market later in the day.

That evening we sat around in a circle and had our last meeting as a full group before we were to go back to the States. We decided one of the things we would do was to go around the circle and "close out" our stay in Nicaragua by talking about something that happened to us that was very important. Before we began, the two women said they wanted to tell us about something that had happened at the market. They proceeded to tell us they saw wall hangings at approximately 5,000 cordobas per rug (there were at the time 28 cordobas to the dollar). The vendors, however, encouraged them to buy with U.S. dollars, saying that they would charge only $15-20 per rug, rather than the $180 or so the rugs would cost if purchased with cordobas. Both women purchased rugs with dollars. One of the women decided that $15 was too little to pay and in trying to be fair gave the merchant more than the price asked.

The problem with that incident was that we had been warned before we went that there was a black market and that Nicaraguans wanted U.S. dollars because the cordoba was declining in value while the U.S. dollar was retaining its value. The merchants wanted U.S. dollars. In this way the people could accumulate money if they wanted to leave the country. Since the merchant could get up to 200–300 cordobas on the black market for one U.S. dollar, it was worth the risk.

The women shared the story for two reasons: first, to warn us that vendors would be going after U.S. dollars and would encourage us to spend them; second, to confess how confused they had been in the market and how they had not even realized what was happening until afterwards.

When the story was told, there was some laughter about what had taken place. Overall it was agreed that it wasn't such a bad thing. The subject was dropped and the circle continued with the original agenda. I was angry about what had happened. By the time the conversation got around to me, I said that although I had something important to share with them, at this point what was most important was what had occurred. (I was going 60 mph in the rocking chair—back and forth.) I proceeded to say that I was so angry that I couldn't even talk about it.

And then, contradicting myself, I tried to say what was wrong, but I couldn't. Instead I kept saying, "I'm so angry, I can't talk about it now, I'll talk about it later." I did get a few things out. I said to the group that if this had happened at the beginning of the trip, I don't think I'd be this angry. But now, after we had witnessed all the hardship, struggle, suffering and death, how could we do this? How could this have happened? However, I suppressed most of my feelings. In part I was disappointed that I was not going to get the rugs. I was not able to pay 5,000 cordobas for a rug and, on the other hand, in clear conscience I could not use U.S. dollars knowing what I knew.

More important, I became aware of something else. Here we were, a group of politically conscious people, who cared enough about Nicaragua to go there, and yet we weren't looking seriously at what had just occurred. For me that was the issue, and the sadness. It wasn't that any one of us couldn't have been seduced into spending U.S. dollars. Any one of us could have gone to the Managua market and plunged into shopping as though we were on Fifth Avenue. It was the idea that on that night, in that room, no one said, "Look at what has happened. We spent this money and isn't it easy to slip back into the U.S. mentality, the materialism and greed, the consumerism." There was no such conversation. We failed to take ourselves seriously by not looking critically at ourselves, our actions.

This was a pivotal event for me. There were two powerful emotions going on simultaneously inside me. On the one hand, I wanted to scream and damn it, and blame everyone else. On the other hand, I wanted to cry out of sheer frustration because I knew that I was capable of the same. I knew for myself the intoxicating moments of wanting material desires fulfilled—whether or not this was the experience of the two women. For the moment, to their disadvantage, they shared my desires and my dilemma. I knew that I would be deluding myself not to realize that I went to Nicaragua to learn about myself as well. The hopelessness I felt about the group's neglect in confronting what had occurred was my own feeling of hopelessness in confronting my own hypocrisy.

In order to insure that my own authenticity would not be violated, I knew I had to eradicate the same mentality that, when the stakes are higher, causes the exploitation our government is perpetrating against Nicaragua and other underdeveloped countries.

With this in mind, the transition back into the United States was not peaceful. As I walked around the Miami airport I was seeing, in some ways, aspects of our culture for the first time. Waiting for the plane back to Boston, it looked as though everyone was eating continuously. The stores displayed colorful and expensive clothes including a $750 cowboy hat. For the first time, I had a real sense of the unjust ways money is spent. In view of a growing understanding of the concept of a global community, it appears unjust—as long as there are hungry people—to *spend $30 toward a six-day visit at a suntanning center, or, more commonly, to spend many dollars on an item destined to become obsolete upon the arrival of a new model. An example is the movement from television, to color television, to color television with remote control, to color television with remote control and a six-foot screen, etc., accompanied by an attitude that defines poverty as the state of not being able to maintain purchasing power to meet rapid technological change.*

—FLO

Amanecida discussed this event upon our return to the States. We agreed that part of our trouble in having this conversation lay in our anxieties about conflict among ourselves. We began, slowly, to sense that these anxieties may be related to the competitive, win-lose, character of our social relations.

The more deeply we probed this and other group experiences, the better we saw how much we do not see about ways in which we literally buy into capitalist assumptions, whether about consumerism or conflict.

Alan Boesak has written: "Community lies on the far side of much struggle and doubt, of mutual trust and courage."[4] The creating of community with one another involves struggle, and it is through struggle that we may begin to understand and experience the transforming power of God in our life together.

We U.S. citizens must not only confront our existing social structures that benefit a minority and burden the majority; we must come to grips with the fact that conflict is a necessary ingredient in life.

Conflict is not a signal for passivity, aggression, or despair. Nor will we ever have sufficient power to meet all of our responsibilities without conflict—that is the nature of human life. Those who aspire to such power die as dictators. Still, our responsibilities—as members of the world community, as U.S. citizens, as sisters and brothers—can be met through conflict.

Conflict is a call to action. The form this action takes in the United States will depend on our understanding of our own society.

The "American way of life" is built on the foundations of individualism which presuppose the rights of individuals but not their responsibilities. Individualism limits the actions of individuals in conflict, but assumes no real relationship among them within which the conflict can be resolved. In this environment, conflict is defined in terms of win or lose. The "resolution" of conflict in these terms must be categorically rejected. It is no resolution at all, but a weapon of violence.

Conflict resolution requires commitment to relationship and the faith that believes in unity within diversity. It requires the resources—our time, our energy, our talents—which we as North Americans most often reserve for our own individual careers, work, and dreams. In individualistic society conversion is too often fanaticism or self-righteousness;

revolution is too often dictatorship; forgiveness is too often powerlessness or despair.

Real conversion, revolution, and forgiveness will happen only when we have come to terms with our differences. When we make a commitment to resolving conflict in our everyday lives, justice will live among us.

—PAT

Cherrie Moraga writes, "The real power, as you and I well know, is collective. I can't afford to be afraid of you, nor you of me. If it takes head-on collisions, let's do it. This polite timidity is killing us."[5] If we are to be agents of change in U.S. society, then we must begin to envision together what sort of a world we wish to create. One woman said at the Christian base community in Estelí, "One does not make peace just by declaring it." We can affirm a world of peace and of justice, but unless we begin to image together in concrete ways how to manifest that world, our affirmation holds little power and may not inspire us to act. Our power to imagine is our power to be co-creators, not simply created.

Ultimately our ability to work together to re-create the world is based in a revolutionary love. This love is practical and visionary. It accommodates conflict. It is the love practiced by Jesus.

It is hard to love because we cannot determine the outcome. Loving has to do with giving up any pretense of controlling other peoples' lives. Dictators do not love those they rule. Manipulators do not love those they control. We cannot love as long as we have high stakes in determining someone else's destiny—even if we believe ourselves to have their "best interests" in mind. As long as we gravitate toward possessions—including *self*-possession, from an individualist perspective—we are incapable of loving anyone, including ourselves and God.

"To give up one's life in order to find it" is not a masochistic slogan or mandate.[6] We who struggle for justice do not ask to be beaten, broken, or crucified. To the contrary, we understand that we are most likely to be violated if we act as if we are alone, isolated, and separate from one another. Our best hope for survival and justice, as well as our greatest joy, is in realizing that we are *together*. This involves realizing the controls we have laid on the world, including ourselves. "To give up one's life" means letting go of the illusions and fear we carry around that prevent us from getting involved with anyone. It means allowing ourselves to participate in a faith rooted in the love that demands solidarity with those in need, risk-taking on behalf of justice, casting our lots with those in every situation who need advocates . . . and welcoming others' advocacy of our own well-being. "To give up one's life" means that we can relax because we can depend on one another. We need not walk in fear of being touched, of causing a fuss, of stirring up excitement on behalf of justice, of generating passion for people and other earth-creatures. "To give up one's life in order to find it" means that we can live as a forgiven/forgiving people.

Throughout Nicaragua we met people who daily are willing to give up their lives in order to find them—who daily are willing to give their lives for their neighbors. Throughout Nicaragua the dead are remembered—those who struggled against the tyranny of Somoza and those who struggle against the tyranny and terror of the contras. To be a Christian in Estelí and other towns and villages of Nicaragua is to put one's life on the line for others because the contras seek, torture, and murder those who practice a faith rooted in the God of justice.

The revolutionary love practiced by Jesus that we saw practiced by the people of Nicaragua made us realize how corrupt the concept and practice of love have become in the United States. Like the notion of forgiveness widely pedaled in the United States, the notion of love is individualized—it is a love confined to one's spouse, children, family, lover. It is a love for those who are like ourselves. Ultimately it is a love that excludes social responsibility and reaps benefits primarily for the propertied, Anglo, individualistic males who dominate the United States. It is a love that suits their needs and desires. It is not the love practiced by Jesus or the people of Nicaragua—a love of neighbor, a love especially of those who are poor and marginalized. The love we saw practiced in Nicaragua is practiced in community and it benefits individuals. It is a love for the poor and marginalized and for friends, children, spouses, lovers. It is a love that reflects spirituality because it emphasizes social responsibility. The love being practiced in Nicaragua means that the hungry are fed, the prisoners are treated humanely, the sick are cared for, human life is cherished.

Against the backdrop of Nicaragua, we saw that the love, forgiveness, and Christianity that predominate in the United States are incomplete. They have been corrupted by individualism. In letting go of lies that have dictated our lives, we call ourselves and one another into right-relation with God. As the people of Israel knew that knowing God is being in right-relation with one another, we *can know* God by acting as God's people—connected, and committed to the value of the whole created earth and all its people.

Appendix A

Letters from Nicaraguan Mothers to Mothers in the United States

When members of Amanecida were last in Nicaragua, in September 1984, several Nicaraguan mothers who have lost children in the struggle against Somoza and the contras asked us to please bring the following letters home with us and to see that they were delivered as "greetings to North American mothers."

Estelí, Nicaragua,
September 17, 1984

Esteemed North American Mothers,

I am the mother of ten children, of whom one was murdered by Somoza's Guard fourteen years ago. Later in the war of liberation, my oldest grandchild and a son-in-law died fighting against those who oppressed us, leaving three children orphaned.

As you can see, several years of struggle and suffering have been the cost of this liberation. Now that we are prepared to reconstruct our homeland, the government over which Reagan presides does not wish to allow us to do that. The United States has been interfering in our affairs for many years.

We know that the aware North American public does not agree with the policy of their president, and that's why we ask you North American mothers to be in solidarity with our cause and not allow your children to come fight against our children. If they do come, this might cause you the greatest pain— that of losing a child. We have to defend ourselves.

Wishing you the joy of genuine peace in union with your children, and confident that we have your support with our cause, I bid farewell.

Fraternally,
Isidora Ubeda

•

Esteemed North American Mothers,

My desire is that you are enjoying the greatest privilege of being a mother: the company of your children.

What greater satisfaction can a mother feel than to see her children grow with the

131

right of all children to recreation and study in peace. This right is being stolen from our children, as a result of the stubborness or capriciousness of the president of the most powerful nation in the world.

I am a mother of six children and I have yet to experience the satisfaction of seeing any of them develop academically. The oldest, having just turned sixteen, and two months shy of graduating from high school, had to graduate into manhood by going to win back the rights which were being taken from us. He died fighting against our oppressors in 1979, having just turned seventeen. The rest of my children, though young in age, have not been able to develop themselves (as all children have the right to), because the aggressions of Reagan have meant that they must defend themselves and work at the same time they are studying.

More depressing is the situation of the peasant children who, despite the efforts made by our revolution, have not been able to enjoy their rights, because the mercenaries of the CIA burn our health clinics, our education centers. We ask you to comprehend our pain and not let your government continue intervening in our affairs. Let us reconstruct our homeland in peace.

Sure of your solidarity, I subscribe myself to you.

Fraternally,
Olga U. deZeledon

•

Mothers of the U.S., Esteemed Companions,

It's pleasing to me to present to you a cordial revolutionary and fraternal greeting. For us, it's a great satisfaction to know that we are not alone, since you are in solidarity with our cause.

It would take a long time to explain exactly how much I've suffered since the time of the Somoza dictatorship, because my child died in 1970. He was detected in a safehouse of the Sandinista Front, which was attacked by three hundred of Somoza's National Guardsmen with every kind of weapon. They left three young people dead there— among them was my son, Leonel Rugama, poet and warrior.

So, friends, if we suffered in the past, it's worse now. We live threatened by the aggression of bands which murder and rape and with the threat of an invasion, as Mr. Reagan suggests. We pray for your help in doing all that's possible to impede such a misfortune. I say this because this would become a generalized war.

Without more to say, I part with hope of your valuable cooperation, and I leave you with much gratitude.

Fraternally,
Cándida de Rugama

Appendix B

What You Can Do

We implore readers to continue educating themselves and others about what is happening today in Nicaragua and elsewhere in Central America and the Caribbean. As we have noted in this book, the critical process of conscientization—learning together how power is used and abused—is essential to good education, honest faith, and effective work for justice.

We urge you also to act now to help stop the assault by the United States government on the people of Nicaragua and to join in the efforts to turn U.S. foreign and domestic policies around so as to benefit the poor and all who are broken by forces of economic greed, domination, and violence.

Listed below are some resources that we have found especially helpful in our educational work and our efforts to act in solidarity with the people of Nicaragua. For an overall listing and critical evaluation of key books, periodicals, articles, pamphlets, organizations and audiovisuals relevant to the situation in Central America, see Thomas Fenton and Mary Heffron, eds., *Latin America and Caribbean: A Directory of Resources* (Maryknoll, N.Y. Orbis, 1986). The work also gives a thorough list of addresses of the sources of material. In what follows, we give some sources' addresses that might be difficult to locate.

SUGGESTIONS FOR FURTHER READING

On Nicaragua, the Rest of Central America, and the Caribbean

An Alternative Policy for Central America and the Caribbean: Summary and Conclusion of a Policy Workshop Held in The Hague, June, 6–25 1983. The Hague, Netherlands: Institute of Social Studies.

Black, George. *Triumph of the People: The Sandinista Revolution in Nicaragua*. London: Zed, 1981.

Bent, George. "Nicaragua—Bordering on Reconciliation: A Miskito Pastor Reflects on the Tension between His People and the Nicaraguan Government" (interview). *Sojourners* 12, (March 1983): 24–28.

Bishop, Maurice, *Forward Ever: Speeches of Maurice Bishop*. New York: Pathfinder Press.

_____. Maurice Bishop Speaks to U.S. Workers: Why the U.S. Invaded Grenada. New York: Pathfinder Press.

Borge, Tomas, Carlos Fonseca, Daniel Ortega, Humberto Ortega, Jaime Wheelock. *Sandinistas Speak: Speeches, Writings, and Interviews with Leaders of Nicaragua's Revolution*. New York: Pathfinder, 1982.

Central America Report. Bimonthly journal of the Religious Task Force on Central

America, 1747 Connecticut Ave., NW, Washington, DC 20009.

Changing Course: Blueprint for Peace in Central America and the Caribbean. 1984. Available from Institute for Policy Studies, 1901 Q Street, NW, Washington, DC 20009.

CIDA (Centro de Investigaciones y Documentación de la Costa Atlantica). *Trabil Nani: Historical Background and Current Situation of the Atlantic Coast.* Available from the Board of World Missions, Moravian Church Office, 69 W. Church St. Bethlehem, PA; also from Riverside Church, Riverside Drive and 122nd St., New York, NY 10027.

Collins, Joseph, with Frances Moore Lappé and Nick Allen. *What Difference Could a Revolution Make?* San Francisco: Institute for Food and Development Policy (see listing of organizations below for address), 1985.

Didion, Joan. *Salvador.* New York: Simon and Schuster, 1983.

Dixson, Marlene and Susanne Jonas. *Nicaragua under Siege.* San Francisco: Synthesis, 1984.

Envío (monthly publication on political, economic, and social developments in Central America and the Caribbean). Available from the Central American Historical Institute, Intercultural Center, Georgetown University, Washington, DC 20057.

Ezcurra, Ana María. *Ideological Aggression against the Sandinista Revolution.* New York: New York CIRCUS, 1984.

Forche, Carolyn. *The Country Between Us* (poetry about El Salvador). New York: Harper and Row, 1981.

Freedom of Expression and Assembly in Nicaragua during the Election Period. New York: Americas Watch, 1984.

Gallo, Jeanne. *Responding to the Rights of the Poor: Nicaragua, the Church, and the U.S.* Boston: Gritaré, Sisters of Notre Dame, 1985.

In Contempt of Congress: The Reagan Record of Deceit and Illegality on Central America. Washington, D.C.: Institute for Policy Studies (see above for address), 1985.

Lappé, Frances Moore and Joseph Collins. *Now We Can Speak: A Journey Through the New Nicaragua.* San Francisco: Institute for Food and Development Policy (for address see below), 1982.

Macaulay, Neill. *The Sandino Affair.* Chicago: Quadrangle, 1967.

McGinnis, James, *Solidarity with the People of Nicaragua.* Maryknoll, N.Y.: Orbis, 1985.

Mueller, Karl A. *Among Creoles, Miskitos and Sumas: Eastern Nicaragua and Its Moravian Missions.* Bethlehem, Pa: Comenius, 1932.

Nicaragua: A Look at the Reality. Hyattsville, Md.: The Quixote Center (see below for address).

Nicaragua: Give Change a Chance. San Francisco: Institute for Food and Development Policy (see below for address).

Noone, Judith. *The Same Fate as the Poor* (biographies of the three Maryknoll sisters who were murdered in El Salvador in 1980). Maryknoll, N.Y.: Maryknoll Sisters.

Randall, Margaret. *Sandino's Daughters: Testimonies of Nicaraguan Women in Struggle.* Vancouver: New Star, 1981.

Report on the Situation of Human Rights of a Segment of the Nicaraguan Population of Miskito Origin. Organization of American States (Inter-American Commission on Human Rights), October, 1983.

Pearce, Jenny. *Under the Eagle: U.S. Intervention in Central America and the Caribbean.* London: Latin American Bureau, 1982.

Shaull, Richard, and Nancy Johns. *Responding to the Cry of the Poor: Nicaragua and the U.S.A.* Omega Press. Available from Johns/Shaull, 156 Maplewood Ave., Philadelphia, PA 19144.

U.S-Nicaraguan Relations: Chronology of Policy and Impact, January, 1981–January,

1984. Washington, D.C.: Central American Historical Institute (see below for address).
Wilde, Margaret D. *The East Coast of Nicaragua: Issues for Dialogue.* Available through Moravian Church Office (see above for address).

Some Resources on Liberation Theology

Related Primarily to Latin America

Brown, Robert McAfee. *Theology in a New Key: Responding to Liberation Themes.* Philadelphia: Westminster, 1978.
_____. *Unexpected News: Reading the Bible with Third World Eyes.* Philadelphia: Westminster, 1984.
Cabestrero, Teófilo. *Blood of the Innocent: Victims of the Contras' War in Nicaragua.* Maryknoll, N.Y.: Orbis, 1985.
_____. *Ministers of God, Ministers of the People: Testimonies of Faith from Nicaragua* (interviews with Fernando Cardenal, Miguel D'Escoto, and Ernesto Cardenal). Maryknoll, N.Y.: Orbis, 1983.
Cardenal, Ernesto. *Flights of Victory/Vuelos de Victoria.* Maryknoll, N.Y.: Orbis, 1985.
_____. *The Gospel in Solentiname.* 4 vols. Maryknoll: Orbis, 1976–82.
Esquivel, Julia. *Threatened with Resurrection: Prayers and Poems from an Exiled Guatemalan.* Elgin, IL.: Brethren, 1982.
Gutiérrez, Gustavo. *A Theology of Liberation: History, Politics and Salvation.* Maryknoll, N.Y.: Orbis, 1973.
_____. *We Drink from Our Own Wells: The Spiritual Journey of a People.* Maryknoll, N.Y.: Orbis, 1984.
Lernoux, Penny. *Cry of the People: United States Involvement in the Rise of Fascism, Torture and Murder and the Persecution of the Catholic Church in Latin America.* Garden City, N.Y.: Doubleday, 1980.
Míguez-Bonino, José. *Doing Theology in a Revolutionary Situation.* Philadelphia: Fortress, 1975.
_____. *Toward a Christian Political Ethics.* Philadelphia: Fortress, 1983.
Peacemaking II: Religious Statements on Central America (Over 60 statements by Protestant, Catholic, and Jewish national bodies voicing opposition to U.S. policy). New York: Inter-Religious Task Force on Central America (see below for address).
Randall, Margaret. *Christians in the Nicaraguan Revolution.* Vancouver: New Star, 1983.
Segundo, Juan Luis. *The Liberation of Theology.* Maryknoll, N.Y.: Orbis, 1976.
Sobrino, Jon. *Christology at the Crossroads: A Latin American Approach.* Maryknoll, N.Y.: Orbis, 1978.

Some Feminist, Black, Asian, and Other Liberation Voices

Baugh, Constance M. *Women in Jail and Prison: A Training Manual for Volunteer Advocates.* New York: National Council of Churches of Christ, U.S.A., Division of Church and Society/Justice for Women's Working Group, 1986.
Brueggemann, Walter. *The Prophetic Imagination.* Philadelphia: Fortress, 1978.
Cone, James H. *For My People: Black Theology and the Black Church.* Maryknoll, N.Y.: Orbis, 1984.
Fabella, Virginia, ed. *Asia's Struggle for Full Humanity: Papers from the Asian Theological Conference.* Maryknoll, N.Y.: Orbis, 1980.
Fiorenza, Elisabeth Schüssler. *Bread Not Stone: The Challenge of Feminist Biblical Interpretation.* Boston: Beacon, 1985.

Gottwald, Norman K., ed. *The Bible and Liberation: Political and Social Hermeneutics.* Maryknoll, N.Y.: Orbis, 1983.

Harrison, Beverly Wildung. *Making the Connections: Essays in Feminist Social Ethics.* Boston: Beacon, 1985.

Heyward, Carter. *Our Passion for Justice: Images of Power, Sexuality and Liberation.* New York: Pilgrim, 1984.

Hope, Marjorie, and James Young. *The South African Churches in a Revolutionary Situation.* Maryknoll, N.Y.: Orbis, 1981.

Hull, Gloria T., Patricia Scott and Barbara Smith, eds. *All the Women Are White, All the Blacks Are Men, But Some of Us Are Brave: Black Women's Studies.* Old Westbury, N.Y.: Feminist, 1982.

Ilunga, Bakole Wa. *Paths of Liberation: A Third World Spirituality.* Maryknoll, N.Y.: Orbis, 1984.

Moraga, Cherrié. *Loving in the War Years: lo que nunca pasó por sus labios.* Boston: South End, 1983.

Ruether, Rosemary R. *Sexism and God-Talk: A Feminist Theology.* Boston: Beacon, 1983.

Sölle, Dorothee and Shirley Cloyes. *To Work and to Love: A Theology of Creation.* Philadelphia: Fortress, 1984.

West, Cornel. *Prophesy Deliverance! An Afro-American Revolutionary Christianity.* Philadelphia: Fortress, 1982.

Wilmore, Gayraud S. and James H. Cone, eds. *Black Theology: A Documentary History, 1966–1979.* Maryknoll, N.Y.: Orbis, 1979.

SOME ORGANIZATIONS AND NETWORKS IN SOLIDARITY WITH THE PEOPLE OF CENTRAL AMERICAN AND THE CARIBBEAN

Caribbean Basin Information Project
1826 18th St., NW
Washington, DC 20009
(202) 462-8333

Central American Historical Institute
Intercultural Center
Georgetown University
Washington, DC 20057
(202) 625-8246

Central American Solidarity Association (CASA)
1151 Massachusetts Ave.
Cambridge, MA 02135
(617) 492-8699

Chicago Religious Task Force on Central America
407 S. Dearborn, Room 370
Chicago, IL 60605
(312) 427-2533

Coalition for a New Foreign and Military Policy
120 Maryland Ave., NE
Washington, DC 20002
(202) 546-8400
(Hotline for information, 24 hrs./day)

Comité de Apoyo Pro-ANDES (Educators in Support of the Salvadoran Teachers'
    Association)
1151 Massachusetts Ave.
Cambridge, MA 02138
(617) 876-4545

Ecumenical Program for Interamerican Communication and Action (EPICA)
1470 Irving St., NW
Washington, DC 20010
(202) 332-0292

Humanitarian Assistance Project for Independent Agricultural Development
in Nicaragua
4318 Michigan Union
530 S. State St.
Ann Arbor, MI 48109
(313) 761-7960

Institute for Food and Development Policy
1885 Mission St.
San Francisco, CA 94103
(415) 864-8555

Institute for Policy Studies
1901 Q St., NW
Washington, DC 20009
(202) 234-9382

Inter-Religious Task Force on Central America
475 Riverside Drive
New York, NY 10115
(212) 870-3383

Michigan Interchurch Committee on Central American Human Rights
4220 W. Vernor
Detroit, MI 48209
(313) 841-4320

Mobilization for Survival/Pledge of Resistance
11 Garden St.
Cambridge, MA 02138
(617) 487-9311

National Network in Solidarity with the Nicaraguan People
2025 "I" Street, NW
Washington, DC 20006
(202) 223-2328

NICA (Nuevo Instituto de Centro América)
PO Box 1409
Cambridge, MA 02238
(617) 497-7142

Nicaragua-Honduras Education Project
1322 18th St. NW, Suite 36
Washington, DC 20036
(202) 822-8357

Nicaragua Interfaith Committee for Action (NICA)
942 Market St., 7th Floor
San Francisco, CA 94102
(415) 433-6057

Nicaraguan Information Center
PO Box 1004
Berkeley, CA 94701
(415) 549-1387

North American Congress on Latin America (NACLA)
151 W. 19th St.
New York, NY 10011
(212) 989-8890

Oxfam America
115 Broadway
Boston, MA 02116
(617) 482-1211

Quixote Center
PO Box 5206
Hyattsville, MD 20782
(301) 699-0042

Religious Task Force on Central America
1747 Connecticut Ave., NW
Washington, DC 20009
(202) 387-7652

Sojourners
PO Box 29272
Washington, DC 20017
(202) 636-36 37

US Out of Central America
2940 16th St., Suite 7
San Francisco, CA 94103
(415) 550-8006

Washington Office on Latin America
110 Maryland Ave., NE
Washington, DC 20002
(202) 544-8045

Witness for Peace
1414 Woodland Drive
Durham, NC 27701
(919) 286-0248

Women's Coalition Against US Intervention in Central America and the Caribbean
475 Riverside Drive
New York, NY 10115
(212) 870-2347

Work Brigades:

Harvest Brigade
Nicaragua Exchange
239 Centre Street
New York, NY 10013
(212) 219-8620

Special Project Brigades
National Nicaragua Network
2025 "I" Street, NW, #117
Washington, DC 20006
(212) 223-2328

Notes

FOREWORD

1. See Dieter Eich and Carlos Rincón, eds., *The Contras: Interviews with Anti-Sandinistas* (San Francisco: Synthesis, 1985). The work contains interviews with contras imprisoned by the Sandinistas.

PREFACE

1. The term "body politic" is developed by Raymond Pelly in his work in progress, *The Resurrection of the Body Politic: A Political Hermeneutic of Christ for Today*. He has discussed this concept of the fundamentally *political* character of human being and action with several of the authors of this volume.

2. This program in Social Pastoral Mission has been accepted in principle by the Episcopal Divinity School's Educational Policy Committee. A proposal for this program is being explored during the 1985–1986 academic year, with a view toward its implementation as a regular component of the seminary's curriculum during the next few years.

3. See the Mud Flower Collective, *God's Fierce Whimsy: Christian Feminism and Theological Education* (New York: Pilgrim, 1985) for an elaboration of the theological and educational value of collaborative research and writing. Carter Heyward was a member of the Mud Flower Collective.

INTRODUCTION

1. On the early feminist movement in the United States, see Alice S. Rossi, ed., *The Feminist Papers: From Adams to de Beauvoir* (New York: Bantam, 1971). For writings from early years of the contemporary movement, see Robin Morgan, ed., *Sisterhood is Powerful: An Anthology of Writings from the Women's Liberation Movement* (New York: Vintage, 1970). For material on ways in which white women betrayed the early aims of feminism, see Angela Y. Davis, *Women, Race, and Class* (New York: Random House, 1981).

2. See Adrienne Rich, "Compulsory Heterosexuality and Lesbian Existence," in Ann Snitow et al., eds., *Powers of Desire: The Politics of Sexuality* (New York: Monthly Review, 1983), pp. 177–205.

3. Feminist resources on sexuality include Evelyn Torton Beck, ed., *Nice Jewish Girls: A Lesbian Anthology* (Watertown, Mass.: Persephone Press, 1982); Rita Mae Brown, *Rubyfruit Jungle* (New York: Bantam, 1977); Beverly Wildung Harrison, *Making the Connections: Essays in Feminist Social Ethics* (Boston: Beacon, 1985); Carter Heyward, *Our Passion for Justice: Images of Power, Sexuality and Liberation* (New York:

Pilgrim, 1984); Audre Lorde, *Sister Outsider: Essays and Speeches* (Trumansburg, N.Y.: Crossing Press, 1982); James B. Nelson, *Embodiment: An Approach to Sexuality and Christian Theology* (Minneapolis: Augsburg, 1978); idem, *Between Two Gardens: Reflections on Sexuality and Religious Experience* (New York: Pilgrim, 1983); Barbara Smith, ed., *Home Girls: A Black Feminist Anthology* (New York: Kitchen Table/ Women of Color Press, 1983).

4. Resources on christology from a liberation perspective include Jon Sobrino, *Christology at the Crossroads* (Maryknoll, N.Y.: Orbis, 1978); Leonardo Boff, "Christ's Liberation via Oppression: An Attempt at Theological Construction from the Standpoint of Latin America," in Rosino Gibellini, ed., *Frontiers of Theology in Latin America* (Maryknoll, N.Y.: Orbis, 1979); pp. 100–132; Leonardo Boff, *Jesus Christ Liberator* (Maryknoll, N.Y.: Orbis, 1978); José Miranda, *Being and the Messiah* (Maryknoll, N.Y.: Orbis, 1979); James Cone, *God of the Oppressed* (New York: Seabury, 1975); Carter Heyward, *The Redemption of God: A Theology of Mutual Relation* (Lanham, Md.: University Press of America, 1982); Carter Heyward, "Being in Christ?" and "Must 'Jesus Christ' Be a Holy Terror?" in *Our Passion For Justice: Images of Power, Sexuality, and Liberation* (New York: Pilgrim, 1984); Rosemary Radford Ruether, *To Change the World: Christology and Cultural Pluralism* (New York: Crossroad, 1981); Tom F. Driver, *Christ in a Changing World: Toward an Ethical Christology* (New York: Crossroad, 1981).

CHAPTER ONE

1. Carlos Manuel, FSLN representative speaking in Estelí, Nicaragua, Feb. 1, 1984.

2. Carter Heyward spent a day at the Anglican Institute with the caretakers, Mary Darkin and Nicholas Cruz. This is a synopsis of a conversation with them.

3. Susan Meiselas, *Nicaragua: June 1978–July 1979* (New York: Pantheon, 1981), p. 76.

4. Augusto Cesar Sandino quoted in Meiselas, *Nicaragua*, p. 73.

5. Humberto Ortega, "Nicaragua—The Strategy of Victory," in Bruce Marcus, ed., *Sandinistas Speak* (New York: Pathfinder, 1982), p. 41.

6. Based on a population of 2.2 million, these statistics were compiled from United States Agency for International Development (AID), the 1971 Nicaraguan census, the United Nations Economic Commission for Latin America, and the Central American Permanent Secretariat for Economic Integration. Reliable, up-to-date statistics were impossible to acquire under the Somoza regime.

7. Richard R. Fagen, *The Nicaraguan Revolution: A Personal Report* (Washington, D.C.: Institute for Policy Studies, 1981), p. 12.

8. Taken from a report of the June 26–July 4, 1984 National Peace Vigil in Nicaragua by the New England Delegation, Witness for Peace. The Rev. Dr. Robert M. Bouthius, Coordinator for New England (RD 2, Box 422A, Ellsworth, ME 24605).

9. Richard M. Garfield and Eugenio Taboada, "Human Services Reforms in Revolutionary Nicaragua," *American Journal of Public Health* 74 (October 1984), no. 10: 1139, 1143.

10. *Financial Times*, September 5, 1983.

11. *El Esteliano*, published by Nuevo Instituto de Centro América (NICA), April/ May 1985.

12. Ibid.

13. Carlos Manuel, speaking in Estelí, Nicaragua, Feb. 1, 1984.

14. Ibid.

15. *The Boston Globe*, March 19, 1985.

16. See Kent Norsworthy and William Robinson, "Nicaraguan Church Hierarchy Moves Central to Internal Counterrevolution," *Frontline* (Oakland, Calif., July 9, 1984).

17. Carlos Manuel.

18. Speech by Daniel Ortega, February 21, 1984, Plaza de la Revolución, Managua, Nicaragua, as quoted by Philip Martinez in "Nicaragua's Road to Elections: The Process, the Opposition, and the U.S.," in *Nicaraguan Perspectives* (Berkeley, Calif., Summer, 1984), no. 8: pp. 27-28.

19. Carlos Manuel.

20. Carter Heyward, "Whose Freedom of the Press?" *The Witness* (Ambler, Pa.: The Episcopal Church Publishing Company) 67, (March 1984), no. 3: 15-17.

CHAPTER TWO

1. The Spanish term *presente*, which in recent years has become a sacred invocation in the Latin American liberation struggle, has no adequate English translation. At funerals and memorial services for those who have been killed by enemies of justice, the congregation often will invoke the company of those who have died by declaring together after each name is spoken, *¡presente!*—which signifies both the imperative command ("Be present!") and the indicative statement of fact ("He or she is present!").

2. Holly Near, "It Could Have Been Me," recorded on *Journeys* (Redwood Records, 1983).

3. Beverly Wildung Harrison, *Our Right to Choose: Toward A New Ethic of Abortion* (Boston: Beacon, 1983), p. 54.

4. Gustavo Gutiérrez, *The Theology of Liberation* (Maryknoll, N.Y.: Orbis, 1973), p. 205; idem, *We Drink From Our Own Wells* (Maryknoll, N.Y.: Orbis, 1984), pp. 95 and 99.

CHAPTER THREE

1. Quoted by Anne Gilson in "Lessons Learned in Nicaragua," in *The Witness* (Feb. 1985): 18.

2. Anne Gilson, originally published in *The Warren Times Observer* (Warren, Pa.), Oct. 16, 1984.

3. For works which portray Jesus as liberator, see Leonardo Boff, *Was Jesus a Revolutionist?* (Philadelphia: Fortress Press, 1971); idem, *Jesus Christ Liberator: A Critical Theology for Our Time* (Maryknoll, N.Y.: Orbis, 1978); and José Miranda, *Being and the Messiah: The Message of St. John* (Maryknoll, N.Y.: Orbis, 1973).

4. *Fe Cristiana y Revolución Sandinista en Nicaragua* (Managua: Central America Historical Institute).

5. Quoted by Anne Gilson in "Lessons Learned in Nicaragua," p. 18.

6. Michael McIntyre, "The IRD: Neoconservative Religious 'Think Tank,'" in Ana Maria Ezcurra, *The Neoconservative Offensive: U.S. Churches and the Ideological Struggle for Latin America* (New York: Circus Publications, 1982), p. 6.

7. Conversation with Bismark Carballo, September 7, 1984. Also see daily issues of *La Prensa*, the newspaper of Nicaraguan conservatives, for allegations of the "be-

trayal" of the church hierarchy and wealthier sectors of the Nicaraguan population by the Sandinistas.

8. Pope John Paul II visited Nicaragua in March 1983. During a Mass in Managua, he said nothing about the accomplishments of the revolution or about the attacks by counterrevolutionaries, but placed repeated emphasis on the authority of the church hierarchy. When he showed no sympathy for the recent loss of 17 young people killed at the border, the people began to chant "We want peace!" Mothers of the 17 pleaded for a prayer for the dead children. The pope's only response was to shout "¡Silencio!" several times. The disrespectful treatment of the pope was spurred by his disrespectful treatment of the Nicaraguan people.

9. Quoted in a letter circulated on IRD letterhead and signed by Chair Edmund W. Robb, Jr. (IRD), Richard J. Neuhaus (director, Center on Religion and Society), and Michael Novak (editor, *Catholicism in Crisis*), dated July 13, 1984.

10. Transcribed interview with Padre Bismarck Carballo, Sept. 7, 1984. Partially quoted by Anne Gilson in "Lessons Learned in Nicaragua," p. 18.

11. Ibid.

12. The Consejo Superiór de la Empresa Privada (COSEP) is a conservative political organization of businessmen in Nicaragua who are allied with the contras in their commitment to oust the Sandinista government. COSEP believes that the Sandinistas are against the best interests of Nicaraguan "free enterprise" (or capitalism). The main voice of COSEP is *La Prensa*, a conservative daily newspaper which regularly publishes anti-Sandinista views and which is also the newspaper supported by the Nicaraguan Catholic hierarchy.

13. In its "Santa Fe Document," the Reagan Administration stated, "U.S. policy in Latin America must begin to counter liberation theology as it is used in Latin America. The role of the Church in Latin America is vital to the concept of political freedom [founded in] private property and productive capitalism."

A secret Vatican document written as papal guidelines on Nicaragua was leaked to a French Latin American news service (DIAL) in June 1983. The document details "How the Church and Christians can face up to a Marxist government and triumph. . . . The fact that the government is an enemy means that the Church must not deposit its confidence in the government or take its statements at face value. . . . A strategy based on strength, unity and firmness has much more of a chance than a strategy that makes an understanding with the government a priority."

A number of liberation theologians, including Leonardo Boff, Ernesto Cardenal, Fernando Cardenal, and Miguel D'Escoto, have come under censure recently by the Vatican for their combining of faith and politics.

14. Meeting with Norman Bent, Moravian pastor who has worked extensively with the Nicaraguan East Coast Miskito Indians, August 31, 1984, in Managua.

15. "Autonomy for the Atlantic Coast—A New Principle of the Revolution," *Envío* (Managua) 4 (no. 45, March 1985).

16. Under the charismatic leadership of Steadman Fagoth, a Miskito ex- intelligence agent of the Somoza regime, the CIA has been steadily recruiting Miskito Indians into the ranks of the contras. Through a contra organization known as MISURA (later MISURA-FDN), which was started with CIA funding and guidance, Fagoth began in 1981 to broadcast on the radio a campaign designed to convince Indians to join him in Honduras to prepare to overthrow the Sandinista revolution. Fagoth preached that the Sandinistas were "atheist communists" who would outlaw Miskito religious practices and confiscate lands. Initially Fagoth succeeded in recruiting many Miskito Indians into

the contra ranks. However, some Miskitos began organizing in support of the Sandinistas. In response to this counter-allegiance, the CIA urged the contras of the MISURA–FDN (Nicaraguan Democratic Force) to begin a series of kidnappings, forced recruitment of Miskitos into the contra ranks, and building up of so-called resettlement camps. In December 1983, 1,000 Miskitos were kidnaped at gunpoint from Francia Sirpe. Seven hundred more were taken from Sandy Bay in March 1984. Young men from Francia Sirpe were sent to the "Center for Miskito Military Instruction," where they spent several weeks training in the use of basic arms and military strategy. The center is run by MISURA–FDN members and three resident U.S. army officers. For two articles on the Miskito Indian situation and the CIA see: William I. Robinson, "Nicaraguan Miskito Indians Confront Counter-Revolution," *Frontline* (Oakland, Calif., Sept. 17, 1984) and "Bordering on Reconciliation," *Sojourners* (March 1983): 24–28.

17. Interview with Berta Zelidon, representative of AMNLAE, in Estelí, Nicaragua, Feb. 4, 1984.

18. Loie Hayes, "Passionate Politics in Nicaragua," in *Gay Community News*, April 28, 1984.

19. Comité Evangelico Pro-Ayuda y Desarrollo (CEPAD), which is the Evangelical Committee for Aid to Development, was born four days after the devastating earthquake in Nicaragua in 1972, largely through the efforts of Dr. Gustavo Parajón. CEPAD was initially an effort by evangelical Christians to provide relief to victims of the earthquake. Realizing the continued need for work with the poor, CEPAD became a major aid and development organization in Nicaragua, supporting over 400 housing, medical, and agricultural projects throughout the country. CEPAD has been supportive of the Sandinistas, and has worked with the government to organize the literacy campaigns. Under the current leadership of Benjamin Cortez (interviewed by some members of Amanecida in August 1984), CEPAD understands Marxism as "a helpful scientific method of analysis of political, social and economic problems." For this reason, CEPAD is often discredited by the Institute on Religion and Democracy in the U.S.

20. Dom Helder Camara, *Spiral of Violence* (London: Sheed and Ward, 1971).

21. See Appendix: letters which we brought back with us written by Nicaraguan mothers to U.S. mothers.

CHAPTER FOUR

1. See Miguel D'Escoto, "An Unfinished Canvas: Building a New Nicaragua," *Sojourners* (March 1983): 14–18.

2. Quoted in Rosa del Olmo, "Remaking Justice and Rehabilitation in Revolutionary Nicaragua," in *Crime and Social Justice: Issues in Criminology* (Winter 1982 issue on remaking justice), p. 103.

3. See, for example, Karl Barth, *Church Dogmatics*, vols. I–IV (Edinburgh: T. and T. Clark, 1957), and especially his chapters on sin and grace for an account of the worthlessness of humanity. Although many early theologians, such as Augustine, hold that humanity is basically good because we have been created by God, the "wallowing in worthlessness" characteristic of much subsequent Christian thought is still commonplace. See St. Augustine, *Confessions*, ed. T.E. Page (Cambridge: Oxford University Press, 1912), Loeb Classical Library, vols. I and II.

4. The "blaming the victim" attitude, characteristic of large segments of society, toward domestic violence, rape, and incest is well-documented in such works as Marie

Marshall Fortune, *Sexual Violence: The Unmentionable Sin* (New York: Pilgrim, 1983). See also Kathleen Barry, *Female Sexual Slavery* (Englewood Cliffs, N.J.: Prentice-Hall, 1979), and Ann Franklin and Wilma Wake, "Betrayal by the Fathers: The Abuse of Women by Fathers and Father-Figures" (unpublished essay, Episcopal Divinity School, Cambridge, Mass., 1985).

5. See Martin Luther King, Jr., *Why We Can't Wait* (New York: New American Library, 1963); Manning Marable, *From the Grassroots: Social and Political Essays towards Afro-American Liberation* (Boston: South End, 1980); and Paula Giddings, *When and Where I Enter: The Impact of Black Women on Race and Sex in America,* (New York: William Morrow and Company, 1984).

6. See, for example, the "Christian" justification of South African apartheid as documented by Allan Boesak, *Black and Reformed: Apartheid, Liberation and the Calvinist Tradition* (Maryknoll, N.Y.: Orbis, 1984); and Desmond Tutu, *Crying in the Wilderness: The Struggle for Justice in South Africa* (Grand Rapids, Mi.: Eerdmans, 1982). See also the "Letter From a Battered Woman" in Del Martin, ed., *Battered Wives* (New York: Simon and Schuster, 1983).

7. For analysis of capitalism in the United States as related to race issues, theology, and food consumption see: Manning Marable, *How Capitalism Underdeveloped Black America: Problems in Race, Political Economy and Society* (Boston: South End, 1983); Jack A. Nelson, *Hunger for Justice: The Politics of Food and Faith* (Maryknoll, N.Y.: Orbis, 1980); and Cornel West, *Prophesy Deliverance: An Afro-American Revolutionary Christianity* (Philadelphia: Westminster, 1982).

8. John Mac Murray discusses the "self-possessed individual" in his books *The Self as Agent* (London: Faber, 1957) and *Persons in Relations* (London: Faber, 1961). Also see Russell Jacoby, *Social Amnesia: A Critique of Conformist Psychology from Adler to Laing* (Boston: Beacon, 1975).

9. The "official" rhetoric of the Pentagon. Quoted in Richard J. Barnet, "Losing Moral Ground," *Sojourners* (March 1985), no. 3: 24.

10. This course was taught by Katie Geneva Cannon at Episcopal Divinity School in Cambridge, Mass., fall 1984.

11. In conversation with Constance M. Baugh, February, 1986, we learned that 1,642 people are on death row. Of those, 1,621 are male and 21 are female. In addition to the 50 who have been executed since January, 1977, 18 have committed suicide and 20 have died in other ways.

12. For an analysis of liberalism see Carter Heyward, "Limits of Liberalism: Feminism in Moral Crisis," in *Our Passion for Justice: Images of Power, Sexuality, and Liberation* (New York: Pilgrim, 1984).

13. Outstanding works on liberation ethics include Katie Geneva Cannon, *Resources for a Constructive Ethic for Black Women with Special Attention to the Life and Work of Zora Neale Hurston* (unpublished Ph.D. dissertation, Union Theological Seminary, New York, 1984); Gerard Fourez, *Liberation Ethics* (Philadelphia: Temple University Press, 1982); Beverly Wildung Harrison, *Making the Connections: Essays in Feminist Social Ethics* (Boston: Beacon, 1985); and Peter J. Paris, *The Social Teaching of the Black Churches* (Philadelphia: Fortress, 1985).

14. See Paulo Freire, *Pedagogy of the Oppressed* (New York: Herder and Herder, 1970), and *The Politics of Education: Culture, Power, and Liberation* (South Hadley, Mass.: Bergin and Garvey, 1985). See also The Mud Flower Collective, *God's Fierce Whimsy: Christian Feminism and Theological Education* (New York: Pilgrim, 1985).

15. Edicio de la Torre, "A Message from the Philippines Struggle," in *Theology in the*

Americas: Detroit II Conference Papers, ed. Cornel West, Caridad Guidote, Margaret Coakley (Maryknoll, N.Y.: Orbis, 1982), pp. 44–50.

16. Carter Heyward, *Our Passion for Justice: Images of Power, Sexuality, and Liberation* (New York: Pilgrim, 1984), p. 1.

17. Conversation with the then Bishop-elect Downs by some members of Amanecida on September 19, 1984, at the Iglesia Episcopal de Nicaragua diocesan headquarters in Managua.

CHAPTER FIVE

1. José Míguez-Bonino, *Toward a Christian Political Ethics* (Philadelphia: Fortress, 1983), p. 112.

2. See Richard Shaull, *Heralds of a New Reformation: The Poor of South and North America* (Maryknoll, N.Y.: Orbis, 1984), pp. 131–32.

3. See Manning Marable, *Blackwater: Historical Studies in Race, Class Consciousness and Revolution* (Dayton, Ohio: Black Praxis, 1981), and *How Capitalism Underdeveloped Black America: Problems in Race, Political Economy, and Society* (Boston: South End, 1983) for a development of these ideas.

4. See Allan Boesak, *Black and Reformed: Apartheid, Liberation, and the Calvinist Tradition* (Maryknoll, N.Y.: Orbis, 1984).

5. Cherríe Moraga, *Loving in the War Years* (Boston: South End, 1983), p. 59.

6. See Matthew 10:39, 16:25; Luke 17:33; and John 12:25.

Contributors

Laura Phyllis Biddle, a student at Episcopal Divinity School, Cambridge, Mass., is a postulant for ordination in the Episcopal Diocese of Virginia and is currently working in a ministry of empowerment with incarcerated and formerly incarcerated women.

The Rev. Florence Gelo, is a co-learner at the Women's Theological Center in Boston, Mass., and a Unitarian Universalist minister.

Anne Gilson, is a recent graduate of Episcopal Divinity School with plans to pursue doctoral work in theology and ordination in the Episcopal Church.

The Rev. Susan Harlow, is a United Church of Christ minister currently working as Minister of Education at the First Congregational Church in Cambridge, Mass.

The Rev. Carter Heyward, Ph.D., is an Episcopal priest and professor of theology at Episcopal Divinity School.

Elaine Koenig, is a student at Episcopal Divinity School with an interest in continuing work in liberation ethics and theology.

The Rev. Virginia Sapienza Lund, is an Episcopal deacon in the Diocese of Michigan and a teacher of feminist theology.

Kirsten Lundblad, a graduate of Harvard Divinity School, is doing occupational therapy with developmentally disabled adults in northern New Mexico. A member of the United Church of Christ, she is a student at The Sunray School of Sacred Studies in Santa Fe.

Patrick Michaels, is a community organizer who teaches piano, coaches singers, and coordinates the musical program in St. James Episcopal Church in Cambridge, Mass. He is married to Laurie Rofinot.

Laurie Rofinot, is a recent graduate of Episcopal Divinity School and a candidate for ordination in the Episcopal Diocese of Minnesota.

Margarita Suárez, a student at Harvard Divinity School, is a Hispanic feminist theologian, activist and organizer who is pursuing ordination in the United Church of Christ.

The Rev. Jane W. Van Zandt, is a graduate of Episcopal Divinity School, assistant to the rector at All Saints Parish in Brookline, Mass., and a staff nurse at University Hospital in Boston.

Carol Vogler, a student at Moravian Seminary in Bethlehem, Pennsylvania, will be ordained in the Moravian Church and hopes to do further work in the church in Nicaragua.

Other Orbis Titles . . .

STEADFASTNESS OF THE SAINTS
A Journal of Peace and War in Central and North America
by Daniel Berrigan
In this poignant and beautifully written account of his recent journey through Nicaragua and El Salvador, Daniel Berrigan attempts to respond, both as a U.S. citizen and as a Jesuit, to the horrors of the U.S.-supported aggression against the peoples of Central America." It is imbued with emotion—Berrigan's sadness upon visiting the church where Oscar Romero was shot, his bewilderment and sorrow over the carnage he encountered, and the strong desire, of both Berrigan and many of the people he met, for peace and the end of suffering. Berrigan stresses the importance of sustaining one another and fighting for peace in a world where nuclear weapons multiply and peasants in Central America continue to be slaughtered. *Steadfastness of the Saints* will be enjoyed by a wide audience, not only for its subject matter, but for the insight Berrigan's perceptions provide.

"Daniel Berrigan looks at Central America from the perspective of 'our' America and his new book is written from both sides of the fence. The victimizers are seen through the eyes of the victims. He never loses sight of the interrelation between Megadeath, made in the U.S.A., and the mutilated corpses of children in El Salvador." *Dorothee Soelle*
no. 447-X   **144pp. pbk.**   **$7.95**

FLIGHTS OF VICTORY/VUELOS DE VICTORIA
by Ernesto Cardenal
In this bilingual collection of poetry Ernesto Cardenal chronicles the Nicaraguan revolution from the insurrection against Somoza, through the triumph of the Sandinista Front, to the reconstruction of the country. Many of the poems are narrative and anectodal and contain stark images of actual events from the Nicaraguan past and present. Others are visions for the future. They are all filled with hope, faith, and the desire for freedom, particularly for the poor. The deep insight they provide into the realities of contemporary Nicaragua—the ongoing struggle for liberation, the problems confronted by the government, and the suffering that continues to exist—could only come from a man so passionately involved in the cause. Few modern poets have attained Cardenal's success in harmonizing the demands of poetry, Christian faith, and the political struggle for justice. *Flights of Victory* will claim the attention of a wide readership.
no. 131-4   **160pp. pbk.**   **$9.95**

THE GOSPEL IN SOLENTINAME
(four volumes)
by Ernesto Cardenal
Four volumes of commentaries on the gospels drawn from Ernesto Cardenal's Sunday dialogues with the farmers and fishermen of the Solentiname community of Nicaragua.

This community was founded by Cardenal in 1966, later destroyed by Somoza's military, and is now in the process of being rebuilt.

". . . guaranteed to provoke reflection, delight, and perhaps dissent." *The Bible Today*

no. 176-4	vol. 1, 288pp. pbk.	$10.95
no. 175-6	vol. 2, 272pp. pbk.	$10.95
no. 174-8	vol. 3, 320pp. pbk.	$10.95
no. 173-X	vol. 4, 288pp. pbk.	$10.95

THE GOSPEL IN ART BY THE PEASANTS OF SOLENTINAME
edited by Philip and Sally Scharper

Thirty-one stunning, full-color paintings depicting gospel stories set in a Nicaraguan context by the peasant artists of Solentiname. The text facing each painting has been excerpted from the four-volume *The Gospel in Solentiname*, the collected commentaries on the Gospel from members of the Solentiname community.

"Rich insights into the meaning of the radical gospel, fresh from the lives of a struggling people." *The Other Side*

no. 382-1	70pp. cloth	$10.95

REVOLUTIONARIES FOR THE GOSPEL
Testimonies of Fifteen Christians in the Nicaraguan Government
by Teófilo Cabestrero

Few people are aware that more than thirty Christian laypeople hold key positions in the Nicaraguan government. In this compelling volume edited by the celebrated Spanish journalist Teófilo Cabestrero, fifteen of these men and women explore their twofold identity as Christians and revolutionaries and the ways in which the Sandinista people's revolution has enabled them to harmonize the political and religious dimensions of their lives. Although the experiences that led these Christians to join the revolution differ, their stories reveal a shared commitment to improve the quality of life for the poor in Nicaragua, a commitment rooted in their belief in the liberation message of the gospel and Jesus' option for the poor. The moving testimonies that make up this book will appeal to a wide readership.

"As a Christian and as a bishop of the church in Latin America, I will say that the confessions of these Nicaraguan men and women have moved me and demand commitment on my part." *Bishop Pedro Casaldaliga, Mato Grosso, Brazil*

no. 406-2	208pp. pbk.	$9.95

MINISTERS OF GOD, MINISTERS OF THE PEOPLE
Testimonies of Faith from Nicaragua
by Teófilo Cabestrero

Teófilo Cabestrero, A Spanish priest-journalist now working in Nicaragua, presents extensive and exclusive interviews with Ernesto Cardenal, Minister of Culture, Fernando Cardenal, Youth Movement Coordinator, and Miguel d'Escoto, Foreign Minister. These three priests in the Nicaraguan government explain how they combine their priesthood and their political commitment.

"The gift of this book is in the intimate nature of its sharing." *Sojourners*

no. 335-X	160pp. pbk.	$6.95

THE RELIGIOUS ROOTS OF REBELLION
Christians in Central American Revolutions
by Phillip Berryman

A well-documented history and analysis of Christian involvement in revolutionary movements in Nicaragua, El Salvador, and Guatemala.

"This is a provocative and important contribution to understanding the role of Catholicism in the struggle for justice in Central America."   *Penny Lernoux*

Phillip Berryman spent more than a decade in Central America, first as a pastoral worker in a barrio in Panama, and later as Central American representative for the American Friends Service Committee.

no. 105-5   480pp. pbk. $19.95

BLOOD OF THE INNOCENT
Victims of the Contras' War in Nicaragua
edited by Teófilo Cabestrero

In this alarming volume, witnesses and survivors of contra assaults on Nicaraguan peasants recount their horrifying experiences. They tell stories of campesino leaders slaughtered for their efforts to aid peasants, women and children forced to witness the murders of members of their own family and then robbed of all their possessions; the brutal slayings of unarmed children and a defenseless, severely retarded man, and the destruction of cooperative communities in which peasants lived and worked to provide food, housing, and education for each other. These are just some of the startling and disturbing accounts presented here. But equally disturbing is the question that is asked time and again throughout the book: "Why does the United States continue to support this aggression?"

no. 211-6   112pp. pbk. $6.95

CRISIS AND CHANGE
The Church in Latin America Today
by Edward L. Cleary, O.P.

"Edward Cleary has furnished an overview of the entire Latin American scene and the church's relation to it that has no equal. . . . This is much more than simply a book about 'liberation theology,' for it positions that phenomenon in the history, culture, ideology, and politics of the region. Any student of church involvement, military ideology, and political-economic currents will profit from this study."   *Robert McAfee Brown,*
Pacific School of Religion

no. 149-7   208pp. pbk. $11.95